SHERMAN'S MISSISSIPPI CAMPAIGN

Sherman's Mississippi Campaign

BUCK T. FOSTER

THE UNIVERSITY OF ALABAMA PRESS
Tuscaloosa

The University of Alabama Press
Tuscaloosa, Alabama 35487-0380
uapress.ua.edu

Hardcover edition published 2006.
Paperback edition published 2015.
eBook edition published 2008.

Typeface: AGaramond

Manufactured in the United States of America
Cover art: Detail from poster advertising the play *Gettysburg*,
Calhoun Show Print, Hartford, CT; Theatrical Poster Collection (Library of Congress)
Cover design: Erin Bradley Dangar / Dangar Design

∞

The paper on which this book is printed meets the minimum requirements of American National Standard for Information Science–Permanence of Paper for Printed Library Materials, ANSI Z39.48-1984.

Paperback ISBN: 978-0-8173-5827-3
eBook ISBN: 978-0-8173-8132-5

A previous edition of this book has been catalogued by the Library of Congress as follows:
Library of Congress Cataloging-in-Publication Data
Foster, Buckley Thomas.
Sherman's Mississippi campaign / Buck T. Foster.
p. cm.
Includes bibliographical references and index.
ISBN-13: 978-0-8173-1519-1 (cloth : alk. paper)
ISBN-10: 0-8173-1519-5 (alk. paper)
1. Mississippi—History—Civil War, 1861–1865—Campaigns. 2. Meridian (Miss.)—History, Military—19th century. 3. Sherman, William T. (William Tecumseh), 1820–1891—Military leadership. 4. United States—History—Civil War, 1861–1865—Campaigns. 5. Strategy—Case studies. I. Title.
E476.14.F74 2006
976.2'05—dc22

2006006858

Contents

Maps

Preface

Civil War journalist-turned-historian Orville J. Victor, in his four-volume history of the Civil War, argued: "The march of [William T.] Sherman through central Mississippi to the Alabama state line was in execution of a masterly design, but little understood at the time, and one which did not receive the notice its importance merited."[1] This is still very much the case today. Few scholars appreciate the importance of the campaign in the scheme of the war, and Civil War enthusiasts have an inaccurate image of it. During February and March 1864 in Mississippi, Sherman first attempted to use hard war on a large scale, and his expedition had a long-term impact on the war's outcome. Sherman's experiences in his march across the Magnolia State shaped and solidified his style of warfare for the rest of the conflict. This was indeed his dress rehearsal for hard war.

Only a handful of publications consider the Meridian campaign in any depth. Richard McMurry's 1975 *Civil War Times Illustrated* article discusses the short-term impact of Sherman's march but is too brief to provide an overall view of the campaign and its repercussions. Only one book-length study exists. Marjorie Bearss's *Sherman's Forgotten Campaign,* published in 1987, provides a blow-by-blow account of the march; however, it does not offer readers any overall analysis. The work is helpful to those who study battlefield tactics and marching orders, but its pages do not provide insight into the long-term importance of the Meridian campaign to the war or its participants.

Publications concerning hard war, total war, or modern warfare sometimes mention this campaign. Two of the best examples are Herman Hattaway and Archer Jones's *How the North Won the War* (1983) and Mark Grimsley's *The Hard Hand of War* (1995). Each monograph appreciates the expedition as the beginning of the Federal army's new, harder style of warfare, but neither provides detail into exactly what Sherman learned here or what the overall significance of the campaign was. Both publications cover their subject well, Hattaway and Jones with the changing of Federal strategy and Grimsley with the modifying of Federal attitudes toward Southern civilians in the war, but they do not create a complete picture of Sherman's campaign.

Similarly, Sherman biographies give this campaign little attention. For example, John F. Marszalek's *Sherman: A Soldier's Passion for Order* (1993) devotes only five pages to it, while Michael Fellman's *Citizen Sherman* (1995), Stanley P. Hirchson's *The White Tecumseh* (1997), and Lee B. Kennett's *Sherman: A Soldier's Life* (2001) barely mention it.

In this work I try to provide readers with a thorough, analytical study that explains the development of Sherman's unique style of warfare, including his attitudes toward civilians, slaves, soldiers, destruction, tactics, and planning. I attempt to show how his style of fighting evolved and what role the Meridian campaign played in that evolution.

Sherman did not develop his style of warfare in a week or even a year. It took the entire course of the war to change him from a commander who sought to exclude civilians from the conflict to a leader who actively searched for ways to terrorize Southern civilians into giving up their cause without injuring their person. In the first three years of the war, Sherman went from protecting Southern civilians and their property to believing that these citizens were ultimately responsible for the war and had to be convinced to stop supporting it. He had spent much time in the South as a U.S. Army officer and as superintendent of what later became Louisiana State University. He had many Southern friends and thus had an attachment to the South and its people. Sherman sought, therefore, a way to end the war with as little bloodshed as possible. His entire war experience, particularly as Ulysses S. Grant's subordinate, provided him with battlefield savvy and tactics to do just that.

While Sherman was in Memphis in 1862 and 1863, guarding the important river town and the Mississippi River, he battled constantly with guerrilla and Confederate cavalry units operating in Mississippi and Tennessee. After exhausting all conventional methods for dealing with these threats, he began to strike at the local Southern towns, which he considered the supply bases for the Confederates. By taking or destroying supplies, Sherman tried to prevent the Confederates from sustaining the fight while simultaneously punishing the citizens for supporting the enemy. Although he experienced limited success with this tactic, Sherman believed that the key to protecting the Mississippi River, a major determinant of Union victory, was to strike at Confederate resources in the Magnolia State. If the Confederates could not find supplies, they could not remain a threat to the river. Sherman, therefore, created a plan to destroy the rail lines in Mississippi, hoping thereby to cripple the state's military value to the Confederacy. In this manner he could remove the state from the Confederacy and end the threat to the Mississippi River. The most important rail junction in Mississippi stood at Meridian, near the Alabama border, its rails connecting the Magnolia State with the rest of the Confederacy. Sherman, therefore, chose the destruction of Meridian as his main objective for the winter of 1863–64.

The other tactics Sherman employed during the Meridian campaign, such as the use of feints and the acquiring of supplies from the countryside, were not new to war. The abandonment of his own supply lines, however, was an innovative idea. Sherman had witnessed Grant's army practically perform this maneuver during the Vicksburg campaign of 1863. When Confederate cavalry destroyed Grant's main supply depot at Holly Springs, Mississippi, and damaged the Mobile and Ohio Railroad in Tennessee, Grant's army subsisted mainly from food and forage gathered from farms along the railroad. Although Grant's army had done this for only two weeks, Sherman (and Grant) thought that his army could carry all necessities (except food) in wagons during his march to Meridian and live off the Mississippi countryside for the entire campaign. Sherman combined all the tactics he had learned during the first three years of the war for one main purpose: to remove the Confederate threat to the Mississippi River. If the Confederate threat were eliminated, Federal officials could remove thousands of garrisoning troops along the river for use on battlefields elsewhere. What Sherman learned about the limitations of the Confederacy and the Southern people during his first large-scale use of hard war provided him with the insight he needed to use his style of warfare on an even larger scale later. Sherman's method of war, under Grant's overall leadership, became the Federal strategy for winning the war. For the remainder of the conflict, the Union army sought to strike at all Southern resources and infrastructure, hoping thereby to destroy the Confederacy's ability and will to keep fighting.

The Meridian campaign was hardly the brutish, purposeless destruction described in Lost Cause mythology. Rather, it was a planned strategy and tactic to end the war as quickly and bloodlessly as possible. Thus it deserves the attention it has seldom received from historians.

SHERMAN'S MISSISSIPPI CAMPAIGN

1 / Sherman's Transformation

During the first year of the American Civil War, William T. Sherman considered proper treatment of noncombatants and their property to be his soldierly duty. He took great care in seeing that his policies and the conduct of his men did not trample upon the perceived rights of secessionist or unionist civilians. He handed out harsh punishment to men who did as little as steal fence rails for their campfires or take liberally from the countryside.[1]

By the end of the war, however, most Southerners saw Sherman as a "brute" for his harsh treatment of Southern civilians and his destruction of property across the Confederate States. His "bummers" became notorious for their ability to strip the land of valuable goods, and Southerners greatly abhorred them. Many historians have credited Sherman with creating the policy of "total war" and being the originator of modern warfare. Although recent works have rightfully concluded that Sherman was not the first general to promote a harsher attitude toward civilians, he nevertheless moved war in that direction to a far greater degree than any of his contemporaries. How and why did Sherman move from one mind-set to the other?[2]

The pivotal circumstances in Sherman's transformation came because of his dealings with guerrillas along the Mississippi River and his participation in the Vicksburg campaign in 1862 and 1863. Because of the partisans' menace to Union depots, communications, and supply lines, coupled with the Confederate populace's support of these raiders, Sherman developed a harsher, more encompassing policy toward Southern civilians. Just after the fall of

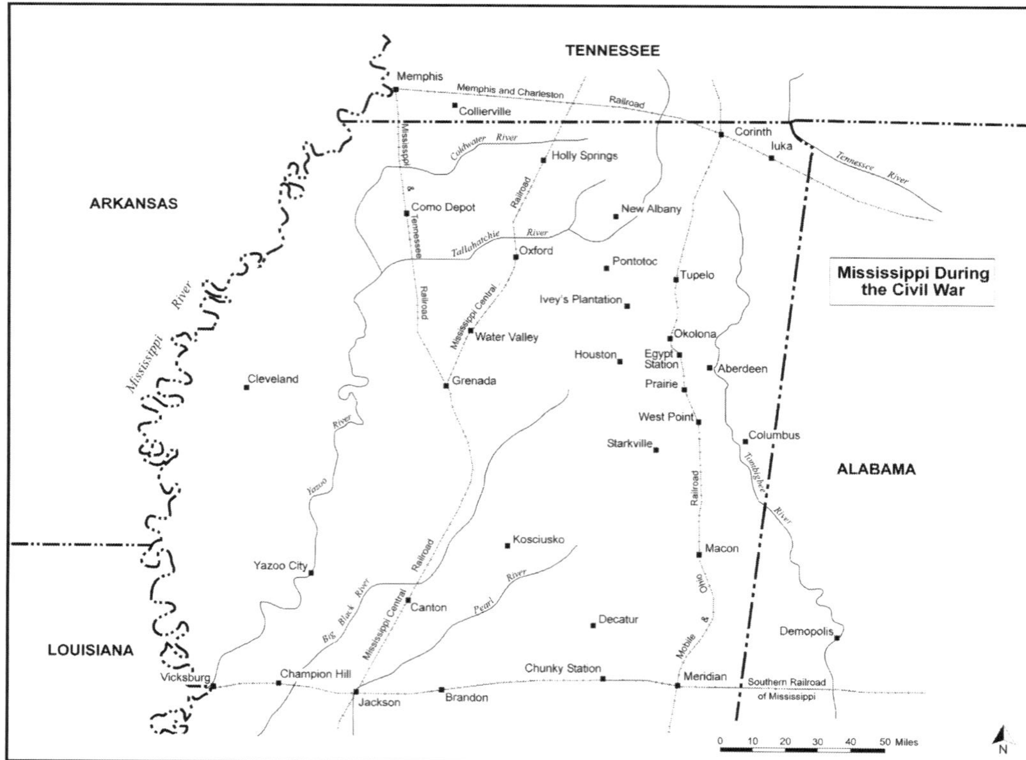
Mississippi During the Civil War
TENNESSEE
ARKANSAS
ALABAMA
LOUISIANA
Memphis
Memphis and Charleston Railroad
Collierville
Corinth
Iuka
Tennessee River
Coldwater River
Holly Springs
Como Depot
New Albany
Tallahatchie River
Oxford
Pontotoc
Tupelo
Mississippi & Tennessee Railroad
Mississippi River
Ivey's Plantation
Mississippi Central Railroad
Water Valley
Okolona
Houston
Egypt Station
Aberdeen
Cleveland
Grenada
Prairie
West Point
Yazoo River
Columbus
Starkville
Tombigbee River
Kosciusko
Macon
Yazoo City
Pearl River
Big Black River
Canton
Decatur
Mobile & Ohio Railroad
Demopolis
Chunky Station
Vicksburg
Champion Hill
Meridian
Southern Railroad of Mississippi
Jackson
Brandon
0 10 20 30 40 50 Miles
N

Vicksburg, while in Jackson for the second time, Sherman conducted a campaign of destruction to render an entire region unusable to the Confederate army. The Meridian campaign, some six months later, was, however, his preliminary attempt to subjugate an entire state and served as his proving ground for later campaigns into Georgia and the Carolinas. Sherman adapted his experiences learned during the first three years of the war into a new technique that he designed to end the war as quickly and bloodlessly as possible. He wanted to remove the enemy's ability and will to fight without the need for the destruction of the opponent's army or the capturing and garrisoning of large areas of the Confederacy.

Although he attended West Point, Sherman did not derive his principles from his experience there. Most professional officers, many of whom had attended West Point, had studied the works of Baron Antoine-Henri de Jomini. Although many historians contend that Jomini's works had little influence on these officers because *The Art of War* was not translated into English until later in 1854, most military tacticians and strategists of the period drew upon this work for their own writings. Jomini contended that the violence between two enemy armies on the battlefield had few limitations but that civilians away from the fighting should not be included. Commenting on acts of guerrilla warfare, he wrote that actions against civilians should "display courtesy, gentleness, and severity united, and, particularly, deal justly." "Absolute war," in his opinion, should remain an action reserved for belligerents, and he made no mention of the expansion of such a strategy to the civilian population. Jomini held that there was a definite wall between warring armies and the common population. His comments about guerrillas also implied condemnation of their style of warfare. Sherman agreed with Jomini that noncombatants should receive different treatment than soldiers.[3]

After the Battle of First Bull Run, Sherman wrote to his wife about the depredations that some of his command had committed. "If he [a private] thinks right he takes the oats [and] corn, and even burns the house of his enemy," he wrote angrily. "No goths or vandals ever had less respect for the lives [and] property of friends and foes." Sherman thought these types of infractions were detrimental to the Union cause. When he became commander of the Department of the Cumberland later that year, he compensated civilians for all property secured for the Federals' military use in the state of Kentucky. He thought this was the best way to keep border state civilians from straying to the Confederate side. A Northern newspaper declared that Sherman's policy had "produced a marked change in favor of the Union cause."[4]

In July 1862, Sherman wrote to Major General Henry W. Halleck about an incident involving a group of guerrillas attacking a forage train. He believed that they were a band of local citizens from the nearby settlement of La Grange, Tennessee, so he ordered that twenty-five of the "most prominent" men from La Grange be captured and sent to Columbus, Tennessee, as prisoners. "I am satisfied we have no other remedy for this ambush firing than to hold the neighborhood fully responsible, though the punishment may fall on the wrong parties," he concluded. Sherman had no way of knowing exactly who was responsible for the attack, but he insisted that the local people knew the guilty parties. If they refused to assist in the apprehension of the culprits, then they would suffer the consequences.[5]

The following month, because of the irregularity of Union supply shipments to the Western theater and the Confederate cavalry's destruction of supply lines and storage facilities, the Federal government began to endorse foraging to offset this shortfall in provisions. General-in-Chief Halleck issued orders to Ulysses S. Grant that read: "As soon as the corn gets fit for forage get all the supplies you can from the rebels in Mississippi. It is time they should feel the presence of war on our side." That same month, the War Department issued General Orders 107 and 108, upholding the idea that, if private property was seized in an "orderly manner" and not "pillaged," its confiscation "for the subsistence, transportation, and other uses of the army" was officially acceptable. The Union army had allowed this type of action before 1862.[6]

Sherman did not like the idea put forth by General Orders 107 and 108. Believing that liberal foraging would lead the men down the path toward outright pillaging, he issued an order that the "demoralizing and disgraceful practice of pillaging must cease else the country will rise on us and justly shoot us down like dogs and wild beasts." He insisted that, while his command was on the move in enemy territory, the cavalry capture and punish any stragglers engaged in destructive activity.[7]

That same month, however, Sherman became concerned about guerrilla cavalry constantly attacking his supply lines and destroying Union provisions. They attacked isolated Federal garrisons and scattered their soldiers. When a larger force moved out to meet the bandits, the partisans dispersed in all directions, mingling with the populace. Sherman, therefore, began to view Southern citizens differently, especially when they lived in areas where the guerrillas operated frequently. "All the people are now guerrillas," he wrote angrily to Grant, "and they have a perfect understanding" of what they were doing.[8]

Sherman decided that if these bushwhackers hid among the local citizens, the Union army should retaliate against those who concealed them. "If the farmers in a neighborhood encourage or even permit in their midst a set of guerrillas they cannot escape the necessary consequences," Sherman warned. "It is not our wish or policy to destroy the farmers or their farms, but of course there is and must be remedy for all evils." Sherman remained steadfast in his belief that wanton destruction of private citizens' property was wrong, but the "exigencies of the war" forced him, he believed, to take a new approach. He continued to insist that, although it was not his "policy to destroy the farmers and their farms," those who resided in the areas around partisan troop activity were "accessories by their presence and inactivity to prevent murders and destruction of property." Therefore, they should properly expect just retribution. Sherman was not the only Union general moving away from the conciliatory stance. Those commanders who contended with guerrillas in Missouri, Kentucky, Tennessee, and western Virginia were also growing tired of the nuisances.[9]

Guerrilla raids on Union supplies and firings upon boats along the Mississippi River continued to anger Sherman when his troops garrisoned Memphis in 1862. In September he wrote his brother, U.S. senator John Sherman, in frustration: "It is about time the North understood the truth; that the entire South, man, woman, and child are against us, armed and determined." Knowing that he had the confidence of his brother, he spoke freely. Sherman loathed the irregular troops' actions, and because the civilian population aided their cause, he grew upset with these people as well.[10]

Sherman did not believe that all Southern civilians were at war with the Union army. The real enemies, he thought, were those citizens who supported the Confederate forces. Because of this aggravation, Sherman began to take his pursuit of guerrillas and the punishment of those assisting them to the next level. The next step consisted of striking at points near to where the attacks had taken place.

Two days after his letter to Senator Sherman, the general ordered Colonel Charles C. Walcutt of the Forty-sixth Ohio Volunteers to the town of Randolph, Tennessee, from where, the day before, bushwhackers had fired upon the Union supply ship *Eugene* as it carried cargo south to Memphis. He instructed Walcutt that he thought "the attack on the *Eugene* was by a small force of guerrillas from Loosahatchie, who by this time have gone back, and therefore you will find no one at Randolph; in which case you will destroy the place, leaving one house to mark the place." Sherman could not capture those directly responsible for the sniping, but, as an example to others, he decided to punish those who assisted in or did not prevent the attack on the boat. "Let the people know and feel that we deeply deplore the necessity of such destruction, but must protect ourselves and the boats," he told his subordinate. "All such acts as cowardly firing upon boats filled with women and children . . . must be severely punished." Sherman considered such bushwhacking beyond the scope of proper military conduct, and thus he felt justified in using any means within his power, including the destruction of civilian property, to stop such actions.[11]

Sherman informed Grant of the action at Randolph and warned that he intended to threaten the enemy with harsher actions if they persisted in their boat attacks: "[I] have given public notice that a repetition will justify any measures of retaliation, such as loading the boats with guerrilla prisoners where they would receive fire, and expelling families from the comforts of Memphis, whose husbands and brothers go to make up those guerrillas." These were not hollow threats. Sherman had already issued a special order empowering the provost marshal to prepare a list of thirty inhabitants. In the event a boat received fire on the Mississippi River near Memphis, ten families from the list would leave the city.[12]

In October an attack on the river craft *Catahoula* compelled Sherman to intensify his retaliation on the wrongdoers. Hoping that harsher action would end the harassment, he sent Walcutt to "destroy all the houses, farms, and corn fields" from Elm Grove Post Office to Hopefield, Arkansas, a distance of roughly fifteen miles. Furthermore, he made good on his promise to expel Memphis citizens. After three subsequent guerrilla attacks along the river, he sent several families out of the city beyond Union lines. These tactics seemed to work; partisan attacks subsided for several months.[13]

While moving south from Memphis down the Mississippi on transports in December 1862 as part of the Vicksburg campaign, Sherman continued his policy of punishing those who sniped at river craft. He penned an order to his men that, if fired upon, the troops should land and "attack the property and stores [and take any supplies] useful to the United States." They should burn "the neighboring houses, barns & c." and dispose of any enemy personnel in the area. The marauders would end their attacks on riverboats, or they and their families and friends would feel the repercussions. Sherman later described his transformation in 1862 to a friend: "[Early in the war,] I would not let our men burn [a] fence rail for fire or gather fruits or vegetables though hungry. We at that time were restrained, tied to a deep-seated reverence for law and property. The rebels first introduced terror as part of their system. . . . No military mind could endure this long, and we were forced in self-defense to imitate their example."[14]

That winter and spring, during the campaign to take the Mississippi River fortress, Sherman learned another important lesson that would prove extremely valuable in his later campaigns and would change the way that he would conduct war against the Confederacy. He had observed the two battling armies at Shiloh earlier that year and saw what bulky, slow-moving supply wagons could do to an army's celerity of movement. "[Don Carlos] Buell had to move at a snail's pace with his vast wagon trains, [while Braxton] Bragg moved rapidly, living on the country," he noted. Sherman remained unsure, however, whether a Union army could live off the hostile country as successfully as the enemy's army had done in its own territory.[15]

By late December, Grant had moved into northern Mississippi from western Tennessee with his Army of the Tennessee, stretching his supply lines to nearly sixty miles from his starting point. A combination of strikes on his supply and communication lines by Confederate cavalry leaders Major General Earl Van Dorn at Holly Springs and Brigadier General Nathan Bedford Forrest at other locations in northern Mississippi isolated the Union force from its base. Grant immediately ordered his men to live off the countryside, hoping that he could reestablish his lines before continuing on the campaign. He was surprised to observe that his army lived well on the northern Mississippi farmlands. He remarked to Halleck that, out to fifteen miles from his principal position, "everything of subsistence of man or beast has been appropriated for the use of our army." Grant later commented in his memoirs, "I was amazed at the quantity of supplies the country afforded. It showed me that we could have subsisted off the country for two months instead of two weeks."[16]

Sherman understood that, without having to guard a supply or communication line, he could free the men previously used to protect that line for use on the battlefield. Furthermore, the Union army could subsist in unfriendly country at the expense of the enemy, while simultaneously removing valuable provisions from Confederate use.

In addition, Sherman came to appreciate Grant's philosophy about the importance of Confederate resources. Grant believed that the destruction of enemy supplies "tended to the same result as the destruction of armies." Sherman had already tried a variation of this tactic when he had punished the Confederate citizens for aiding the guerrillas and destroyed their supplies, thereby keeping such goods from the irregulars' use. Now he understood that he would have to take his actions even further to obtain his desired goal—the end of attacks on the Mississippi River.[17]

In April 1863 the Federal government would set forth a distinction between civilians and combatants inhabiting the Confederacy in its General Order 100, "Instructions for the Government of Armies of the United States in the Field." Article 22 read in part that there is a "distinction between the private individual belonging to a hostile country and the hostile country itself, with its men in arms. The principle has been more and more acknowledged that the unarmed citizen is to be spared in person, property, and honor as much as the exigencies of war will admit." The key factor was war necessity, and as Article 28 pointed out, there was also a right of retaliation. General Order 100 only served to further outline what General Orders 107 and 108 had defined in 1862.[18]

In keeping with the Federal government's mind-set, Sherman believed his troops should take all precautions not to disturb the property of those civilians who did not participate in or aid guerrilla action. In the spring of 1863, after another bushwhacking incident near Greenville, Mississippi, Sherman ordered Brigadier General Frederick Steele to clear the area of partisans and any Confederate regulars. "If planters remain at home and behave themselves, molest them as little as possible," Sherman cautioned, "but if the planters abandon their plantations you may infer they are hostile, and can take their cattle, hogs, corn, or anything you need." Steele should consider any cotton, except that marked with "C.S.," as private property and leave it unmolested. The Union troops, despite Steele's attempts, "burned up everything there was to eat on the plantations," leaving nothing for the "peaceful inhabitants" as Sherman had instructed. Steele's overzealous troops' destruction of private property typified what often happened on these raids. Soldiers, either away from their officers' eyes or because of official neglect, often took liberties as a means of revenge or to collect luxuries for themselves.[19]

When Steele offered to return some of the acquired goods, Sherman agreed, stating: "War at best is barbarism, but to involve all—children, women, old and helpless—is more than can be justified. Our men will become absolutely lawless unless this can be checked."[20]

When Grant marched on the capital of Mississippi in May 1863, his men once again lived successfully off the land. Grant did not intend to hold Jackson. Instead, he wanted to remove any militarily beneficial materials from the city and rid the area of any Confederate troops, thus protecting himself from a rear attack after he moved on Vicksburg. After he had driven out the Confederate forces, Grant fanned out his men across the city to "collect stores and forage, and collect all public property of the enemy [and to destroy] the river railroad bridge and the road as far east as possible, as well as north and south."[21]

Sherman sent his men to set fire to piled rails and ties, twisting the heated iron in order to render the rails useless, making "Sherman neckties." He ordered the destruction of "presses, sugar, and everything public not needed by us," but he cautioned again that "the private rights of citizens should be respected." When Sherman received word that the provost marshal condoned the taking of store contents unnecessary to the subsistence of the troops, he ordered Brigadier General J. A. Mower to look into the matter. "The feeling of pillage and booty will injure the morals of the troops, and bring disgrace to our cause," he warned. Sherman considered the object of his actions to be the removal of supplies from the enemy's use while simultaneously utilizing them for his own troops' welfare. He still respected the rights of private citizens and destroyed only public property. Grant continued to order the region around Vicksburg stripped "to prevent an army coming this way from supplying itself." He sent Sherman back to Jackson after the fall of Vicksburg to retake the city from General Joseph Johnston's army, which had reoccupied the capital.

As during his first visit to Jackson, Sherman went about destroying and confiscating supplies from the area in and around the town. He also caused Johnston to retreat. This trip to Jackson proved different from any other attack on a city during the war. Sherman, even though not immediately threatened or in need of supplies, continued to destroy railroads, collect and demolish supplies from the town and the countryside, and burn the remaining factories and cotton. Grant had ordered Sherman to "leave nothing of value for the enemy to carry on the war with." Sherman took these orders to the extreme, reporting to his superior that his men were "absolutely stripping the country of corn, cattle, hogs, sheep, poultry, everything," and that he used the fields of newly sprouted spring corn for pasture or cut them for fodder. "The wholesale destruction to which this country is now being subjected is terrible to contemplate," he continued, "but it is the scourge of war . . . and weakening the resources of our enemy [is] being executed with rigor." He wrote triumphantly: "Jackson, once the pride and boast of Mississippi, is now a ruined town." Sherman also remarked happily that after his two successful raids on the capital, "Jackson ceases to be a place for the enemy to collect stores and men from which to threaten our great river." This was the first step that illustrated Grant's and Sherman's belief that the Union army needed a new type of strategy to win the war.[22]

It is important to note that in the preceding months, Sherman had tried diligently to end the guerrilla attacks along the Mississippi River with a series of precise retaliations. Then, he had attacked the settlements near the points of these assaults, destroying property and insisting that the local populace either were the guilty party or, at the least, were aiding the attackers. Next, he increased the area of his retaliation to encompass not only the immediate vicinity of the harassment but some miles around the place, still searching for partisans and their supporters. Now, Sherman attempted to render an entire region thoroughly and systematically unusable to the Confederate army and the guerrillas. In all of these actions except one, Sherman took great care not to disturb non-militarily significant private property of those not directly involved in the war. In Jackson he had changed his view concerning private citizens and their property. Grant had ordered him to make the area unusable, and he complied, destroying and confiscating both public and private property. To ensure the security of the Mississippi River, Sherman now had to attack a larger, more encompassing area of the Confederacy.

In September 1863, Sherman laid out his emerging philosophy in a long letter to Halleck. He believed that the Federal government should deal with each sector of the population and the rebellion as a whole. In general, he thought that "every member of the nation is bound by natural and constitutional law to 'maintain and defend the Government against all its opposers whomsoever.' If they fail to do it they are derelict," he said, "and can be punished or deprived of all advantages arising from the labors of those who do." He contended that the United States and its representatives had the right to "remove and destroy every obstacle—if need be, take every life, every acre of land, every particle of property, everything that to us seems proper . . . [and] that all who do not aid are enemies, and we will not account to them for our acts." This latter line was reminiscent of his statement in August 1862, when he had warned that those who resided in the areas near partisan troop action were "accessories by their presence and inactivity to prevent murders and destruction of property." He summed up his attitude in one line when he wrote to his brother near the end of December: "The Army of the Confederacy is the South." This time, however, he meant all Southern residents, not just those living close to guerrilla activity. Sherman would continue to issue orders in an attempt to keep his troops from outright pillaging as they marched through the South, but the private property of Southern civilians was now in peril of Federal confiscation and destruction if deemed profitable for Confederate use or useful to the Union.[23]

As 1864 began, Sherman continued to grapple with the guerrillas who unrelentingly attacked locations along the Mississippi River. While in eastern Tennessee he sent General Grenville Dodge on a mission to "hunt the pests that infest our country. Show them no mercy and if the people don't suppress guerrillas, tell them your orders are to treat the community as enemies." In January, while on a trip down the Mississippi to investigate another river attack, he heatedly wrote: "For every bullet shot at a steamboat, I would shoot a thousand [cannon into every] hapless town on Red, Ouachita, Yazoo [Rivers], or wherever a boat can float or soldiers march." Four days later he ordered Brigadier General A. J. Smith to western Tennessee from Columbus, Kentucky, in preparation for the approaching Meridian expedition with orders to "punish the country for permitting the guerrillas among them. Take freely the [supplies and animals] of the hostile and indifferent inhabitants," and inform them that if "they permit their country to be used by the public enemy they must bear the expense of the troops sent to expel them."[24]

Sherman also worried that Richmond had designs on wrestling control of the Mississippi River away from the Union army in order to reunite the severed pieces of the Confederacy, undoing all that the Union army had accomplished in the previous months. He had heard news about the reconcentration of Confederate forces in the Magnolia State and had become intent on ridding Mississippi of enemy forces before his expected spring campaign eastward into Georgia. A great number of the thirty thousand paroled troops from Vicksburg had entered into partisan and regular service throughout the state, enhancing the number of enemy troops already there. "To secure the safety of the navigation of the Mississippi River I would slay millions," he declared. "On that point I am not only insane, but mad."[25]

Sherman intended to cut Mississippi from the eastern section of the Confederacy, much like Grant had isolated the Trans-Mississippi with his victory at Vicksburg and General Nathaniel Banks's capture of Port Hudson. In order to free up thousands of garrisoning troops along the Mississippi, discourage guerrilla raids, and remove valuable military resources from Confederate grasp, Sherman would burn, confiscate, and destroy corn, hams, railroads, depots, warehouses, and any other items that might aid the enemy's cause.

By these actions, Sherman also hoped to dishearten Mississippians, who had already shown signs that they were becoming unhappy with the war. In the latter part of 1863, Sherman had learned about a series of town meetings and petitions all across the state "to consider the question of abandoning the Confederacy." Although he had initially dismissed the reports as nonsense, he still believed that some in the region were growing tired of the conflict. If not, he would persuade them into feeling that way.[26]

One must remember that Sherman had happily lived in the South and had made numerous close and lasting friendships. He believed, therefore, that it was better to attack and destroy material than citizens. He planned to travel across the state, punishing the population for aiding the bushwhackers, tearing up railroads, confiscating and destroying corn and other supplies, and thereby crippling the enemy's ability and will to fight. He would break the Confederate will without a serious loss of life to either side. If successful in Mississippi, Sherman would intensify his activities, saving lives while simultaneously obtaining effective results. The Meridian campaign, therefore, would act as the final dress rehearsal in Sherman's evolution of a new philosophy of prosecuting war.[27]

On the eve of his foray into Mississippi, Sherman sent a lengthy announcement to Major R. M. Sawyer in Alabama and instructed him to read the message to the civilians there "so as to prepare them for my coming." He explained that in European conflicts, from which the United States had obtained its principles of war, the people had remained neutral and had been free to sell their goods to either combatant. Therefore, he concluded, "the rule was and is, that wars are confined to the armies and should not visit the homes of families or private interests."

However, he contended, in Ireland when the English occupied the land to end a revolt, the citizens were driven off their native lands and a new group of people introduced. Sherman believed that the American conflict was like the latter. He argued, therefore, that since the Southern population's "provisions, forage, horses, mules, wagons" went to the enemy's army, "it [was] clearly our duty and right to take them, because otherwise they might be used against us." If any noncombatant should create chaos or communicate with hostile parties, the Union army would arrest, banish, and punish the guilty party. "The Government of the United States has . . . any and all rights which they choose to enforce in war—to take lives, their homes, their lands, their everything." The South had "appealed to war," Sherman cautioned, "and must abide by its rules and laws. . . . Satan and the rebellious saints of Heaven were allowed continuance of existence in Hell, merely to [feel] their just punishment. To such as would rebel against a Government so mild and just as ours was in Peace, a punishment equal would not be unjust," he declared. Thus, the citizens of Mississippi would receive the Sherman of 1864, who believed in destructive war, not the one of 1861, who had gone to great lengths to protect all private property within his lines.[28]

The Meridian campaign was the next step in Sherman's evolving attitude toward the prosecution of war. The expedition demonstrated to Sherman and other Federal commanders the successful way to conduct "hard war." Its importance rested more in its impact on Sherman's military policy toward Southern civilians and the Union strategy to win the war than on immediate military ramifications in Mississippi.

Sherman had undergone a complete change of attitude toward the Southern populace and the army's dependence upon secure supply and communication lines. His dealings with guerrillas in Kentucky, Tennessee, and Mississippi had hardened his resolve toward nonbelligerents. His experience with Grant during the Vicksburg campaign had given him the confidence to strike at those who supported the partisan factions deep within their territory without fear of his troops starving for want of goods. Sherman could support his own armies with his enemy's assets. He had come to believe that the best way to end the war was to strike mightily at the enemy's resources, rendering them useless for the further prosecution of the war. These experiences, and what he would learn along the muddy roads from Vicksburg to Meridian, would allow him to wreak more havoc on an enemy population's supplies and psyche than any other general in the Civil War had before him.

2 / The Plan

After retaking Jackson in the summer of 1863, Sherman had thought about moving down the railroad track toward Meridian, a small town of about four hundred people, located about one hundred miles east of Jackson near the Alabama border. This bustling community contained warehouses, storehouses, depots, an armory, a hospital, and other pertinent military items. It served as a hub for Confederate traffic between Mississippi and the rest of the eastern Confederacy. The Confederacy used the Mobile and Ohio Railroad and the Southern Railroad of Mississippi, which intersected at Meridian, to shuttle into the Magnolia State vast amounts of men and supplies. Additionally, these lines worked as an important interior route to transfer Confederate troops from one front to another quickly and efficiently.[1]

At the time, Sherman decided that because of the hot summer weather and the exhaustion of his men, he should postpone any movement on Meridian. Simultaneously, however, he became determined to rid the state of its guerrilla elements and other Confederate forces who harassed river traffic and posed a threat to the Mississippi River itself. Convinced that a strike at Meridian could stymie these Confederate forces, at every opportunity he pressed his request to take the town. His plan suggested the possibility of an amphibious assault near Mobile, a large cavalry raid, numerous feints, or a march of more than twenty thousand infantry straight across 150 miles of enemy territory.[2]

Ulysses S. Grant, Sherman's superior, had bigger plans than Meridian, but an attack on the Mississippi town would fit nicely into his larger strategy. Grant sent letters to Henry W. Halleck on several occasions in July and August suggesting an attack on Mobile. Grant believed that the Alabama city could provide an excellent base for his operations into the Confederate states further east, where he could hit some of the South's manufacturing and supply sectors. Mobile could provide the southernmost anchor for another split of the Confederacy. The important port city had become, with the Union victories at Shiloh and Corinth, the only rail link, besides Meridian, from Mississippi to the eastern Confederacy.[3]

Halleck thought Texas was a more important target, so he did not provide Grant with the approval he wished, reflecting President Abraham Lincoln's belief that Texas was especially important to U.S. interests. The president wrote Grant in August that "an expedition against Mobile . . . would appear tempting, were it not [for the] recent events in Mexico." Emperor Napoleon of France had made threatening remarks about the possible annexation of Texas into Mexico, a country he had nearly conquered after several years of struggle. Lincoln wanted to show a strong American military presence in the Lone Star State. Neither Halleck nor the president, however, realized that the low river level at that time of year would prevent any serious Union army movement into Texas. Although Grant did not secure permission to attempt a capture of Mobile in the summer of 1863, the importance of the city never left his mind, and he hoped that Sherman would have an opportunity to attack the city later on.[4]

As early as August 1863, therefore, Sherman had begun to make plans for a move against Meridian. He ordered a map containing his intended route. The map included information on Meridian in Mississippi as well as Demopolis and Mobile in Alabama. He hoped to move across Mississippi as soon as his men were rested and the cool fall weather had arrived.[5]

When word came in September that Confederate general Braxton Bragg had cornered General William Rosecrans at Chattanooga, Sherman thought that the best way to relieve his colleague was to direct an attack on Mobile through Meridian, making a "powerful diversion." He argued that, if the Army of the Tennessee moved rapidly across Mississippi and Alabama, Joseph Johnston would have to take large numbers of men from Bragg's army in order to counter the move in Alabama. Sherman believed that Rosecrans could hold the line in Tennessee and "doubt[ed] if our re-enforcements [could] reach him in time to do good."[6]

The following month, while at Corinth, Mississippi, Sherman wrote to J. A. Rawlins that if Meridian and Enterprise, Mississippi, were stripped of their garrisons, and Mississippi Confederate general Stephen D. Lee's cavalry had moved into Tennessee, Federal divisions garrisoning Natchez and the Big Black River near Vicksburg could move swiftly to Meridian, wrecking the railroad junction there. He contended that such a move would "paralyze" all Mississippi and Mobile. What Sherman did not know at the time was that Joe Johnston had reached Meridian and was working on organizing a force of Vicksburg parolees to retake their city. In the end, however, Johnston never moved on Vicksburg, and Sherman did not voice his opinion to Halleck or Grant and prepared to leave for Chattanooga.[7]

Just before leaving Mississippi, Sherman gave instructions to Major General James B. McPherson, one of his favorites, commanding the Seventeenth Army Corps at Vicksburg, to hold the place "with the tenacity of life." He suggested that McPherson look to future movements for the destruction of the railroads at Meridian or between Canton and Grenada. He believed Meridian especially was of "vital importance."[8]

While in Tennessee in mid-November, Sherman finally decided to mention to his superiors his idea for an immediate attack on Meridian. He wrote to Halleck that a force should hit Meridian and Selma. Again, Sherman thought that he could relieve some of the pressure from the Chattanooga area by launching a strong attack farther south. Halleck ignored the suggestion.[9]

After the stunning defeat of the Army of the Cumberland at Chickamauga in late September, Rosecrans had moved his army into the city of Chattanooga. Bragg pursued the Union army with his Army of Tennessee and cut its supply lines in hopes of starving it into submission. Bragg hoped to follow his victory at Chickamauga with another maneuver that would rout the Army of the Cumberland and reverse the Confederate position in Tennessee. Grant traveled to Chattanooga to break the stalemate and save the Union's position in Tennessee. With a three-day-long battle that sent the Army of Tennessee in full retreat toward Dalton, Georgia, Grant broke the siege.[10]

After re-securing eastern Tennessee for the Union, Grant believed his next step should be Atlanta. This large city served as a major rail hub between the lower Confederacy from Mississippi to Florida and the Gulf Coast states.

If Union forces could take Atlanta, the move would isolate significant Confederate territory from the government in Richmond and prevent the supplies of the southernmost farmlands from reaching the Confederate capital. Grant began to make preparations for a move from Chattanooga against Atlanta.[11]

Grant's first concern remained the Mississippi River, however. He needed the extra men, now garrisoning locations from Memphis on the Mississippi River to Yazoo City on the Yazoo River, to strengthen his main force for a march into Alabama and Georgia. In order to use these men, the Federals needed to clear Mississippi of Confederate forces so that those soldiers could not attack Grant's vulnerable lines along the Mississippi River and into western Tennessee. If a great enough concentration of Confederates could reach the larger towns along the great river, they might retake the waterway, once again disrupting Union shipping. Grant simply could not risk the hard-won prize of Vicksburg.

Just before Christmas 1863, Grant moved his headquarters to Nashville and left General George H. Thomas, commander of the Department of the Cumberland, at Chattanooga. Grant called a meeting of his main subordinates to discuss plans for the winter campaign and for taking Mobile and most of Mississippi.

Prior to leaving for a visit to his family for the holidays, Sherman received word that Grant wanted to see him. He was also to place his men along the railroad from Stevenson to Decatur, Alabama, and from Decatur up to Nashville, repairing and guarding the rail lines there. Sherman now planned to suggest to Grant his long-considered plan for striking the Meridian rail lines.[12]

Sherman, Philip Sheridan, John A. Logan, and Grenville M. Dodge, among others, met with Grant in Nashville on December 21. Grant believed that if the Federals gained control of Mobile they could effectively cut off Alabama and Mississippi from the rest of the Confederacy, freeing men for his march to Atlanta. He intended to send thirty thousand men from Chattanooga to New Orleans to attack Mobile in a combination sea and land movement. He agreed that Sherman should move from Vicksburg to Meridian, destroying the railroad as he went, and join him near Mobile. Dodge was to take two divisions, join with William Sooy Smith's cavalry in Nashville, and cut across northern Alabama into Mississippi, likewise destroying supplies and rails. Dodge's objectives also included the detection and routing of Nathan Bedford Forrest's cavalry, known as excellent hit-and-run fighters. If Grant's army could not quickly take Mobile, Grant would leave the city besieged and march into the interior of Alabama, perhaps as far as the state of Georgia. If he could not move that far, at least this grand movement would lay the groundwork for a subsequent attack on Atlanta.

Before the officers could prepare for this winter campaign, however, word came from Washington that it was out of the question. Lincoln felt uneasy about draining men from Chattanooga with Confederate James Longstreet still hovering in eastern Tennessee. Only if Grant could eliminate Longstreet, Lincoln said, could he organize his campaign against Mobile.

Grant traveled to Knoxville to assess the situation. General John G. Foster informed Grant that he was sure that he could keep Longstreet from advancing past his present position. Grant agreed with Foster but realized that this holding action meant abandoning the winter campaign plans. In addition, Grant did not believe that the benefits gained from an advance on Longstreet would offset the "hardships upon [the] men, and the disqualifying effects it would have upon them and [the] war material for a spring campaign." Union forces at Knoxville had already repulsed Longstreet's army of twenty thousand men in November, and by the time Grant visited there the Confederate army on the distant front contained only twelve thousand cold and hungry soldiers. Grant, who learned this information much later, always regretted not having driven Longstreet out of eastern Tennessee. At the time, however, he decided to look to Sherman to remove the danger of Confederate forces in Mississippi. The Meridian campaign received new attention.[13]

While in Nashville, Sherman and the other commanders accepted an invitation to dine with General Gordon Granger. Granger's mother-in-law, a staunch Southern supporter, berated Sherman for his foraging tactics. Sherman listened quietly, holding in his emotions until finally he had had too much. He sternly rebuked the angry woman: "Madame, my soldiers have to subsist even if the whole country must be starved to maintain them." If one army had to starve, he argued, it would not be "the army that is loyal." Sherman would forage from the country to sustain his army at any cost. Southern citizens were the enemy, and they had to pay the price of war. His thoughts remained firm on that.[14]

Having completed his plans, Sherman traveled home for Christmas and enjoyed time with his family. He still missed Willy, the eleven-year-old son who had died during a visit to his father in Vicksburg and Memphis in 1862.

The loss never seemed far from Sherman's mind. He spoke often of Willy in letters to his wife, the country along the Mississippi River frequently reminding the general of the young lad.

That cold late December in Lancaster, Sherman penned his feelings in a letter to his brother John. As always, but especially because of his sorrow over Willy, Sherman contemplated his position in society and in the regular army. He did not want fame and heroic status, he said, because such status came with too many dangers. If a famous person made a mistake, no matter how small, it brought immediate dishonor or unwarranted criticism. Sherman did not want to be in a position to have to worry about making little mistakes. He wanted to prosecute his war and leave any criticism (referring to his battle with the newspapers) until after the hostilities ended. Then, "the real men of war will be determined [and] the army will determine the questions." His peers alone would judge him. Those who only wished to sell newspapers certainly would not.[15]

In preparation for his expedition, Sherman kept information about it as vague as possible to reporters. He carried harsh feelings toward the press for its rabid attack on his actions during the first two years of the war. For his new form of warfare to work, Sherman needed secrecy; it would be disastrous if the Confederacy learned of his plans for Mississippi from a newspaper article. Furthermore, Sherman wanted freedom from press condemnation. Exercising his power to do so, Sherman banned newspaper reporters from his expedition. He made an exception for the *New York Herald*'s De B. Randolph Keim, whom Sherman liked. He listed him as one of McPherson's aides.[16]

As the new year dawned, Sherman prepared to return to Tennessee and then Mississippi to complete preparations for his Meridian expedition. He learned that Forrest, whom the Union cavalry had pursued since October, was presently in northern Mississippi. Stephen A. Hurlbut, at Memphis, reported that his cavalry had worn itself out chasing after Forrest and partisan fighters. There were also, at present, two divisions of regular Confederate infantry in Mississippi—William W. Loring's division at Canton with around six thousand men and Samuel G. French's division in Meridian of unknown number. Hurlbut's news seemed to confirm Sherman's suspicions about Confederate intentions to retake the Mississippi River. Furthermore, the report induced him to plan the addition of more men to the ragged Federal cavalry forces at Memphis before he used them for his trip through Mississippi.[17]

Sherman reached Memphis on January 10, 1864, and checked into the Gayoso House, the city's leading hotel. It had taken him four days to reach the Tennessee city from Cairo because heavy ice clogged the river, forcing the steamboat to travel carefully. Sherman met with Hurlbut and explained that he intended to make an army of twenty thousand men from Hurlbut's garrisoning forces at Memphis and McPherson's at Vicksburg.[18]

Hurlbut, the only Northern general born in South Carolina, had journeyed to Illinois as a young man and become involved in politics. He liked bantering with his friends in the confines of a warm office while sipping on strong spirits, but he did not care for commanding troops in the field, especially during the cold winter months. He had been given the rank of brigadier general because of his status as a leading Republican politician and statesman. The adopted Illinoisan was quite content to remain a garrison commander in Memphis for the duration of the war and allow his political clout, not battlefield ability, to advance his career. Sherman had heard rumors of Hurlbut's drunkenness and corruption, but he found no evidence to substantiate the allegations. Neither he nor Grant held Hurlbut in very high esteem as a military commander, however, and Sherman did not need any mistakes in Mississippi from the political general. Therefore, Sherman would make a special effort to travel throughout the Meridian expedition with Hurlbut's corps, directing it as if it were his own.[19]

Sherman proposed leaving Vicksburg in February to march to Meridian for the purpose of destroying the railroad there. He instructed Hurlbut to organize one cavalry and two infantry divisions of five thousand men each from the Sixteenth Army Corps. The cavalry division should join William Sooy Smith's cavalry, which had recently arrived at Memphis. Sherman understood that with the reduction of its garrison by fifteen thousand men, the important river commerce center would stand weakly defended. As a result, he ordered garrisons all along the Mississippi River north of Vicksburg reduced and the men sent to the areas in and around Memphis. He also ordered the abandonment of Corinth and Fort Pillow. Troops there were to return to Memphis with all the public property they could transport. Sherman told Hurlbut that he was headed to Vicksburg and ordered the completion of all the preparations within ten days. He also wrote McPherson and informed him that he would visit his command in a few days.[20]

Sherman particularly requested General A. J. Smith (no relation to William Sooy Smith, the cavalry commander), whose infantry garrisoned Columbus,

Kentucky, to join the mission. Smith, a Pennsylvanian and West Point graduate, had distinguished himself as Halleck's cavalry chief in 1862. He had received the rank of brigadier general of volunteers in March 1862 and had commanded a division of infantry under Sherman at Chickasaw Bayou. Known for his fighting spirit, Smith had impressed Sherman. Now, the commander wanted him to join the march to Meridian.[21]

Sherman told A. J. Smith that only three wagons per regiment would be allowed on the trip and that baggage had to be kept minimal. "[Bring] all stockings and army shoes . . . mule shoes and nails [and] Spencer rifle ammunition" available, he ordered, and report on the condition of the men's clothing items, such as "drawers, shirts, stockings, and shoes." Sherman intended to move with great celerity on the march from Vicksburg to Meridian. The men's clothing and equipage had to be in good condition at the start of the march because Sherman would maintain no supply lines. For more than a month the men would have only what they carried with them in their haversacks or what the regimental wagons could procure from the country.[22]

Even though he had long argued for an attack on the Meridian railroads, and Grant had offered proposals for the taking of Mobile, Sherman had not definitively laid out his plans. He had only mentioned that he wished to destroy the railroads at Meridian so that the guerrillas could not receive supplies from the rest of the Confederacy. He hoped to stop any bushwhacking along the Mississippi River. He had dealt with isolated incidents of irregular attacks, but because of what Hurlbut had told him about Loring and French, he worried now that a larger enemy force might lurk in the state. The destruction of the Meridian railroads, along with those in Jackson, could effectively retard any large Confederate infantry force from operating in the Magnolia State and thereby eliminate any significant threat to the Union's hold on the Mississippi River.

It was not until January that Sherman, for the first time, outlined his exact intentions. He planned to gather as many infantrymen and artillerists as the region could spare and move from "Vicksburg direct on Demopolis or Selma" while a significant cavalry force moved from Memphis until it reached the Mobile and Ohio Railroad. The cavalry would travel down the railroad to Meridian, where it would meet with Sherman's main force. This action, he explained, would "force the enemy to let go of their hold on Dalton or endanger the loss of Selma, and perhaps Mobile." He and Grant agreed that Union forces in Chattanooga should feint toward Confederate-occupied Dalton or at Longstreet in Tennessee to hold Confederate forces there. Many of the men, under the command of Generals Thomas and Dodge, had reached veteran status and had taken advantage of their reenlistment furloughs, reducing the commands' numbers. Grant believed that, because of these fewer numbers and with Longstreet to their front, he could do little with the troops there other than order a feint.[23]

Grant informed Halleck of Sherman's intended move in Mississippi on January 15. Knowing that Halleck wished an action to the west of the Mississippi River, he explained that Sherman's twenty-thousand-man force was larger than any that could proceed west of the river, and that the Red River, at that time of the year, was too low to navigate. Because of these conditions, Grant had decided to "direct Sherman to move out to Meridian . . . and destroy the roads east and south of there so effectually that the enemy will not attempt to rebuild them during the rebellion." Grant expected Sherman to return after he completed the work in and around Meridian "unless the opportunity of going to Mobile with the force he has appears perfectly plain." Grant had created grand plans for taking Mobile on two earlier occasions, and now, it seemed, the best opportunity for capturing the city might present itself through Sherman's accomplishments in Mississippi. Grant reiterated to Halleck his earlier plan that Mobile could serve as one of two launching points, along with Tennessee, for his spring campaign toward "Atlanta and Montgomery." Grant believed that Sherman's success might open the door to the entire lower Confederacy east of the Mississippi state line.[24]

Sherman clearly never intended to attack Mobile. He agreed with Grant that the port city was important, but he did not consider such a move possible in February 1864. He later wrote, however, that "if [he] had ten more regiments, [he] would be tempted to try Mobile, but as it is," he would only attempt to take Meridian and Demopolis and possibly Selma.[25]

While at Vicksburg for a meeting with McPherson, Sherman wrote to Nathaniel Banks, commander of the Department of the Gulf, to explain his plans. He informed Banks that the Meridian movement would present the illusion that its intended object was the taking of Mobile. He requested that Banks feint at Pascagoula, Mississippi, while Admiral David D. Porter send gunboats to the area around Mobile to keep up "the delusion and prevent the enemy drawing from Mobile a force to strengthen the points aimed at by me." If Banks could keep up the ruse for a week and allow Sherman to wreck Meridian's railroads, Mobile would lose communications with the "interior save by the Alabama River, and would to that extent be weakened," he argued. Sherman also promised to send, no later than early March, available troops to Banks for his Red River campaign. He would later reiterate his pledge to send troops for the westward movement to Frederick Steele, commander of the Department of Arkansas.[26]

Sherman's instructions to the young and energetic McPherson mirrored those he had given to Hurlbut in Memphis. He ordered McPherson to gather two mixed divisions of ten thousand men, with infantry, artillery, and cavalry out of the Seventeenth Corps' twenty-one thousand, to combine with Hurlbut's two divisions coming down the river from Memphis. McPherson was to provide pontoons and materials for moving both commands across the Big Black River and assemble enough equipment and rations for his two divisions' march. Sherman wanted McPherson to make sure that his artillery contained "at least two 20-pounder Parrotts, or 3-inch Rodman Guns." He wanted just enough artillery along, but not so much as to encumber the army's swift movement across the state. As it developed, McPherson's cavalry would serve as the only Union horsemen in Sherman's immediate vicinity for the entire expedition.[27]

Sherman needed experienced cavalry to protect his infantry from enemy horsemen. He understood the danger that "Mounted Devils" and "Wandering Arabs" presented. As it turned out, the brigade of cavalry he took along in his main column conducted most of the skirmishing on the expedition.[28]

Colonel Edward F. Winslow was the commander of McPherson's cavalry brigade. A businessman from Maine, Winslow had served until April 1863 in Arkansas and Missouri, commanding cavalry brigades in both the Fifteenth and Seventeenth corps, Army of the Tennessee. Wounded at Mechanicsville during the Vicksburg campaign, he had recovered in time for the Canton expedition later that year. Fighting in the Western theater for the first three years of the war had hardened Winslow to fighting Confederate horsemen. He would need that experience as the leader of Sherman's cavalry escort into Mississippi.[29]

Another section of McPherson's army, the Pioneer Corps, would also provide important service. McPherson sent Chief Engineer Andrew Hickenlooper to construct a bridge across the Big Black River. Hickenlooper had been so proficient in his work during the Vicksburg campaign that he had earned an award for his labor there. One of his most significant feats had been building a bridge across the Big Black River out of cotton bales, so he was no stranger to the area and to the challenges of the state's streams, swamps, and rivers. For the Meridian campaign he created a map detailing the country from Vicksburg to the Tombigbee River which Sherman routinely used to deploy and guide his troops movements. Beyond this, the Pioneer Corps would construct miles of corduroyed roads, repair bridges, destroy rails, and advise the command about terrain features.[30]

The weather had warmed since late December, and the large ice flows in the Mississippi had been reduced to tiny chunks. As Sherman steamed up the mighty river on his return from Vicksburg to Memphis, he fought the shuddering boat to pen a legible letter home to his wife. The success of the operation, he explained, would come from his ability to keep his objective secret from the enemy, "otherwise, [we] may be checkmated." However, he insisted, "we must in war risk a good deal," and he could "do more on the Mississippi than any general officer in the service except Grant." It was up to him to end the Confederate presence in Mississippi, and he was anxious to begin the process.[31]

Before he reached Memphis, Sherman took the time to write one more letter to his brother. He described his impending expedition and reiterated his thoughts about fame and how he hated celebrity status and the treatment that came with it. Whether he cared for the attention or not, Sherman considered himself a fairly successful general, and he used his confidence as a shield. In his view, no small setback would harm his position, so he could afford to take a calculated risk in the campaign. In a more philosophical strain, Sherman explained that he thought people had the "natural right to a separate Government provided they had the power to enforce it." The South had asserted that right, and now it had to face the test of war to sustain its right to maintain its independence. Furthermore, Sherman argued, "during this test Laws are silent, argument fruitless and arms can alone decide." Until the war ended, "all other questions should be waived." "We may do anything that weakens them and strengthens us," he concluded. Sherman's Meridian expedition would serve to achieve both goals, weakening the Confederacy by taking supplies and destroying infrastructure, and strengthening the Union's position by removing the Confederate threat from the Mississippi River and clearing any significant enemy forces from the river to the Alabama line.[32]

On January 17, in response to Grant's letter explaining Sherman's proposed Mississippi movement, Halleck quizzed Grant about Sherman's intentions. "Does he fully understand your plans," Halleck questioned, "and is that part of your proposed winter campaign?" Halleck was still concerned about Longstreet's position in Tennessee, and he also wanted all spare troops sent to Banks for his Red River campaign in Louisiana.[33] Halleck had heard rumors of a Confederate buildup, and he worried about what the enemy planned. Grant ignored Halleck's inquiries. He had few choices for action that winter. He had thousands of men performing garrison duty across the Western theater. Furloughs had reduced his effective numbers to a dangerous low. His best chance for taking Mobile that winter was with Sherman, and the subjugation of Mississippi would contribute to his plans to take the important Southern city, even if Sherman did not capture it that winter. Furthermore, he believed in Sherman, and he did not care for Banks. Sherman's movement promised more success than any that Banks led.[34]

Sherman reached Memphis on January 21 and went about his preparations for moving Hurlbut's Sixteenth Corps down the river to Vicksburg. He contacted Admiral Porter and requested all the light-draft boats the admiral could spare to transport his troops south. Sherman also wanted to ensure that Sooy Smith had completed arrangements for his move out of Memphis to his departure point at Collierville, Tennessee. He wanted Smith to leave Collierville on February 1 and meet him at Meridian on February 10. He ordered him to destroy public property and supplies along with the rails of the Mobile and Ohio Railroad from Okolona, Mississippi, south to Columbus.[35]

Sooy Smith had brought twenty-five hundred cavalrymen with him to Memphis from Chattanooga. Sherman intended to take part of Hurlbut's seventy-five hundred horse soldiers, combine them with Sooy Smith's force, and create a unit of around seven thousand riders. The other three thousand would remain around Memphis and assist in the protection of the city. With this large a command, Sherman believed that Sooy Smith would outnumber Forrest almost two to one.[36]

Although Sherman respected Forrest's ability, he loathed the damage that the Confederate had perpetrated on the Union supply and communication lines. Forrest and Earl Van Dorn had proven especially troublesome when they had destroyed Grant's supplies at the Holly Springs station during the Vicksburg campaign. Sherman wanted Sooy Smith to obliterate Forrest's command on the way to Meridian if the opportunity presented itself. If Forrest allowed the Union cavalry force to travel unmolested to Meridian and made a run at Memphis, Sherman had completed arrangements for Ralph P. Buckland to assume command of the garrison (thirty-two hundred men) and some organized citizens to protect the city from such an attack. Buckland had commanded a brigade under Sherman at Shiloh and Vicksburg, and Sherman knew that he could trust him to guard Memphis adequately.[37]

On January 27, Sherman issued final orders. Hurlbut was to move the Sixteenth Corps down the upper Jackson road to the Big Black River and ready a bridge for crossing at Messinger's to the east. McPherson was to take the Seventeenth Corps to the Big Black railroad bridge and prepare to move east. Sherman instructed his army not to carry any "tents or luggage" except what they could carry on their backs or horses. The wagons of each regiment would carry only food and ammunition. Sherman believed that a supply of ten days' meat rations and thirty days' rations of salt, coffee, and sugar, with a few cattle driven along behind the army, would suffice for the thirty-day journey. He cut the number of artillery pieces to half of the usual and ordered the guns double-teamed with two hundred rounds per gun allowed. Sherman reminded his officers that he expected the expedition to move quickly and that they should leave behind anything that proved detrimental to swift travel.[38]

As Hurlbut's corps traveled down the Mississippi toward Vicksburg, many remarked about the pleasant weather. Ice had filled the river just a few weeks before, but now green fields and groves of budding peach trees lined the shores. "The country had the appearance of June in the north," one New Yorker commented, "while the weather was so warm many of the men were bathing." The scene along the riverbanks was silent and eerie—plantations deserted, fences gone, houses burned, with a multitude of naked chimneys along the water. The river had seen much conflict, and now the troops were taking the battle deep into the interior.[39]

While traveling down the Mississippi for the second time in a week, Sherman began thinking about the gamble he was about to undertake. "Our armies are at the lowest point, and so many are going home as reenlisted veterans," he remarked, "I shall have a less force than should attempt it." He had canceled all furloughs until after the end of his Mississippi expedition, but many of the officers had allowed their soldiers to leave for home before they received his orders. Sherman insisted that he faced two main hazards. First, if the enemy recognized his plans, they could reinforce Meridian. Second, poor roads could prevent his army from moving quickly enough to succeed. He wondered if he had enough men to deal with the Confederate force now in Mississippi, because if Richmond sent additional troops his army might be routed before he could safely withdraw.[40]

Grant reminded Sherman that although he left any movement past Meridian to his discretion, Sherman was neither to risk the loss of his army nor weaken it so much that it could not participate in the upcoming spring campaigns.[41] Sherman had made preparations to thwart any Confederate attack on towns along the Mississippi, but he had drastically stripped the largest towns of their garrisons. If the Confederates understood the situation and could act upon it—in Memphis, for example—they might strike at a weakened point on the great river. Sherman ran a great risk; now, as the expedition's starting point neared, he had begun to more deeply appreciate the hazards.[42]

Meanwhile, on January 15, Grant ordered Thomas, with ten thousand men of the Army of the Cumberland, to concentrate against Dalton. He had learned that Johnston at Dalton had sent two divisions to Mobile and two divisions to Longstreet. Grant knew that if he could defeat Johnston at Dalton, Longstreet could not stay in eastern Tennessee, and Grant sorely wanted Longstreet out of that area before the spring campaigns commenced. He also sent General John M. Schofield, who now commanded the Army of the Ohio, with more troops to eastern Tennessee to occupy Longstreet further.[43]

Four days later, Grant sent word to Thomas at Chattanooga about Sherman's intended route. He instructed Thomas to "keep up appearance of preparation of an advance from Chattanooga" to hold Confederate forces in his front. Logan would send whatever force he could forward from Bellefonte, Tennessee, toward Rome, Georgia. If the Confederates believed that the Union was preparing to advance from Tennessee eastward, they would either reinforce their troops there or at least not send them to strengthen Sherman's opposition in Mississippi.[44]

The day before he reached Vicksburg, Sherman sent a letter to Halleck explaining his preparations for the expedition and what he intended to accomplish. While he would send the cavalry from Collierville and lead the infantry from Vicksburg, Sherman intended to send Colonel James H. Coates with the Eleventh Illinois and the Eighth Louisiana Infantry force, along with gunboats under Lieutenant Commander E. K. Owen, up the Yazoo River as a "diversion to threaten Grenada." He wanted to confuse and hold the reported enemy force in that region as long as possible before they discovered his departure from Vicksburg. Sherman promised that after his Mississippi expedition he would send troops to aid Banks, Steele, and Porter in their attack on Shreveport and Texas during the Red River campaign.[45]

Sherman informed Coates and Owen that after they had encountered the enemy at Yazoo City or Sartartia, they were to go up the Yazoo River as far as Greenwood and destroy every boat and skiff available to the enemy. The group should also visit all navigable tributaries of the Yazoo and collect all the Confederate cotton they could find and send it via transports to Memphis for sale. The proceeds would go to loyal steamboat owners who had suffered losses from guerrilla attacks. He reminded his officers that Southern planters would either "be active friends or enemies" and that those who chose the latter must "feel that war may reach their doors." He insisted that Coates and Owen not burden themselves with firewood or provisions but rather secure these items in the countryside. "The enemy must not only pay for damages inflicted on our commerce," he argued, "but for the expenses incurred in the suppression."[46]

By 1864 the Federal military's attitude regarding noncombatants had passed through several phases. Mark Grimsley, in *The Hard Hand of War,* contends that Union military policy toward Southern civilians had gone through two stages before 1864: it was "conciliatory" from April 1861 to June 1862 and was then "pragmatic" from the summer of 1862 to January 1864. Sherman's Meridian expedition led the Federal military into its final change in policy, to "hard war," which lasted until the Confederate surrender. Sherman's attitude toward waging destructive war, therefore, mirrored that of the entire Union military hierarchy.

A number of factors influenced the "conciliatory" policy: most Northerners believed that making war on Southern civilians would be counterproductive; international law formed an outline for the proper treatment of civilians; and historically, the ill treatment of enemy civilians had backfired. The success of the conciliatory policy depended on three key points: the Northern soldiers had to leave civilians alone; the civilians had to leave the troops alone; and the South had to come back toward the Union. Such a policy was not realistic. The large scale of the hostile area, the South's continued stubborn resistance, and the Northern government's inability to enforce rigid rules created a need for new policies.

Moreover, the continuous Southern bushwhacking and the difficulty of supplying troops in the Western theater forced the Federals to alter their philosophy to a "pragmatic" approach. This program served to support the unionists, punish the pro-secessionists, and ensure that the neutrals remained inactive. It manifested itself in both the Confiscation Acts and Union commander John Pope's orders to "live off the land." As this new program spread to the Eastern theater, the promulgation of the Emancipation Proclamation dealt a deathblow to the conciliation policy because it symbolized that "the North would crush the rebellion by any means necessary."[47]

With the promotion of Grant and Sherman, the Federal policy changed again. The Union military command structure had adhered to two different strategies to end the war up until 1864, and both of these had failed. One was the idea that Union victory would come from the total destruction of the Confederate army. This strategy did not work, because both military powers exhausted themselves in their attempt to eradicate each other. Thus, the victor could never follow up his success because he was as weak from any battle as was his enemy. Territorial acquisition was the other Federal strategy, but the Confederacy was too large and the Union army was not large enough to garrison simultaneously all of the captured land and remain on the offensive. By 1864 Grant and Sherman had come to the realization that the best way to defeat the enemy was through a "strategy of exhaustion."[48]

They believed that the North needed to disrupt communications, live upon the stores of the enemy, and block the supply lines in the South. Hence the quickest way to victory was to take away the Confederacy's ability to wage war, which depended upon Southern civilians. These ideas further embodied themselves with the adoption of General Order 100, the authorization of the destruction of public and private property while simultaneously emphasizing humanity. Using careful planning, utmost efficiency, and unmatched discretion, Sherman's Meridian campaign exemplified the proficient use of the "hard war" policy that helped the North to win the war and shape warfare thereafter.[49]

Both Grimsley and historians Herman Hattaway and Archer Jones argue that Grant and Sherman decided in late 1863 that the best way to implement the strategy of exhaustion was through the use of large raids. Hattaway and Jones point to Grant's plan to take Mobile deep behind Confederate lines as evidence that Grant had changed his strategy in late 1863. Although he did change to a "strategy of raids" in early 1864, he did it because of the success of Sherman's Meridian expedition. Grant's plan to take Mobile still included garrisoning troops to remain there to protect the port city from Confederate counterattacks. Supplies would come from the sea, which the Union controlled. Grant did not intend to hold Mobile temporarily; he hoped to garrison it and use it as a base for spring operations. He had told Halleck in January 1864 that Mobile could serve as one of two launching points, along with Tennessee, for his spring campaign toward Atlanta and Montgomery. Because Grant's plan called for a permanent garrisoning force, the plan to move on Mobile cannot be considered a raid.[50]

Sherman's march to Meridian was a raid, although he disliked having it called that. He never intended to garrison Meridian or the interior of Mississippi; he simply wanted to destroy the railroads and return to Vicksburg. Since Sherman's expedition was temporary, he did not have to depend exclusively on supply or communication lines. His army could take supplies and foodstuffs from the Southern populace, thus serving two purposes: supplying the army and removing the goods from Confederate use. The Union army did not have to leave behind thousands of garrisoning troops, because once the mission had been accomplished, Sherman's army would return to Vicksburg.[51]

Furthermore, Confederate troops in northern Georgia could not start their operation to regain lost ground in Tennessee while Sherman was in Mississippi. This was another benefit of the "strategy of raids" that Hattaway and Jones outline. Since Confederate leaders would remain on the defensive because of a Federal raid, they would be reluctant to attempt any offensive maneuvers while the raid continued.[52]

Sherman had "hard war," not conventional war, in mind when he headed into Mississippi. He knew that death was a part of war, but he also wanted to keep bloodshed to a minimum. There was another way to wage war and keep casualties low while simultaneously defeating the Confederacy. That was to strike hard at the enemy's resources, rendering them useless to that enemy. If the war visited the Southern people at their doorstep, they would be less enthusiastic about continuing the fight. Sherman would strike fear into the citizens and leave them on the verge of starvation. He could spare their lives and the lives of their soldiers while the United States won the war. Southern people, whether from fear of the Union army or the lack of goods, would induce their government to end the war.

Although he condoned this new type of warfare, Sherman did not send his army to destroy all the goods in the state of Mississippi indiscriminately.

In August 1863, after the second capture of Jackson, he arrested and court-martialed three soldiers for burning a cotton gin without orders. "I should have executed [them] on the spot," he wrote angrily to John Rawlins. "The amount of burning, stealing, and plundering done by our army makes me ashamed of it. I would quit the service if I could, because I fear that we are drifting to the worst sort of vandalism. The burning of this building in no way aided our military plans."[53]

This final sentence demonstrates clearly Sherman's attitude toward prosecuting hard war during the Meridian expedition. He supported the destruction of any building, equipment, or supplies of use to the Confederacy, but he would not tolerate activity that "in no way aided" the Federal military plans to injure the Confederacy. Foodstuffs from civilian pantries and stores were needed to feed his hungry army, so Sherman allowed the entering of residences and private property to secure rations for the soldiers' use. He did not excuse, however, the taking of nonmilitary items such as jewelry, clothing, and silverware. He considered it stealing, and on several occasions he issued orders against it. With such a large number of Union soldiers scattered in all directions across the Mississippi countryside, however, it was difficult to police their individual actions. Besides, such chaos only convinced Confederates even more to stop the war, so Sherman was not completely opposed to it.

By the first of February, Sherman had completed all necessary preparations for his campaign. The plan called for the use of Union forces from throughout the Western theater. He had gathered twenty thousand infantry, sixty pieces of artillery, and a small force of cavalry. His southern (right) wing contained portions of the Seventeenth Army Corps under the command of James B. McPherson. These troops included Mortimer D. Leggett's Third Division, Marcellus M. Crocker's Fourth Division, Alexander Chambers with the Third Brigade from the First Division, and a small cavalry brigade under Edward F. Winslow. Winslow would command his force as a corps and report directly to Sherman. The Sixteenth Army Corps would start as the north (left) wing under the command of Stephen A. Hurlbut. It contained A. J. Smith's Third Division and James C. Veatch's Fourth Division. Sherman ordered the First Division of the Sixteenth Corps under James M. Tuttle to remain in Vicksburg as a city garrison. Some of Tuttle's men later cooperated with Smith as he left Collierville, but they returned to camp by February 15. The two columns were to depart from Vicksburg and travel on either side of the railroad until they reached the far side of the capital city of Jackson. There they would merge into a single column, continuing on to Meridian to destroy the rail yards there.[54]

Sooy Smith was to leave simultaneously from Collierville on February 1 and move across to Meridian through Pontotoc, Okolona, and Columbus, Mississippi, to rendezvous with Sherman on February 10. The two merged forces would move to defeat the Confederate army under Lieutenant General Leonidas (Bishop) Polk, stationed at Meridian, and then continue into Alabama. Coates and Owen would move up the Yazoo River, creating a diversion while Sherman's main column left Vicksburg. Nathaniel Banks and David D. Porter would send gunboats and infantry to Pascagoula and Mobile, fueling the rumor that the Union's main objective was to take the Alabama port city. Thomas would strike at Dalton, Logan would strike at Rome, and Schofield would feint into eastern Tennessee, creating confusion and keeping the Confederate forces in those areas from strengthening their brethren further south.

All these movements, Sherman believed, would baffle the Confederate forces in Mississippi, Alabama, and Georgia and increase his chances of success. If he could cross 150 miles of enemy country and demolish a valuable enemy supply base, Sherman could essentially remove Mississippi from the war. Furthermore, he would complete the task without a vulnerable supply line and without having to fight a substantial number of enemy troops. He would feed his army from the hostile territory while simultaneously consuming and destroying valuable enemy provisions, making it impossible for any significant Confederate force to operate there. As Sherman set out on February 2, he had an ambitious goal to accomplish.

It looked as if Sherman had perfectly timed his march of destruction across Mississippi. Just the previous year, a drought in the middle and lower sections of the state had ruined the corn and wheat crops, but relief had come in the spring of 1863 with a bountiful wheat crop; the harvest of corn had been so large that prices had dropped across the state. Mississippi corncribs and barns, from Jackson to Meridian, now stood full, and the railroad warehouses overflowed with Confederate supplies. Sherman's army marched in the face of the largest Mississippi harvest during the war.[55]

3 / "We Whipped Him Handsomely"

By the beginning of 1864, the Confederacy's early hopes for a quick victory had vanished. With the loss at Gettysburg in the East and crushing Federal victories at Vicksburg, Port Hudson, and Chattanooga in the West, Southern civilians began to reexamine their attitudes toward the war. Confederate casualty reports listed their fathers, sons, and brothers. The scarcity of provisions and enormously inflated food prices resulting from the Confederacy's prosecution of the war hit civilians hard at the kitchen table. The 1861 concept of a tranquil independence for the Southern states was not the reality of 1864 for its people. A "nudge" from William T. Sherman might very well push Southern civilians to give up their cause and stop providing support for their army. Southerners would worry more about protecting and feeding their families and less about supplying the army.[1]

As Sherman had hoped to leave Vicksburg by February 1, he worked hard to coordinate all the troops, equipment, and horses coming into the city. If things went as planned, he would take Jackson before the Confederates even realized he had left Vicksburg. With a little luck, he could be halfway across the state before General Leonidas Polk could maneuver his Mississippi army into position to intercept him. The first few days of his campaign would indeed set the tone for Sherman's experiences in Mississippi, with the Union army moving swiftly and strongly forward, meeting minimal resistance.

The Confederates would remain confused throughout the campaign and would continue to make poor decisions. Polk, new to his command in Mississippi, would miss an opportunity to concentrate his forces near Jackson. Despite information to the contrary, he would continue to believe that Sherman was headed to Mobile, to which Polk would mistakenly maneuver his men. Just when his army needed his leadership most, Polk would even travel to Mobile and leave William W. Loring in charge of the Mississippi army. There were no reinforcements available to Polk from any source other than Mobile, so he lost valuable time before gathering troops from the garrison there.

In December 1862, Confederate President Jefferson Davis relieved Joseph E. Johnston from the command of the Army of Mississippi and sent him to Dalton, Georgia, to assume control of the Army of Tennessee, a force of about thirty-six thousand effective troops. Johnston was in charge of the Department of the West during the Vicksburg campaign. When the Federal pressure on Vicksburg increased in the winter of 1862, a frustrated President Davis and Secretary of War James A. Seddon urged Johnston to take over John C. Pemberton's command there. Instead of traveling to Vicksburg, however, Johnston, blocked by James McPherson's corps, remained at Jackson with his Army of Relief and begged Pemberton to evacuate Vicksburg to avoid a siege. When the "Gibraltar of the West" fell, many Southerners, including President Davis, blamed the loss on Johnston. When Braxton Bragg failed to follow up the Confederate victory at Chickamauga, the Confederate high command searched for a general to replace him as head of the Army of Tennessee, which had now fallen back to Dalton after its loss at Chattanooga. Johnston wanted the position, and his advocates pressured the president to appoint him to the post. When Davis decided finally to send Johnston to Dalton, he ordered him to regain the territory that the Confederacy had lost in Tennessee. The Army of Tennessee, in its new commander's opinion, did not have enough men to accomplish the order, so Johnston's army wintered at Dalton while Johnston begged Richmond for reinforcements.[2]

Leonidas Polk, an Episcopal bishop and good friend of the president, took command of Johnston's army in Mississippi, renamed the Army of Mississippi. He was a North Carolinian and son of a war hero of the American Revolution. Polk graduated from West Point in 1827, where he was the first cadet to proclaim his faith and be baptized there. After graduation he resigned from the military and studied at the Virginia Theological Seminary, gaining ordination as an Episcopal priest in 1831. In 1841 he had become bishop of Louisiana and lived briefly in the state. By 1854 he had moved to a twenty-seven-hundred-acre plantation in Bolivar County, Mississippi, where he farmed and worked on the creation of the University of the South, an Episcopal-affiliated institution in Tennessee. When the war broke out, Polk contacted Davis, expressing concern about the safety of the Mississippi River Valley. Davis invited Polk to Richmond for a visit, during which time the bishop accepted Davis's invitation to serve as a major general in the Confederate army. Polk then commanded troops at Belmont, Perryville, Stones River, and Chickamauga, never distinguishing himself on the battlefield. He regularly blamed his mistakes on subordinates, and many of his peers believed he was ineffective as a battlefield commander. Because of Polk's personal problems with Bragg during the battles at Stones River and Chickamauga, Davis had decided to transfer Polk to Mississippi.[3]

Polk established his headquarters at Meridian that winter and labeled his command the Department of the Southwest. His army consisted of two divisions of infantry under William Wing Loring at Canton and Samuel G. French at Brandon and a cavalry corps under Stephen D. Lee, scattered from Jackson to the Yazoo River. Nathan Bedford Forrest's cavalry, although under Polk's command, roamed northern Mississippi.[4]

Before the command change, Johnston had ordered Polk to halt Federal navigation along the Mississippi River. In taking command, therefore, Polk set about repairing the Union-caused damage to the railroad between Meridian and Jackson and visiting his department to ascertain the feasibility of fulfilling his instructions. On December 24 he met with French and the two rode together to the Meridian depot, with Polk planning to go to Enterprise to check the rail lines. He told French to go to Jackson to repair the rails and rebuild the bridges there. French set about completing the work despite the intense winter cold.[5]

French's division traveled back to Meridian during the first week of January, but it was delayed for two days because of the shortage of railroad engines. French repaired most of the rail lines between Jackson and Meridian, but the lack of engines retarded the Confederate infantry movements, a problem that would continue to plague Polk from this point on.[6]

Polk believed his force was too small to face any sizable Union army and decided, therefore, to await further orders from Johnston and Davis before he did anything. When he learned that Bragg was returning four brigades that Johnston had sent him before the battle at Missionary Ridge, the bishop asked Davis to send the brigades to the Department of the Southwest. He insisted that Grant would not move against Johnston until the spring. "Johnston will be unemployed," Polk argued, and "in that case [he can] well spare all four." He worried that the enemy might try to move on Mobile, and he knew he needed more men to garrison that port city. As it was now, Mobile contained only about ten thousand troops. After a flurry of letters between Dalton and Richmond, Davis compelled Johnston to send the brigades to Polk. Polk, in turn, sent two brigades to Dabney H. Maury in Mobile, both men nervous about Federal gunboats moving in for an attack on the city.[7]

Johnston had informed Davis that taking the offensive without sufficient reinforcements would be impossible and that he had "neither subsistence nor field transportation enough" to march. Longstreet in Tennessee had only twelve thousand men, and Johnston, with only thirty-six thousand himself, needed an additional ten thousand. The terrain in middle and eastern Tennessee, he complained, was too rough and mountainous for his army to cross. Johnston had suggested that the best chance for retaking Chattanooga was through northern Mississippi, but even that action required reinforcements. Johnston concluded that the best way to reclaim Tennessee was to "beat the enemy when he advances, and then move forward," taking the offensive. But without more men, Johnston said, he could not and would not move.[8]

Polk believed that the enemy was preparing to advance in force soon, so he canceled all furloughs and sent the wounded and sick officers to the Officer's Hospital at Lauderdale, Mississippi. He also decided to send his army to fortify defenses at key locations in the state while he traveled to Mobile to inspect matters there. He ordered Loring to build works just north of Canton to protect the railroad there and to connect them with the works in Jackson, which French was rebuilding or constructing for the first time.[9]

Loring, a Floridian, had served in the regular army during the Mexican War, where he had participated in all of the major engagements, losing an arm in the conflict. He had resigned his U.S. Army commission in May 1861 at the rank of colonel and joined the Confederacy as a brigadier general. After a lackluster showing as a commander during the first three years of the Civil War, he had come under Polk's command in Mississippi as a division commander at the rank of major general.[10]

French, a graduate of West Point and a native of New Jersey, was also a Mexican War veteran. He had resigned from his position in the Quartermaster Department in 1856 to run his wife's plantation near Vicksburg and served in the state militia as chief of ordinance. He had accepted a commission as major of artillery in the Confederate army after hostilities broke out in 1861, and for the first three years of the war he served in the East. In the summer of 1863 the Confederate War Department sent him back to Mississippi with Johnston to combat the Federal assault on Vicksburg, thinking that his knowledge of the location might lend assistance. French remained in Mississippi after the fall of Vicksburg and came under Polk's command when the bishop took control of the Confederate army there. Both French and Loring had witnessed Johnston's retreat at Jackson in front of Sherman's advancing army in the summer of 1863. Each wondered if Polk would do the same thing.[11]

By the time Polk took command of the Army of Mississippi, Loring's and French's divisions were greatly reduced in number. When Johnston commanded the army at Jackson during the Vicksburg campaign, Loring's division contained seven infantry brigades, but in February 1864 it contained only three—Winfield Featherston's, John Adams's, and Abraham Buford's. French's division had consisted of three brigades, and now it contained only two—Matthew D. Ector's and Francis M Cockrell's. Most of the absent brigades had joined the Army of Tennessee to reinforce Bragg at Chattanooga. Unfortunately for the Confederacy, they did not reach the battlefield in time and joined the retreating Army of Tennessee as it moved to Dalton.[12]

As part of the Army of Relief, Polk's men had garrisoned Jackson, waiting for the order from Johnston to march westward and save Pemberton's besieged army from defeat. Instead, they remained in the capital as Vicksburg fell. When Sherman moved to Jackson for the second time that summer, Johnston's army retreated from the city and left it to the Union army. Downtrodden and angry about the decision, the Confederate soldiers again watched another Mississippi city fall to the enemy. When news came that Sherman was marching into the Magnolia State again in February 1864, the Confederate soldiers may have believed that God had granted them another opportunity to avenge the capture of their land and looked forward to meeting the Union army in battle.

While the Confederates constructed earthworks, the western side of the Big Black River was abuzz with Federal activity. Upon returning from Mobile, Polk found waiting for him scouting reports that the enemy from Memphis and points further north had begun concentrating at Vicksburg. Polk wired Davis on January 26 that the enemy intended to "move probably from Vicksburg, Yazoo City, and perhaps Natchez at the same time." Confederate troops, therefore, had to prepare quickly.[13]

Stephen D. Lee, informed of the buildup, sent cavalry units to Benton to guard the Yazoo River and the Mississippi Central Railroad, to Brownsville to observe the Big Black River crossing east of Vicksburg, and to Rodney, a tiny settlement of less than three hundred citizens, near Natchez. Forrest, meanwhile, sent scouts across northwestern Mississippi to keep watch for any Federal movements out of Memphis. When the Confederate horsemen reached the Big Black River, they discovered the air filled with the hammering and chopping of Andrew Hickenlooper's bridge construction crew.[14]

At Canton, Loring suggested to Lee that "in the event of Mobile not being threatened" he should send all "forces to Jackson and Brandon." Brandon, a little town of about seven hundred people just east of the capital down the Southern Railroad, was, as one Federal soldier described, "a pretty little town . . . [with] some very pretty residences and a fine court house." Brandon had, however, fallen into disrepair because of the hardships of war. One of its citizen noted that they had not had any nails in two years.[15]

Loring also recommended to Polk that they destroy the railroad between those two points. Polk, meanwhile, was worried about the number of men he could muster to withstand the Union invasion. He determined that without adequate reinforcements to his twelve thousand infantry in Mississippi, he could not confront the Union army with anything but cavalry. Scouting reports told Polk that his enemy had more than twenty thousand infantry concentrated at Vicksburg with another five thousand to seventy-five hundred marching from Memphis. Therefore, even before Sherman's expedition left Vicksburg, Polk decided that his best course of action was to fall back into Alabama. Unsure of himself, however, he lingered in Mississippi in case the Federals sent a smaller force than he had predicted. Still, he planned to use the railroad to fall back to Meridian and beyond if pressed too strongly.[16]

Polk sent an urgent request to Johnston at Dalton for aid against cavalry raids in Alabama. Johnston, however, citing his own lack of cavalry, refused to send any horsemen to Polk. Unless the president ordered it, Polk would not receive any assistance from Johnston.[17]

On February 1, Polk made final arrangements to meet Sherman's advance from Vicksburg. He ordered Lee to destroy the railroad from Vicksburg to Jackson (some of the same railroad that the Confederate infantry had just repaired), hoping thereby to deter the enemy advance. "Let it be done thoroughly," he cautioned. French fortified Jackson, while Loring remained at Canton. Polk made no attempt to combine his two infantry divisions. The bishop sent word to Maury at Mobile to send two brigades to him if he saw no immediate threat on the port city. The seriousness of the Federal threat passed down through the hierarchy of command until it began to concern the infantrymen. Not knowing exactly what enemy commander they faced, one Missourian commented: "If Grant succeeds in cutting us off from the Department of Virginia, we will have to resort to guerila [*sic*] warfare." If that occurs, he declared, "may God have mercy on the women and children for the Federals will not."[18]

Throughout the final week of January and into the first days of February, Union forces continued to pour into camps near Vicksburg. The 124th Illinois Regiment, for example, had traveled by train from their post southeast of Vicksburg. Upon their arrival around noon, they marched into town and reported to Mortimer D. Leggett, their division commander, and James B. McPherson, their corps commander. After they participated in a drilling contest with other regiments in their brigade and were awarded the title of "Banner Regiment," the 124th Illinois boarded trains for the campgrounds near the Big Black River. As they waited they drilled and paraded, passing the time before the order to move inland was given.[19]

Sherman's men, like their commander, were primarily from the Midwest. They had left their farms to answer Lincoln's call for soldiers to stop the rebellion. Illinoisans, Iowans, Indianans, Ohioans, New Yorkers, Wisconsans, Missourians, with a smattering of Tennesseans, Kentuckians, Pennsylvanians, and men from New Jersey filled the rosters of the Sixteenth and Seventeenth corps. Most of them had fought beside Sherman before they had reached Vicksburg that February 1864. After Shiloh, Corinth, and Iuka, Grant reorganized the Army of the Tennessee into the Fifteenth, Sixteenth, and Seventeenth corps before the Vicksburg campaign. While participating in capturing the important river city, the Federal soldiers had tromped with Sherman through the dismal swampy lowlands during his failed attack at Chickasaw Bayou in December 1862. He had also led them to victory at Jackson when he had helped wrest the city from Confederate hands in July 1863. Sherman's army had experienced the highs and lows of war under their commander. Most of the soldiers liked serving with "Uncle Billy," and they were willing to journey confidently into Mississippi with him.[20]

The volunteer soldiers of the Sixteenth and Seventeenth corps may not have looked and drilled like West Point graduates, but they had experienced success on the battlefield, and they carried with them a fierce sense of self-reliance and pride because of it. By 1864, three years of hard campaigning had worn the men into haggard, scraggly, bearded veterans who believed that parading made little difference to a soldier's performance in battle. Most followed orders out of respect for the officers, not from fear of punishment.[21]

Sherman's officer corps, like his foot soldiers, had a great deal of experience. Most had enlisted in the first two years of the war and had risen through the ranks to receive their commissions. Sherman, like Grant, chose to surround himself with competent young officers whom he could trust. He pushed ineffectual officers toward retirement and replaced them with capable men. Sherman commented about his assemblage of high-quality officers with experience: "[They] accomplished many things far better than I have ordered."[22]

Officers and men got along well because of the style of the western army. Because many of the officers had once been enlisted men themselves, they appreciated what their soldiers were enduring. The greater discipline found in the eastern armies was rarely found in the West. Men appreciated their commanders' performing their duties without the pageantry often associated with rank. "The discipline of this army," one trooper wrote home, "is not so strict in matters of trifling importance to cause hard feelings towards our superiors. Rank is not royalty in Sherman's army."[23]

Another important characteristic pointing to success was that, by 1864, new recruits, when they first entered the service, joined veteran regiments. Unlike during the first three years of the war, the Federal government had almost completely ended the formation of entire regiments from newly enlisted soldiers. Instead, the War Department tried to place the "green" soldiers in with veterans so the "new men would, by association with the veterans and under the instruction and care of veteran officers, soon [become] efficient and reliable." This "merging" process sped up the rate at which the men adapted to army life and prevented the existence of entirely new regiments to create problems for the rest of the army.[24]

Sherman left Vicksburg, therefore, with an army of self-reliant and experienced veterans. They knew him and respected his command. He felt the same about their ability as a fighting force. Uncle Billy was one of them; he would just as soon banter with his men around the campfire as talk with any officers at the meeting table.

Some of these regiments had the good fortune to receive new armament. Edward F. Winslow's cavalry, for example, received hundreds of new Sharp's carbines. These weapons provided a faster rate of fire than did other small arms, and the cavalry could use the weapon effectively from the mounted position. Some of Stephen A. Hurlbut's units also acquired new arms before leaving Memphis. The Seventeenth New York traded in their old Enfield rifles for newer Springfields just prior to boarding boats bound for Vicksburg.[25]

Late on the afternoon of January 30, a group of transports filled with wide-eyed soldiers rounded the last northern bend of the Mississippi River before arriving at Vicksburg. The soldiers scrambled to the bow to catch their first sight of the river city. That summer, the name Vicksburg had been prominent in newspaper headlines. Now the soldier readers were going to get a personal look at the "Gibraltar of the West." Deckhands on the *Rose Hamilton* unfurled Old Glory, and musicians struck up "Dixie" as they steamed by the bluffed heights. Upon reaching shore and depositing their equipment at their camps near the town, many of the soldiers requested passes so they could explore the mystical Confederate bastion that had held out for so long. Many were shocked at the holes in the banks where frightened families had lived during the siege, protecting themselves from bombarding Union guns. A member of the 117th Illinois commented: "There is not a hill near Vicksburg that is not hollow." Hurlbut's men also drilled and paraded over the next two days, their first such military activity in several months. Garrisoning Memphis for the last several months, many of Hurlbut's soldiers, fattened on ample rations and light duty, had not marched any distance for some time. The soldiers also readied themselves by cleaning their gear, weapons, and clothing, a practice that, like drilling, had been ignored for many weeks.[26]

The teamsters matched mules to wagons and went about shoeing the animals and repairing broken fixtures. Officers vied for extra horses but found that few worthwhile mounts were available. With guns cleaned, tattered socks mended, and baggage stored, many of the men wrote home. Word had it that an extended period of time, perhaps a month or more, would pass before they would have another chance to post a letter. They assured father and mother, wife or girlfriend that they would write as soon as the expedition ended. Most had no idea where the officers would lead them, but they knew it might be some time before they returned.[27]

Rumors swirled throughout the camps about their objective—was it Mobile, Jackson, Shreveport, Meridian, or some other distant place? "We do not know how far, nor to what place the expedition is bound," a Illinois cavalryman wrote, "nor whether there is a prospect of any fighting to be done." Judging from the rations they carried—twenty days' worth of salt, meat, and hardtack in their regimental wagons, and ten more days' worth in the supply wagons—and from the order not to carry tents or baggage, they deduced that they would soon be moving fast over a great distance for at least thirty days. The men were anxious to get under way. Since Sherman had halted all furloughs until his expedition ended, the soldiers wanted to finish this campaign so they could visit their loved ones.[28]

Bad weather hit Vicksburg the night of January 30 and continued the following day. Many of the men suffered from the cold, especially those from Hurlbut's corps, who had not carried their tents with them from Memphis. Men became sick from the winter weather chills and from smallpox. The officers ordered the infected soldiers to remain in camp and not travel into town.[29]

On the first of February, the weather grew warm once again and the men's spirits lifted. Sherman sent orders to his army to prepare for departure. Most of the two corps moved out of the campgrounds to locations further east, near the Big Black River, bivouacking just west of the waterway. As they passed through the old fortifications and across the ground that their brethren had fought so valiantly to capture, many remarked in awe at the sight.[30]

Sherman interrogated a spy he had sent out two weeks earlier to obtain the locations and strength of the enemy in Mississippi. He learned that Polk, commanding from Meridian, had a division of infantry under Loring at Canton and another under French at Brandon. Lee's cavalry division stretched from Yazoo City to Jackson, with Forrest's command located somewhere in northern Mississippi. As far as Sherman could ascertain, "General Polk seemed to have no suspicion of our intentions to disturb his serenity."[31]

Sherman also received word from Grant that George H. Thomas was maneuvering to attack the enemy just north of Dalton and that John A. Logan had started his move on Rome. Grant reported that the Confederates were concentrating at Mobile from points further east. A spy had informed him that Johnston had sent at least a division toward Meridian and Mobile and that his entire army might retreat from Dalton as far away as the Etowah River. Sherman knew that, if Johnston's and Polk's armies joined, their combined force would greatly outnumber his own. He decided, however, that the expedition had to continue. If the two enemy forces did unite, he would have assistance from Logan, Thomas, and Nathaniel Banks. Sherman considered it unlikely that Johnston would move to reinforce Polk, unless heavily pressed, and the number of men Thomas commanded did not amount to a sufficient sum to dislodge the Confederates from Dalton. He concluded, therefore, that Johnston's command would not move en masse to support Polk.[32]

On February 2, Federal troops continued arriving on the banks of the Mississippi to link up with those already camped along the Big Black. As they marched, some of the men struck up a tune and sang their way into camp:

> We're going home,
> We're going home,
> We're going home,
> To die no more.

When they grew tired of that rendition, they turned to "John Brown's Body," ending the recital with great shouts of "Hallelujah," which echoed from hill to hill. Despite all this fanfare, Sherman was unhappy with what he saw of Hurlbut's corps, garrison troops at Memphis for close to six months, and told his wife: "Hurlbut's command had been so long in town that it is good for nothing as soldiers." Sherman did not expect to meet a heavy Confederate resistance early in the march, however, and guessed that by the time that he did in Meridian, the men of the Sixteenth Army Corps would be in fighting shape.[33]

Brigadier General James M. Tuttle, a defender of the Hornet's Nest at Shiloh, arrived late, his men scrambling up the Vicksburg shore around 3 A.M. on February 2. Sherman had already enlisted a reserve brigade from McPherson to take his place, so he ordered Tuttle to remain behind in the Big Black campground to protect the bridge, the railroad, and the city from attack. Sherman also told Tuttle to gather thirty to forty wagons filled with bread and salt and to keep them ready in case they were needed in the interior. While Sherman conversed with Tuttle, he awaited word from Colonel Benjamin F. Coates, in charge of the Yazoo River feint.[34]

This feint started on February 3. Lawrence Sullivan Ross, the Texas cavalry officer, immediately moved to block the Union expedition and repulsed it after five days of intermittent skirmishing. While Coates led the Federals up the Yazoo, Sherman started his men across the Big Black—Hurlbut at Messenger's Ferry on a pontoon bridge and McPherson on a temporary bridge near the Southern Railroad bridge, about six miles below.[35]

The sun rose bright and warm, and the roads began to dry from the earlier rains. A gentle breeze blew, making marching pleasant. "The little birds were hopping from branch to branch singing their beautiful spring songs," a Hoosier commented, and "everything appeared to cheer us on to deeds of daring and bravery." The men were in high spirits. The brigades moved from their campgrounds to their rendezvous points at the river crossings throughout the day, some traversing the river, fighting some of the deep mud holes that littered the low river-bottom roadway.[36]

Sherman's army would march through six Mississippi counties on its way to Meridian: Warren, Hinds, Rankin, Scott, Newton, and Lauderdale. Warren County, with Vicksburg as its county seat, had river commerce and the business associated with the river, such as shipping, boat repair, and dock work. It boasted more than one hundred thousand acres of improved farmland in 1860, and farmers harvested a fair amount of corn, peas, sweet and Irish potatoes. Twenty thousand cattle had roamed the delta prairies in the county, and thirty-four thousand hogs rooted through the rich earth. Warren County produced thirty-six thousand bales of cotton in 1860, about half the amount of the Mississippi county that produced the largest cotton crop of sixty-four thousand bales. The outbreak of the war and the long siege of 1863 had damaged the county's agricultural system, both armies destroying or consuming large amounts of its agricultural infrastructure and goods. For three years, cattle were driven off and slaughtered, mules and horses confiscated, gristmills, sawmills, barns, and warehouses burned. By 1870, five years after the war ended, Warren County contained only forty-five hundred cattle and fifty-five hundred hogs, a telling sign of the hardships that war had produced for the state of Mississippi. Many of its young men, as in many other counties across the South, had left their homes to join the war, leaving many of the farms untended during the four-year conflict. The Union army started off from this ravaged county across five more Mississippi

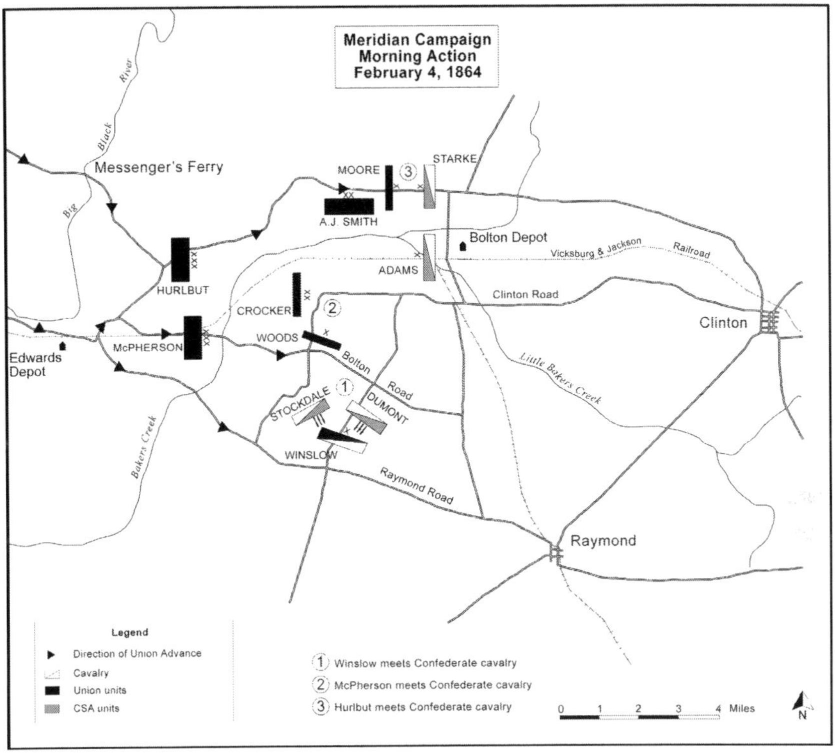

counties that had felt much of the same hardships. Sherman, however, was determined to press the civilian population even harder and destroy as much militarily important material as he could in order to compel Mississippians to end their support for the Confederacy.[37]

Winslow's cavalry crossed first at the railroad bridge, assuming the advance of the Seventeenth Corps. The horsemen moved ahead of the column to secure the bridge at Bakers Creek, near Champion Hill, the site of the old battlefield. After they had traveled about a mile from the bridge, the cavalry received fire on its flanks. They skirmished briefly near Wilson's Creek with a small force of mounted scouts from Wirt Adams's brigade, neither side taking casualties. The enemy disengaged, fell back, and did not bother the Federals anymore that evening. The scouts informed Adams of the enemy movement, so he took his brigade from Raymond and traveled to Edwards Depot road that night. By four o'clock the next morning, Adams had passed through Bolton and taken a position about a mile west of the town. He sent men forward to locate which road the enemy was moving on, the Raymond or the Bolton road.[38]

Wirt Adams, a Kentuckian, had served in the army of the Republic of Texas in 1839 and had moved to Mississippi as a planter. While a state legislator in 1858 and 1860, he became friends with Jefferson Davis, who, after the formation of the Confederate government, offered Adams the position of postmaster general. Adams declined, however, choosing instead to form and lead a cavalry regiment in Mississippi. Primarily fighting in the Magnolia State and Tennessee under Stephen D. Lee, Adams received the rank of brigadier general for his action during the Vicksburg campaign. He was determined to halt the Federal advance into his adopted state.[39]

McPherson's infantry camped for the night in a long line from Edwards Depot back to the Big Black River. Hurlbut's men, after they had built the pontoon bridge at Messenger's Ferry late that afternoon, had camped on both sides of the river. Some of the troops, satisfied with their first day's march, reflected on their officers. Hurlbut and Sherman had ridden through the Sixteenth Corps that afternoon, and one fellow remarked: "We have confidence in Hurlbut and Sherman." All agreed that they had started on a long campaign, and they were content with their superiors and trusted their judgment. The chill of the beautiful, cold, clear night made many men crowd together in small groups to keep warm. With no tents, they covered themselves with leaves or huddled close to the campfires for warmth. That night the Mississippi meadows resembled patches of fireflies, the flames dancing from thousands of fires.[40]

The next morning at 6:30 A.M., Winslow's cavalrymen climbed into their saddles and started for the Raymond road on McPherson's right. Passing near Champion Hill, they paused a while to reconnoiter. Winslow heard bugles sounding and saw a line of enemy cavalry drawn up in his front. Adams, from his position near Bolton Depot, had learned of Winslow's advance and had sent two regiments of cavalry under Colonel F. Dumonteil and Major Thomas Stockdale to stop the four regiments of Union cavalrymen from getting at his left flank from the south. The Confederates waited about a mile from the Clinton road junction. Upon seeing the Union cavalry approach, Dumonteil's cavalry fired, but Winslow kept coming. Stockdale hit the Federals on the left flank, and after a great deal of maneuvering, Winslow positioned his troops to repulse the charges successfully. The Union horsemen moved up the main road, steadily progressing toward Bolton Depot, losing sixteen men killed and captured. Dumonteil and Stockdale fell back out of sight, leaving several men on the field, and made little attempt at stopping the Federal advance until later that afternoon.[41]

The rest of the Union army had moved out that morning with McPherson's infantry on the Bolton road and Hurlbut north of the Southern Railroad on Messenger's Ferry road. The Seventeenth Corps crossed Bakers Creek, a small, steep-banked body of water that they had to bridge, about four and a half miles east of Edwards Depot, and moved onto the Clinton road. Upon reaching Champion Hill, McPherson encountered Robert C. Wood's Mississippi cavalry of Adams's command (eight hundred men) and two artillery pieces, all on the eastern slope of the old battlefield. McPherson had fought here during the Vicksburg campaign the summer before. Large trees lay broken and twisted, reminders of the fierce battle that had occurred there and "the terrible missiles which laid many a brave soldier wounded and lifeless upon the bloody field." He rode to the head of his column, and after viewing the enemy's position he remarked that he would soon "rout them out of that [position]."[42]

James Birdseye McPherson was a good friend and confidant of Sherman. Although born into poverty, McPherson had received the friendship of an influential businessman, who had assisted him in gaining entry into West Point. He had graduated in 1853 at the top of his class and had become known as a talented young engineer. McPherson received the attention of Grant while serving as his chief engineer during the march on Forts Henry and Donelson. The War Department had promoted McPherson from colonel to brigadier general, then to major general, on Grant's requests. In January 1863, Grant had placed McPherson in command of the Seventeenth Corps, where he later played a significant role at Champion Hill during the Vicksburg campaign. Sherman, like Grant, admired McPherson and believed him to be a highly capable officer. He is "a noble, gallant gentleman and the best hopes for a great soldier," Sherman noted. The thirty-five-year-old McPherson stood just under six feet tall, with a "dark complexion [and] dark eyes," and touches of gray speckled his brown hair. Other officers considered him agreeable and unpretentious. Most of his soldiers, while considering him courageous, disliked his attempts to discourage pillaging among the ranks. Considered handsome by many observers, McPherson had an appeal to the ladies. By 1864, however, he had already given his heart to a Mary Hoffman

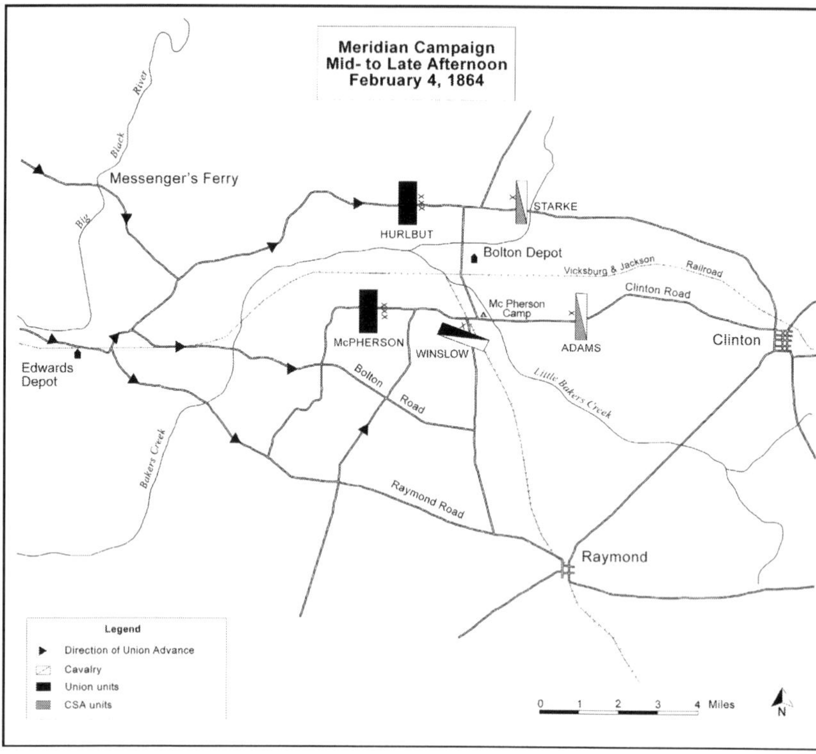

of Baltimore, and he confided to Sherman that he hoped to marry her after returning from the Meridian expedition.[43]

Not long after McPherson arrived, a Confederate officer on a white horse came riding hard across the field. McPherson ordered his men to hold their fire, thinking that the rider carried dispatches. The horseman came within "easy range, coolly drew his revolver" and fired at the Union officers. The shot ricocheted off a tree branch and rolled "harmlessly" across the ground. Some of the blue-clad soldiers returned fire, at which time the officer shouted: "You may shoot, you damn Yankees, but you can't hit me anyhow." The rider quickly turned his horse and rode hard for the opposite side of the field with Federal bullets flying after him. No shot hit its target, and the white horse carried its rider out of musket range and into the Confederate lines. For the rest of the day, as the Federals advanced, they could see the officer riding wildly up and down his lines, waving his sword violently and encouraging his men. Union soldiers fired shot after shot, but the officer remained uninjured.[44]

McPherson sent forward two brigades—about two thousand men—from Marcellus M. Crocker's Fourth Division, Crocker advancing a heavy line of skirmishers while the rest of the division followed. The unit moved steadily forward, driving the enemy cavalry for the rest of the day—a distance of about ten miles. They lost about six men during the day's fighting. Late that afternoon, the Federals came across the white steed lying dead by the side of the road. When they inquired about the horse's owner, nearby citizens said that they thought it belonged to Wirt Adams. No one knew for sure.[45]

On the far right, when Winslow again met Dumonteil's troops, drawn up in a line among some scattered trees on Walton's plantation near Bolton Depot, he ordered his men to charge. After a brief but intense clash, the four regiments of blue-clad cavalry drove the single enemy regiment from its position, sending the Confederates across Bakers Creek late that afternoon. With McPherson moving to Bolton Depot from the west and Winslow from the south, Adams had to withdraw across the Bakers Creek bridge before the Union troopers could flank him. He settled his men into camp at the Thomas plantation, about a mile to the rear, and positioned heavy skirmishers to protect the roadway, having taken ten casualties in the day's fight.[46]

While McPherson and Winslow were battling the Confederates from Champion Hill to Bolton Station, Hurlbut's corps, with Sherman along, was also fighting the enemy cavalry. Moving that morning along the Bridgeport road, they made good time. Around 11 A.M. the corps began to hear the boom of artillery fire from McPherson's clash with the enemy at Champion Hill to the south. Hurlbut's men grumbled about missing the fight. All they had seen were a few pickets near Queen's Hill, which they had driven off with great ease. Just then, an enemy cannon from Peter B. Starke's cavalry fired into them from about a mile down the road to the front, sending the Federals scrambling for cover. Starke had placed his lead forces in a defensive position about two miles northwest of Bolton Depot on Joseph E. Davis's plantation, while he remained with reserves near the crossroads and Reynolds' Ponds about a mile to the west. Three regiments of Confederate cavalry and a battery were atop a hill, ready to defend their ground at the Davis plantation.[47]

Peter Burwell Starke had served in the Mississippi State Senate in 1862. Originally from Virginia, Starke had commanded the Twenty-eighth Mississippi Cavalry as its colonel since 1862. The horsemen, as a part of Joseph Johnston's Army of Tennessee, had served in Mississippi during the Vicksburg campaign and had retreated with their commander before Sherman when he marched on Jackson after the river city fell. When Polk took command in Mississippi, Starke served under Lee in the Army of Mississippi's cavalry. He now was positioned in front of Sherman's infantry with one brigade of cavalry, searching for a way to halt the massive Federal advance.[48]

Union colonel Risdon Moore's Third Brigade, about twelve hundred men, moved forward in the lead, hoping to dislodge the Confederates from their position. Moore's artillery, the Seventh Independent Light Artillery, covered the infantry's advance. A member of the Confederate First Mississippi described the Federal movement: "A heavy line of skirmishers advance steadily in battle-array, evidently despising the smallness of our force." At the head of their lines trotted a little dog, "as if they simply meant only to set him on us to show their contempt for our cavalry." A "few well aimed shots" sent the dog running, but the question still remained: "We could never learn whether the dog was the 'mascot' of some regiment or merely a 'scalawag' deserter from the loyal dogs of the state." The Federals drove the enemy cavalry from their positions, inflicting ten casualties and taking fourteen, and continued moving steadily forward. Starke and his men withdrew eastward toward Clinton, and Hurlbut's corps halted at Reynolds' Ponds near nightfall. As darkness fell, the Union officers tallied their losses—sixteen killed, forty wounded, and seven missing. The Federals were unsure how many Confederates had fallen but remembered seeing several gray-clad fighters lying dead along the road at Bolton's Depot and near Champion Hill.[49]

As McPherson's corps settled into camp for the night near Bolton Depot at the junction of the Bolton, Clinton, and Raymond roads, some soldiers had a chance to record the day's events in their diaries. "The woods are afire all along the Black River to this place, fences burning, and also several houses and cotton gins burned," one Iowan noted. Sherman had promised to visit Mississippi with destruction, and now he was delivering on that promise. Foragers took public and private property, or they set it on fire. Yet, Sherman remained steadfast in his protection of innocent Southern civilian lives. When word spread that a widow had suffered a fatal musket shot near Bolton Depot, he rode to the location personally. He found three small, ragged children in the cabin and yard dazed and confused over the loss of their mother. None of the soldiers knew where the shot had come from, but the woman had died instantly, and the men had found the children clinging to her dead body when they arrived. Sherman ordered a notice placed on the cabin door specifying the cause of the woman's death and contacted a neighbor to care for the children.[50]

Civilian death was not what Sherman had wanted when he took up the strategy of destructive war. In fact, he had hoped that this new type of warfare would save lives on both sides, military and civilian. Robbing the Southern countryside of provisions would cause the Confederacy to end the war for want of provisions and goods. He could burn, damage, and demolish supplies without the need of a pitched battle, thereby reducing casualties. If Polk's infantry did not meet the Union army on the battlefield, that was fine with Sherman. He was not after the Army of Mississippi, only the railroads, warehouses, supplies, and foodstuffs in the state. This woman was dead, however, and Sherman did what he thought appropriate for the circumstances.

Southern women frequently found themselves in dangerous positions during the Civil War. Depending upon their station in life—poor farmers, middle-class or wealthy plantation and townswomen, or slave women—each met different challenges and hardship throughout the conflict. When their men left home to join the army or a guerrilla unit, poor farm women remained to care for the farm and children. Most of them did not have the money or means to travel to a "safe" city further south. The farming lifestyle of many Mississippians left the women on isolated farmsteads far from any neighborly assistance. Sometimes such isolation proved beneficial for the women, because they could provide for their families while avoiding the rising costs of goods and rent that many of their urban counterparts endured. Isolation, however, left their homes open to foraging parties or bands of guerrillas. Deserters from the Confederate army posed one of the greatest threats to secluded farmsteads. By August 1863 there were five thousand Confederate soldiers absent without leave, many of them roaming the Mississippi countryside.[51]

As Sherman's army marched from Vicksburg to Jackson, an area where the majority of army maneuvering had been for the first three years of the war in Mississippi, many families were absent from their farms and had escaped into cities or to another state to live with relatives. From Brandon, about fourteen miles east of Jackson, however, the rural populace had experienced few, if any, visits from the Union army, and the small farms had many women-led families living on them.

Some of the Union soldiers took pity on the poor Southern women, often left destitute after the army had passed. During the Meridian expedition, a member of the 117th Illinois Infantry Regiment, for example, was touched especially with the plight of a woman and her nine children living in a tiny house along the side of the road. "Soldiers took all their provisions," he commented sadly. "I gave them all the crackers I had in my saddlebags." Some of the families, however, received no relief from war's torments and had to scrape what living they could from the land, as Sherman intended.[52]

Some poor farm women living along the route of march, not having seen either army and having little to lose in the way of valuables, often gathered along the roadway to watch the Federal soldiers march by. An Iowa infantryman observed a group of women who came to sit and watch the army pass: "They sat still and talked with the soldiers left behind." He noticed that two of the women had newborn babies, and they suckled them while they talked to the soldiers. "They did not seem to have the faintest idea that there was any impropriety in sitting flat on the ground, suckling babes in public and letting the soldiers sit around them," he said with astonishment. The Iowan, like many of the Northern soldiers, thought that these rural women were "perfectly ignorant" people.[53]

Many middle-class or wealthy Mississippi women had the funds to travel away from the advancing Federal armies and went to live with friends and family or board in a hotel away from the action. Those who remained behind often carried a deep resentment toward Union soldiers. Because of their status in the community as "high class" women, their attitudes toward their "barbaric" treatment from invading Federal troopers made many of them lash out in verbal rage. Their attitudes made their property prime targets for foragers and pillagers looking for a way to return the ladies' "kindness." Secessionist women's verbal abuse, however, was not the only reason for "Yankee Wrath" upon them. Soldiers knew that plantations and fine homes held rich stores of goods. If a Mississippi woman treated the troopers poorly, her behavior only added justification for soldier actions. "In our regiment as in all others there are men of very low principle," a Federal soldier commented. He watched as a group of Federal soldiers "broke into a trunk belonging to the lady of the house." The woman had no power to stop the pillaging, so she fell to her knees and began to pray. She asked the "Almighty Ruler" to "have mercy on the Yankee Villains," but the soldiers paid her no attention. "I know that the soldiers of our army do many things that would shock the sensitive consciences, but war is very different from peace," the Illinoisan concluded.[54]

Sherman, after all, wanted to compel the Southern people to stop providing provisions for the Confederate army. In some instances, nonetheless, his soldiers left families with enough food for their own sustenance. In other instances, the soldiers stole nonmilitary items too. They had little sympathy for the wealthy Mississippians they encountered.

Mississippi slave women underwent a harsher experience than white women. The Civil War brought with it a great deal of uncertainty for female slaves. Federal soldiers meant salvation from the bonds of slavery, but they could also bring rape and molestation. During the Vicksburg campaign, a white plantation mistress watched in horror as Federal soldiers took turns raping her young house slave. The rape of slave women occurred throughout the South, but such violence was apparently extremely rare. Federal soldiers were not the only troopers who committed such atrocities either. Lawless bands of guerrillas or isolated Confederate soldiers were guilty as well. If slave women managed to join a Federal column, the soldiers often forced them to cook and wash without compensation. Still, African-American women flooded into Sherman's lines throughout the campaign, facing uncertainty and enduring hardships, choosing the possibility of freedom rather than continued slavery. Sherman leaves no record of his attitude at the time toward these refugees, but he later noted that he disliked dealing with the throngs of former slaves that followed his already encumbered army.[55]

Sherman's army, wet with sweat from the day's marching and fighting, became chilled when night fell. The soldiers huddled together and built fires from fence rails, an action quite common for both armies. It had become so common in some areas that travelers could pass along miles of road before they saw one split rail where once the road-edge fences had been stacked six feet high. Such fire builders were rarely punished.

Just before dark on February 4, McPherson's lead elements had noticed that the Confederates had taken a new position on a hill to the east overlooking Bakers Creek. They knew that the next day would bring another skirmish. Early that evening, Lieutenant Colonel James K. Proudfit of the Twelfth Wisconsin made his way to the Union picket line on the west side of Bakers Creek bridge with a "queerly dressed stranger" at his side. "Boys, here's a Rebel that I don't want with us," he explained. "I am going to send him through the lines out to where he belongs." Proudfit sent the man across the bridge, and before he reached the enemy lines the odd-looking individual turned off the road and slipped into a stand of tall grass that reached up to the edge of the Confederate position. Early the next morning the "Rebel" returned cold and wet, carrying information about the position and number of the enemy troops. The Union men then realized: "He was a spy."[56]

That same day, Johnston sent an urgent message to Polk requesting that he send reinforcements to Rome immediately, specifically requesting Loring's division. "If you have a brigade nearer Rome send it, I entreat you, in advance of Loring," he begged. Johnston feared a strong Union advance was imminent, and he wanted more men to confront them. Polk, however, was looking down the barrels of Sherman's many guns, so it was impossible for him to send half of his infantry to Rome. He needed more men himself, not fewer. Polk simply ignored Johnston's dispatch.[57]

Reveille sounded early that February 5 morning, and as soon as the light shone bright enough to see, McPherson had his corps in motion along the Clinton road just south of the Vicksburg and Jackson Railroad, Leggett's Third Division in the lead. Four cannons, including the 10-pounder rifled Parrots, covered the advance of Benjamin F. Pott's Second Brigade and Jasper A. Maltby's Third Brigade.[58]

Wirt Adams's dismounted cavalry (eight hundred men) sat atop the hill about eight hundred yards to the east of Bakers Creek bridge, his artillery pieces in position to shell the Federal approach along the main road. He hoped to halt them as they tried to cross the narrow bridge. The Confederate cannon fire, however, fell short of its intended target until the Federals were already halfway across. The Second Brigade crossed the bridge with the Third Brigade quickly following. They formed a battle line on the left and right of the roadway and stretched themselves out along the creek. They advanced slowly toward the Confederate-held higher ground.[59]

When the Yankees came within range, the graycoats' entire line showered them with musket fire. A Wisconsin volunteer described the scene: "The site was not only enlivening and exciting, but beautiful. Clouds of smoke arose after the volleys of musketry and rolled off white and fleecy in the bright sunshine." He soon realized the seriousness of the moment when he observed the ambulances bringing "back the dead and dying" and reported

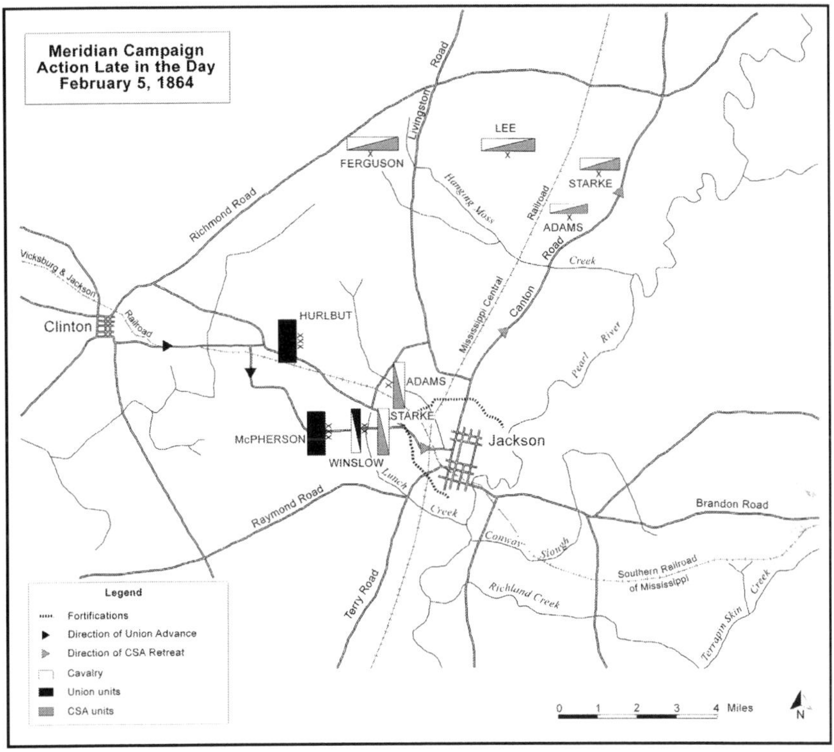

that the "gate by the roadside where the Rebels had made their stand was all bespattered with human brains."[60]

Scouts in the Union Signal Corps spotted the enemy artillery, and the Federal guns fired into that position. The entire skirmish lasted about an hour. One of the veterans in the rear turned to a new recruit and commented about the loud sound of cannonading and musket fire: "Them fellows in front are getting their veterans bounty." "Yes, in hard money, too," came the reply. "Can't you hear them plank it down on the table?" Facing superior numbers and more accurate artillery, the butternuts retired toward Clinton along the Clinton road. As Adams neared that village he received orders from Stephen D. Lee to stand and hold the Seventeenth Corps in check until Starke, who was battling the Sixteenth Corps on the Bridgeport road, could retreat there.[61]

While McPherson's infantry drove Adams's cavalry along the Clinton road, Sherman and Hurlbut, after about an hour of light skirmishing, had driven Starke from his position just north of the Vicksburg and Jackson Railroad on the Bridgeport road. A little before noon, the Sixteenth Corps pressed Starke where the Bridgeport and Clinton roads converged on the town of Clinton. McPherson, advancing parallel to Hurlbut, ordered his artillery to fire at Starke as he moved toward Clinton. Receiving fire from two greatly superior forces, Starke fell back to a position two miles east of Clinton on the Clinton-to-Jackson road, while Adams attempted to hold the Seventeenth Corps in check. Adams soon joined Starke at his location, redeploying to a defensive position on a slight rise in the eastern edge of a long field in the area called the "Tombstone," where he covered the enemy advance along the road.[62]

Starke received orders to withdraw from his location and take position in the works on the west side of Jackson. Before he could complete the move, however, he discovered that Winslow's cavalry had already passed the western breastworks. Starke reported the information to Lee, who was now in Jackson. Lee then sent Starke to cover the road from Jackson to Canton in case the enemy moved northward from the capital city. The way to Clinton was now wide open; no Confederate forces were in position to deter the Federal advance into the town.[63]

Sherman's army marched into the nearly abandoned Clinton with "bands [playing] and colors flying." "Clinton is at present a very dilapidated-looking place, being visited once before and partially destroyed by our army," a Federal marcher noted. A fine Female Seminary, housed in a beautiful building, stood vacant, "poorly patronized these times."[64]

Winslow's cavalry entered the town from the Raymond road just ahead of the Union infantry. When the cavalrymen reached the outskirts of town, they noticed the enemy's rear guard leaving Clinton eastward. Sherman called his officers together and outlined his next move. McPherson's corps would bear south in an attempt to reach a plantation road that led directly to Jackson between the Clinton and Raymond roads. Hurlbut would follow the main Clinton and Jackson roads into the city.[65]

At 1 A.M., Samuel French at Jackson had sent an urgent dispatch to William Loring in Canton describing the mess he was in. He explained that he had only about sixteen hundred men, the rest of his division having not yet arrived. He could not hold the position without reinforcements. He also concluded that unless Loring had already started for Jackson, the enemy would reach the capital prior to his arrival. Loring replied that he would move south of Canton to Madison Station, cross the Pearl River, and move eastward toward Morton beyond Brandon. French decided to fall back as well.[66]

French busied his command with loading stores and shipping them to Meridian. Around midmorning he received a dispatch from Lee, assuring him that the cavalry would cover his retreat from the city and Loring's move across the Pearl River at Culley's Ferry. After the infantry had moved safely east of the Pearl River, Lee would stay between Canton and Jackson in the hope that the enemy army would pass that way. He could then gain access to their rear. French agreed with Lee that abandoning Jackson was the only Confederate option: "It would be useless to give battle against such odds."[67]

Polk sent a message to Loring: "Detain the enemy as long as possible from getting into Jackson." The commanding general had found reinforcements at Mobile and was just then leaving for Meridian. He promised to come to the front as soon as he could with six thousand infantry. Loring replied to Polk's message: "It is impossible to comply. The enemy 25,000 strong, entered Clinton this morning." Polk's reinforcements were too little, too late.[68]

Sherman planned to occupy Jackson before sundown. McPherson's corps came upon Adams's dismounted cavalry two miles beyond Clinton. Winslow's cavalry moved forward and kept the Confederates' attention until the infantry came up. McPherson then deployed a strong skirmish line, his artillery firing over the soldiers' heads at the batteries. As the infantry advanced steadily across the wide-open field toward the Confederate position, McPherson ordered the Union cavalry to disengage. Although the skirmish did not last long, it was fierce. A member of the Twentieth Illinois hyperbolically remarked that the action was "one of the most desperate hand to hand conflicts ever witnessed on this earth. From all parts of the field you could hear the groans of wounded and dying." Neither side lost more than fifty men during the entire day. Adams's cavalry withdrew, but they quickly re-formed at the end of another open field about six miles west of Jackson.[69]

Hurlbut's corps arrived around three o'clock that afternoon, positioning itself on the Confederate right. Sherman acted immediately. He ordered Winslow to move around to the right, flanking the Confederate cavalry in an attempt to get into the city before being discovered. He told Winslow that he did not believe the Confederates would "seriously defend Jackson." The commander wanted the capital in his hands by the end of the day, if possible, because "the possession of it by tonight would be worth five hundred men to us." He depended upon Winslow to capture and secure the Pearl River pontoon bridge before the Confederates could destroy it. The enemy cavalry, Sherman believed, would use the bridge to leave the city. While the cavalry left to execute their orders, the infantry continued forward. Andrew Hickenlooper of the Pioneer Corps was impressed by what then transpired:

> At this junction point I witnessed one of the most beautiful and interesting sights I had ever seen. The enemy evidently supposing that General Hurlbut's column was the advance of our forces had here massed their entire cavalry force in an immense cotton field and clearing. The advance of our column suddenly appeared upon their [left] flank and from a totally unexpected quarter. A battery was hastily brought forward and opened upon this dense mass of the enemy effectively but without producing panic or confusion. Their perfection of discipline, graceful movements and apparent ease with which they formed into columns of divisions at a trot, and left the field before we could bring our infantry forward, was a sight which elicited the hearty applause of our men.[70]

With Hurlbut pressing on the right and McPherson coming up on the left and center, the Confederates had to retreat while they still had that option. "In a twinkling they mounted, and moved like a whirlwind through the yet open space to the south and escaped," an Ohioan observed. A member of the 124th Illinois said: "Our whole force was in sight at this time, both corps. It was a most imposing and beautiful spectacle to see the different divisions and brigades in line of battle, with colors flying, the artillery in position, and the signal flags waving. It was the pomp of war, and it stirred within me feelings that are indescribable."[71]

Winslow's cavalry had circled wide right around Adams's left flank, as Sherman had ordered it to do. A wooded area concealed their movements as they passed the end of the Confederate line. After a few miles, the blue-clad horse soldiers emerged from the underbrush and into a road in view of Jackson and in front of its outer defenses. Reaching that position, the lead horsemen paused for further orders while the rest of the men came up. They heard the noise of enemy troops moving toward their position from the west. Within a few minutes, they witnessed a "sight before them not often within the experience of a soldier." It was Adams's and Starke's cavalry. While retreating along the Jackson road, Adams had run into Starke before the latter could get under way for the Canton road. The two had merged and now headed toward Jackson together, within rifle shot of Winslow's undetected unit. The gray column of fours stretched out before the admiring Federals from inside the city to out of their sight to the west. "They filled all the space in view, and there was no telling the number." Actually, there were about thirteen hundred horsemen.[72]

The Fourth Iowa dismounted at the order: "Prepare to fight on foot!" The Eleventh Illinois remained mounted on the left of the line, awaiting an opportunity to charge. Two James rifled cannons were brought into position and readied to fire. A group of Confederate officers noticed the commotion, but before they could react the Union artillery opened up, causing great confusion in the Confederate ranks. Adams's men rode toward the fortifications and took cover, while Starke's unit backed off the main road into a wooded area north of the roadway. Winslow took the opportunity to send the Eleventh Illinois in at a charge toward the enemy in the woods, with the Fourth Iowa advancing at a run toward the fortifications. The rest of the cavalry followed mounted.[73]

Starke's cavalry scattered and retreated northward at the approach of the charging enemy. Cut off from the capital, they re-formed in the rear and headed cross-country toward the Canton road where Lee had ordered them earlier. They spent the rest of the night riding around Jackson, finally joining Lee around midnight four miles north of the city.[74]

Initially met with fierce fire from Adams's soldiers, the Iowans stormed the earthworks and toppled into the ditch. By the time they reached the rear of the fortifications, the enemy gunfire had ceased. They climbed up the final bank to see the cavalry riding hard for the center of town. As night fell, Winslow remounted his men and they dashed into Jackson searching for the bridge across the Pearl River that Sherman had ordered them to capture and hold.[75]

French, after sending all the stores eastward to Meridian, had crossed the river on the pontoon bridge around 4 P.M., moving toward Brandon. After ensuring that the column was indeed under way, French, along with his staff, returned to Jackson. Riding into the capital, he learned that the enemy had control of the western part of the city. He wheeled about and raced toward the bridge, ordering it to be cut free. As one of his staff cut the ropes, a rider rushed up shouting that Adams's cavalry had to use that bridge to escape. French ordered the bridge retied, but as soon as the men did it they noticed enemy cavalry lining up on the far bank. Adams's horsemen would have to find another route out of the city. The rope was cut once again.[76]

When Winslow's cavalry finally located the bridge, they noticed that the retreating Confederates had severed its western end, and the current had pulled it downstream. The bridge lay on the opposite shore covered with gray soldiers hacking wildly at its timbers. A few Union shots caused the enemy soldiers to scamper into the brush. In the dim light, Winslow noticed the outline of a Confederate supply train and ordered two of his mountain howitzers to fire on it. Before long the enemy scrambled out of sight, leaving the town and the bridge to the Union cavalry.[77]

By sundown, McPherson's lead unit, Leggett's division, had reached a position about two and a half miles from Jackson with the rest of the command scattered between there and Clinton. McPherson sent word to his officers, requesting volunteers to travel with him to Jackson in support of Winslow's cavalry. Manning Force offered the First Brigade, and McPherson accepted. The Yankee troops marched into Jackson "to the music of 'The Girl I left Behind Me,' colors flying." "One woman waved a lighted lamp as we passed," one soldier commented, "and a little boy sang 'Hurrah for the Yanks.'" The First Brigade deployed behind the fortifications on the Canton road just before midnight, while the rest of the corps bivouacked for the night between Clinton and Jackson, the soldiers exhausted from their long march. The capital of Mississippi, for the third time, was under the control of the Union army.[78]

Even before they had reached Jackson, the Union army had encountered large numbers of slaves. Many of the soldiers noted how the plantations had become larger and the soil "better" since they had departed Clinton. Warren County, the starting point for the march, contained a little over thirteen thousand slaves in 1860. Because of the Federal military activity surrounding the Vicksburg campaign, many African Americans had fled their masters for the safety of Union lines. Many remained enslaved, however, and when Sherman's army arrived, blacks had another opportunity to leave home. A Wisconsin volunteer observed that hundreds of contrabands joined the Federal columns, "seem[ing] to think that to go with us meant to be free." All ages, sizes, shapes, and conditions of slaves—young boys, aged and decrepit grandmothers, mothers with children, and middle-aged men and women—

came into Union lines. "There were crippled people being helped along the road by those who wanted to take this chance for liberty, but would not leave the grandfather or grandmother behind to die alone."[79]

Some of the blue-clad soldiers concluded that the slaves probably "suffered more during their ill-advised escapade than they ever did in bondage." They left their plantations without food or water to join the long, blue line to freedom. They did carry with them, however, the "simple faith that somehow, in some way, 'Massa Linkum' could and would make it all right." Collecting provisions was especially difficult for the fleeing people because they followed the immense Union army, which left the countryside bare of goods. More than one freedom seeker fell out on the roadside too weak to walk any further. But they remained undeterred and kept coming.[80]

Sherman did not like the encumbrance to his column that the fleeing contrabands presented. The slaves were no longer working for their former masters, however, and that pleased the Union general. He would comment to his brother after the Atlanta campaign that military operations would have been constrained if the Union army had tried to assist the mobs of black refugees. Perhaps he believed that in Mississippi. As long as they did not get in the way, however, contrabands could tag along, but Sherman did not attempt to make the march any easier for them. Still, he was satisfied with the disruption to the Mississippi economy that their escape created.[81]

Sherman's army had fought elements of the enemy continually for three days and had driven them back steadily. "[We] whipped him handsomely and utterly disconcert[ed] his plans," Sherman said. Loring and French had failed to concentrate at Jackson before he had reached the capital. Sherman's cavalry had saved the pontoon bridge across the Pearl River, so he could even send his pontoon train back to Vicksburg. "Entered Jackson on the night of the 5th. We captured about 30 prisoners and 1 gun, killed about 20, and wounded at least 50. Our loss is about 10 killed and 25 wounded," Sherman wrote contentedly to Ralph Buckland back in Memphis. He also sent a message to Tuttle at the Big Black River, stating that the army would cross the Pearl River the following day and destroy the bridge there. Sherman was moving ever forward and totally cutting himself off from his communication line.[82]

By midnight on February 5, Sherman's army had marched nearly halfway across the state of Mississippi, taking three days, encountering no opposition but an extremely outnumbered enemy cavalry unable to do more than detain the Federals a few more hours. The Confederate infantry had yet to fire a shot at Sherman. Instead, French had evacuated Jackson moving east for Brandon, Loring had left Canton headed east for Morton, and Lee's cavalry had been beaten and scattered from the Big Black River to Jackson. Concentrating the Confederate forces would take a considerable amount of time and effort, and, as swiftly as Sherman was moving down the Mississippi byways, the Southerners had an insurmountable task to unite their forces into a defensible position. They had to merge, however; neither Loring nor French commanded enough troops to meet Sherman alone.[83]

Should Polk not have worked to concentrate his forces at Jackson earlier? He had sent French to Jackson in late January to rebuild and construct fortifications there. Simultaneously, he had sent Loring to do the same at Canton. When he received word that Sherman had left Vicksburg headed east, he should have sent Loring from Canton to assist French in garrisoning Jackson and supported them with reinforcements from Mobile, but he chose not to do so. Instead, he decided to travel to Mobile to secure reinforcements, leaving all decision making to Loring.

Polk knew that he would not receive any assistance from Johnston at Dalton in time to meet Sherman at Jackson because, only a few days previously, Johnston had insisted that Polk send him reinforcements. Clearly, Johnston would send no assistance without direct orders from the president. Even if Davis gave such an order, there was no chance of the troops reaching Jackson in time. Simultaneously, Longstreet was dormant in eastern Tennessee and could not send reinforcements, and Polk could not further weaken Mobile, as he had already reduced the garrison strength there to less than three thousand troops.

When Polk had heard of Sherman's departure from Vicksburg, he had considered withdrawing into Alabama if the Union army contained twenty-five thousand soldiers, as earlier scouting reports had advised. He still believed that the Federal advance was part of a plan to take Mobile, so he chose to wait before deciding what to do. He wanted to understand exactly what Sherman was after. Was it Mobile or something else? This uncertainty only benefited Sherman's movements and boded ill for Confederate Mississippi. Sherman's diversions and feints were working.

4 / "A Miss Is as Good as a Mile"

As William T. Sherman thought about leaving Jackson for Meridian, he expected to see William Loring's and Samuel French's divisions along with Stephen D. Lee's cavalry force over the next rise in the road. Sherman did not know where Leonidas Polk would choose to make his stand, but he believed that the bishop would not let him pass without providing opposition somewhere.

Polk's maneuvers, however, were unpredictable. He first hoped to concentrate his forces just east of Morton, seventeen miles east of Brandon on the Southern Railroad. He hurried his men to this junction of rail and road to repel Sherman from the state. Suddenly, Polk split his forces in the face of the superior Union foe, sending half his troops to Mobile and the other half into a retreat toward the Alabama line. After a few more days, the bishop decided to try to stop Sherman, not through a frontal assault on the Union column but by defeating the heavy cavalry force coming down from Collierville, Tennessee, to cooperate with the Federal infantry. Polk's actions demonstrated that he was thoroughly confused, and the results indicate that he was completely wrong.[1]

On his march from Jackson to Tallahatta Creek, Sherman continued to develop his strategy of raiding, particularly when Polk's cavalry attempted to cut his supply and communication lines but found that none existed. This development supported Sherman's theory about the importance of marching without a supply line. Furthermore, Andrew Hickenlooper's actions during the entire march bolstered Sherman's belief that the efficient work of the Pioneer Corps could contribute to a successful campaign. Lastly, by the time the Union army reached Tallahatta Creek, Sherman understood that his Mississippi plan, calling for feints at other locations in the immediate area, had worked to keep the Confederate generals and government guessing about his intentions. All of these occurrences and ideas helped shape Sherman's evolving style of warfare.

Hickenlooper had the Pioneer Corps up and moving early on February 6 to complete the reconstruction of the pontoon bridge across the Pearl River, a task that would take until midafternoon. Although Edward F. Winslow's cavalry had halted the Confederate destruction of the bridge the night before, it needed significant repair before the Union army could use it.[2] While the Pioneer Corps labored hard on the bridge, the rest of the army slowly trickled into Jackson over the course of the day. McPherson's Seventeenth Corps had the lead, and Hurlbut's Sixteenth Corps moved closer to the capital, the men camping and resting, waiting for the bridge to be rebuilt. They sent out foragers, who returned with wagons ladened with meats and grains.[3]

Hurlbut caused a sensation among the men when he came through their ranks on his way to visit Marcellus Crocker's Third Division headquarters in Jackson. "The Boys fell in after him . . . and he was surrounded by a multitude of the 4th Division," an observer commented. Hurlbut made a short speech, telling the men of his pride in serving with them and adding that "nothing would grieve your old commander as to hear of one of you departing from that discipline I used to teach you." Hurlbut, a politician at heart, could make a good speech, and his soldiers appreciated his effort. They cheered their general.[4]

Hinds County, in which Jackson was the major city, was a productive agricultural area. In 1860 the county produced a million bushels of corn and fifty-five thousand bales of cotton. The county's rich, dark soil produced a bountiful yield. The Pearl River ran through the middle of the county, providing the farmers access to water during even the driest months. Most of the farms were more than a hundred acres in size, with almost a hundred plantations over five hundred acres. The state capital at Jackson served as the county seat as well and provided rail connections to markets for the agricultural produce. Industries associated with cotton production were located in and around Jackson. Cotton belt manufacturers, cottonseed gins, flax factories, and storage warehouses were found throughout the city. With an economy based primarily on agriculture, Hinds County had, in 1860, twenty-two thousand slaves, more than any of the six other counties that Sherman's army would march through on its way to Meridian.[5]

Sherman had brought destruction to Jackson on two earlier occasions, so he was surprised to find the railyards and industries still operating. Once again he sent his troops to destroy the capital city's public property. A Federal marcher described the scene in Jackson as he marched into town: "It was truly a vivid picture of war to see the streets filled with armed men, squares of large brick buildings on fire, furniture of every description, from rocking-cradles to pianos, clothing, books, in fact almost every article of domestic utility and ornament, piled upon the sidewalks. Women and children running hither and thither, pictures of the most abject despair."

The Confederate troops had carried as much of the supplies and equipment out of Jackson as they could, including a large amount of private property that Confederate stragglers had stolen from citizens' homes. "Nearly all of the large buildings here have been burnt," an Illinoisan commented, and "there are a good many buildings being burnt today, and the Soldiers are doing a big business of the foraging line." "It was a heap of ruins," another soldier wrote. In exaggeration, many observers called the town "Chimneyville," alleging incorrectly that nothing but bare chimneys stood throughout the city.[6]

Although Sherman made it clear to his soldiers that they were to destroy only public property, several private homes burned throughout the day and the following night. "During the day at least twenty houses were burned in sight of our camp," Private Benjamin Hieronymous observed, "some of them splendid palace-like mansions of the rich southern slave-holding aristocratic planters." He concluded that the "devastation and waste which an army makes in passing through a country is awful." Better property than lives, Sherman thought.[7]

"A new burning has been inflicted on this afflicted town," Sherman wrote his wife. Most public property that he had left intact after his earlier visits was now consumed in fire. The statehouse, however, remained standing. Mississippians would not rebuild their capital city as quickly this time as they had after Sherman's earlier visits. Streams of white refugees had flowed out of the capital after the Union army had first visited there in 1863, reducing its prewar population of thirty-one hundred significantly. In anticipation of the Union army's arrival for a third time, the roads had long been filled with travelers once again. "The distress of the people of Jackson was very great at the approach of the enemy," an observer wrote the *Montgomery Mail,* "and the roads leading east were crowded with fugitives."[8]

Upon Hickenlooper's completion of the bridge across the Pearl River that afternoon around 3:30, Alexander Chambers's Third Brigade led the Seventeenth Corps across and traveled another two miles before discovering that the retreating Confederates had burned two more bridges on their way to Brandon. The Third Division's Pioneer Corps spent the rest of the night repairing the bridges, while the army bivouacked where they stood.[9]

Several of the Confederate cavalry brigades had made their way northward toward Canton, where Lee waited for the passing of Sherman's army. He was lingering between Canton and Jackson hoping to combat the enemy advance toward the north. He had also covered Loring's flight across the Pearl River toward Morton. "Dead horses and broken down wagons" littered the road north from Jackson, signs of the Confederate withdrawal. Around midday, Lee's cavalry met Union cavalry foragers on the Canton road. After a brief skirmish, the blue-clad cavalrymen retired back to Jackson and did not attempt to travel northward for the rest of the day. By the late afternoon of the sixth, because he believed that the enemy had no intention of moving toward Canton in force, Lee sent a regiment of his cavalry to Brandon to support French and watch the Pearl River crossing at Jackson. He readied the other three brigades to cross the Pearl if a Union force left Jackson and moved eastward. If the enemy passed him, Lee planned to attack his rear.[10]

Lee told French, however, that the enemy force coming into Jackson numbered nearly thirty thousand men and that French's small force could not "give them battle." By nightfall, French, at Brandon, had received word from Polk that he was sending four more brigades as fast as possible. Polk had decided that with the "emergency now in [his] front," he could spare the men from garrisoning Mobile. French fell back further east, past Brandon toward Morton, to concentrate his forces with those of Loring and the reinforcements that Polk had promised.[11]

At Morton, Polk had decided to make the stand that Sherman was worried about. He sent a message to Nathan Bedford Forrest urging him to send the majority of his northern Mississippi cavalry to a location near Grenada, 150 miles north of Jackson, and there combine his cavalry with Lee's. He should then sweep down and disrupt Sherman's communication and supply lines from Vicksburg and Jackson. This would "force him [Sherman] back to the Mississippi River," Polk contended. He also planned to move all his infantry to Morton. Polk calculated that the Lee and Forrest attacks would weaken the Union army, and, with his infantry, he could then complete the job.[12]

Before sunrise on the seventh, Federal drums called for the men to fall in. They slowly roused, shivering from the morning's chill. McPherson's Seventeenth Corps moved out of Jackson with the daylight giving a clearer view of the destruction that had taken place the day and night before. As Union soldiers crossed the pontoon bridge over the Pearl River, one turned back and looked at the city: "The place looks like destruction," he said. Many of the town's citizens came out into the streets to watch as the enemy army left. A young black boy banged out a tune on a discarded piano. Papers fluttered across the dirt streets. Smoke continued to rise from the smoldering remnants of buildings. McPherson's corps headed toward Brandon, the seat of Rankin County, through the Pearl River Swamp, known for its deep mire.[13]

Hurlbut's Sixteenth Corps had moved east from positions that unit held between Jackson and Clinton. It came into Jackson and waited for McPherson to get well under way. While in the city, Sixteenth Corps foragers had a difficult time finding any subsistence in the ravaged town because the Seventeenth had cleaned the citizens out of most of their provisions. "Cornbread was about all [we] could find," commented a disgusted private. Sherman and his staff rode through the ranks evaluating the situation. Many of the men dropped what they were doing and straightened up, their chests pushed out in a proud display. "It was his first raid," one New Yorker commented, "and it was our good fortune to be with him." In one final action, the Union army destroyed the pontoon bridge after the last man had crossed to the east.[14]

Sherman's army traveled relatively unmolested along the road to Brandon. One Union soldier commented about how the landscape had changed from the area west of Jackson: "The country between Jackson and Brandon is very good, and there are many fine plantations." Rankin County, like Hinds, relied heavily on agricultural production. Most of its farms were more than fifty acres in size, and the county had three plantations of more than a thousand acres. There were more slaves than whites in Rankin County in 1860, illustrating its dependence upon black labor. In the area east of Jackson, the Mississippi citizenry had not seen Federal troops other than when Grierson's Raid came through briefly during the Vicksburg campaign.[15]

Winslow's cavalry and Lucius Rose's detachment from the Signal Corps served as a screen on the left edge of the Union lead column. These men battled briefly with about fifty Confederate scouts on the way to Brandon, and they raced through the city chasing the retreating horsemen. Surprisingly, neither side incurred a loss. Winslow's horsemen returned that night to camp with the infantry near town.[16]

Lead elements of McPherson's Seventeenth Corps marched into Brandon that afternoon with their drums beating. They camped about a mile east of town. McPherson ordered a detail of men to destroy the railroad, and the rest of the afternoon consisted of burning crossties, warping rails, and demolishing nearby bridges and culverts. Foragers discovered a "large quantity" of cornmeal stored in a warehouse, which they burned after removing its contents.[17]

Some of the men recognized the blackened foundations of buildings that their cavalry had burned the summer before. Fires again visited the little town, which contained slightly over a thousand people, and many buildings burned, including the jail. "The town all laid in ashes. Great destruction of property," an Ohioan commented. "This place like Jackson was none the better nor richer for our occupation, foraging and fire doing fearful work, and as usual attacking the loveliest and costliest first," another fellow observed. "Before we came to camp there, it had some fine brick blocks, railroad depots, etc., which are now *non est* [non-existent]," one fellow commented.[18]

An observer later wrote to the *New York Tribune* about what he had witnessed at Brandon: "The work of destruction was most thoroughly done. The houses of prominent rebels were burned. Every horse and mule that could be found was seized upon, and the number became so great that a special detail was made to care for them. In fact, everything of an edible nature was levied upon and made an item in our commissariat. Thousands of blacks came into our lines. The railroad track was torn up, and every wagon, bridge, and depot was burned." One soldier kept it simple: "[Left] Brandon purified as by fire."[19]

J. J. Thornton, a Mississippi state representative who had voted against secession, owned a drugstore in Brandon, and Federal soldiers pillaged its contents. "A large number" of abandoned homes were torched in Brandon, one Federal soldier remarked, even though "there were strict orders issued against it by the Commanding Generals." Stragglers had started most of the house fires, he concluded. The boys of the Fifteenth Iowa "jayhawked" some wagonloads of tobacco and passed the trophies out to their comrades, enlivening the mood in camp.[20]

Among the other prizes the Federal soldiers found at Brandon were several Southern newspapers. One soldier read one of them out loud to the others around the campfire. "It made a startling announcement to the Southern public, that the 'Yanks' had added another animal to their menagerie in the person of 'Beast McPherson,'" he stated. The Southern newspapermen, it seemed, had now extended their hatred for Sherman to his subordinates as well. "The General felt badly," the same trooper commented. McPherson had suffered criticism from some of his men because he insisted that they should not pillage and plunder—the very thing that the newspapers now accused him of doing.[21]

The Confederates spent the next two days rushing to Morton, a small town on the Southern Railroad, not much more than a depot, a drugstore, two or three railroad buildings, two stores, and a few scattered houses. French's division reached the city and found Loring there. He ordered his soldiers to join in the construction of breastworks on a natural rise. Polk sent his wife and daughter back to Asheville, North Carolina, and hurried to join his soldiers on the front lines. Mrs. Polk wrote to her family that it was "the first time General Polk showed great concern about the eventual outcome of the war."[22]

Earlier that morning, a Confederate scout near Clinton had sent a message to Polk concerning the enemy's objective in Mississippi: "They do not try to conceal that their destination is Meridian, to cut our communications with Mobile." Polk discounted the message and continued to believe that Sherman was headed to Mobile via the Mobile and Ohio Railroad. Although the railroad intersected the Southern Railroad in Meridian, Polk believed that Sherman was determined to move southward away from the Southern Railroad before he reached that junction. The enemy forces at Yazoo City and those in eastern Louisiana might strike across the state and join with Sherman somewhere between Meridian and Mobile and then make a run at the port town. Therefore, Polk insisted, the Union army would not enter Meridian. Many of his subordinates did not agree. Stephen D. Lee wrote to Loring that he believed the enemy's destination was indeed the Mississippi city.[23]

Polk now requested troops from P. G. T. Beauregard in Charleston and

Joseph E. Johnston at Dalton in the event that the Union army attacked the Alabama port city. "I have not an adequate force for the defense of Mobile," he argued. Beauregard answered Polk two days later: "Regret cannot assist you. My force is quite limited." Johnston did not even bother to respond.[24]

After the Union army had left Jackson, Peter B. Starke's cavalry brigade had fallen in behind them, while Wirt Adams and Lee had taken positions on the Federal flank. They spent the day searching for an opportunity to harass the lumbering army as it traveled the road to Brandon. Except for capturing a few stragglers and skirmishing with the rear guard, the Confederate cavalry had a difficult time finding any vulnerable openings. "The enemy moved in good order, well closed up, with wagon trains [well protected]," a frustrated cavalry commander noted. As night fell, the Confederate cavalry regrouped and awaited orders. Tomorrow might bring the opening they had hoped for all day.[25]

On February 8, McPherson's Seventeenth Corps marched out of Brandon toward the northeast. Hurlbut's Sixteenth Corps, which had camped further from Brandon than McPherson's Seventeenth, marched into the town around midday, and the men foraged for provisions. It was not good to follow another corps, because most of the forage and food were already tucked away in the leaders' haversacks. In Brandon, however, a deserted commissary depot provided enough supplies for both corps, and the men obtained meal, salt, sweet potatoes, sugar, molasses, and a small amount of bacon. They also found a printing office that their brethren had bypassed and broke the place apart, similarly destroying a Confederate recruiting office and some other public buildings.[26]

As Hurlbut's men fell in that afternoon and proceeded to march toward Morton, a cleanly dressed fellow passed the column on foot. "I guess that's some fool chaplain," one soldier remarked. "He looks like it and very likely he jayhawked those clothes, for they are too good for a soldier," another shot back. The man paid no attention to the banter and continued walking until a group of mounted officers approached with a riderless horse in tow. When the infantrymen asked about the fellow on foot, the reply came as a shock. "They then told us that he was Gen. Sherman, so that was our first opinion of the best general we ever served under." They swore to never talk out of turn again. As Sherman was rarely described as well dressed, this occurrence provides insight into just how dirty and disheveled his soldiers must have been.[27]

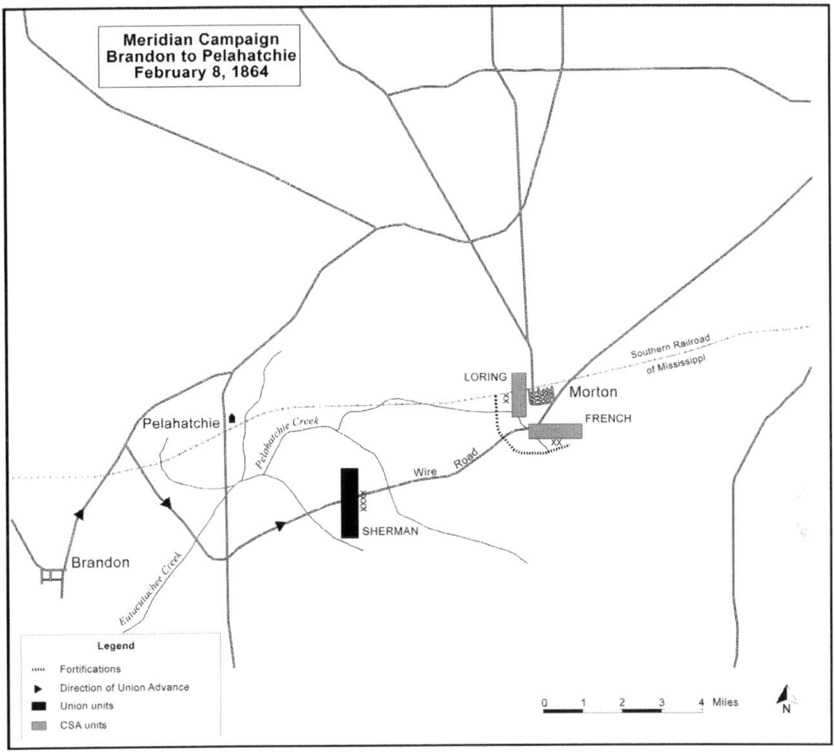

Hurlbut's corps continued on toward Morton, halting a few miles west of town for the night. McPherson's infantry had already camped at Line Creek, about four and half miles from Morton, with the cavalry about two miles in the front. The soldiers, huddled together for warmth against the cool night air, discussed the march. "By this time it became apparent that we were on 'Uncle Billy Sherman's' raid toward the heart of the Confederacy. We were bound for Alabama or Georgia; possibly Mobile [or] Savannah; certainly Selma," an Iowan prophesied.[28]

Just after dark, McPherson ordered Hickenlooper to take a twenty-man cavalry force to destroy a railroad bridge to the north, on the other side of a swamp. "This seemed like a very easy and simple matter," Hickenlooper later wrote in his memoirs, "but a more difficult task was never assigned to me." A moonless night and dense forest canopy made navigation almost impossible. The thick underbrush soon caused Hickenlooper to abandon his horses and walk his men single file through the tangle until he finally reached the bridge late into the night. Walking along the tracks were two local men, who "were the worst frightened men I have ever seen, supposed they were to be hanged and begged pitiously [*sic*] for their lives." The two men informed Hickenlooper that the Confederates had moved out of Morton that night. They happily showed the Federals the way to the bridge. Hickenlooper released them after he concluded that they were harmless. After they destroyed the bridge, Hickenlooper's little band retraced their steps and arrived back at camp as dawn broke over the horizon. "I reported to the General in a very wet, bedraggled and sorry looking plight," Hickenlooper said. Word soon arrived from McPherson's advance unit that the Confederates had indeed abandoned their fortifications.[29]

Around midnight in camp, while Hickenlooper was feeling his way through the swamp, the Union cavalry, only two miles from Morton, had enjoyed music from distant Confederate bands. While they listened, a courier appeared from McPherson with written orders. McPherson instructed Winslow to form at first light and feel out the enemy's position to his front. If Winslow called for it, McPherson promised he would send the infantry against such positions. Reports from the pickets also came in throughout the night reporting enemy movement. Sherman, hearing the news, continued to plan for a pitched battle the following day.[30]

Loring, still in command at Morton, had indeed decided to take the fight to the Federals. That morning, he instructed French to place his division in line of battle about two miles west of the city. The Missouri Brigade had reached Morton that morning after a cold journey, most of the way spent on open flatcars. They joined French's division on the line. Loring would use his division for support, and Lee would strike at the enemy from the rear and upon his flanks.[31]

By this time Polk had reached the town of Lake Station, twenty miles east of Morton, at which point he ordered Baldwin's brigade to go back to Mobile. He also ordered Francis Shoup's command, a partial brigade of Confederate parolees at Enterprise, Mississippi, to travel to Mobile. Polk insisted that T. F. Sevier at Meridian send transportation to Morton to carry four brigades along with five batteries back to the Alabama city. Polk's plan had not worked. Lee could not find a vulnerable opening in the enemy army's rear or flank. He could find no supply or communication line to compel Sherman to fall back to Vicksburg. The enemy was living off the land, and they were traveling in such force and compactness that the Confederate cavalry could cause but little harm.[32]

The Meridian campaign's success depended upon the Union army's ability to travel quickly to its objective. In Mississippi, the army needed to reach Meridian, complete its destruction of the railroads, and return to Vicksburg before the Confederates could send reinforcements to Polk. In this instance, Sherman's larger army could easily handle the smaller Confederate Mississippi force, forcing it to retire or defeating it on the field. Sherman's decision to dispense with a supply line and live off the land enabled him to move his army from Vicksburg to Brandon with celerity. He made the right decision.

Simultaneously, Sherman did not have to place a protective force along the line back to his supply base. Traditionally, the further an army advanced, the weaker it became because of the draw on troops to maintain the line. Now, Sherman could advance as far as he wished without fear of decreasing his strength as he marched. His army could forage off the land, ending the need for a supply line to provide victuals for the march. Here was a tactic he had first seen during Grant's Vicksburg campaign.

The rear lines of an army are always its most vulnerable points. Throughout combat history, severing supply and communication lines had always caused an invading army to return to its base for want of goods or information. As Sherman's army continued toward Meridian, however, it had no supply line, so the classically exposed position did not exist. When Lee's cavalry could not find Sherman's supply or communication lines, the weaker Confederate army had no choice but to continue retreating in the face of a superior enemy.

Loring and French met with their officers that afternoon. They decided that since they were indeed facing a superior enemy force, they had no choice but to continue to fall back and wait for the two thousand men that Polk had promised from Mobile. More infantry, along with Lee's cavalry also reinforced, might allow the Confederates to turn and fight Sherman's advancing column. Unfortunately for them, they did not know that Polk had already ordered some of the infantry brigades back to Mobile. The best opportunity for meeting the Union army passed because of miscommunication and poor leadership from Polk. Whether Loring and French stood at Morton and waited for reinforcements or fell back and waited further east, it did not matter. Support was not coming. Without it, the Confederate army had little chance of a victory against such overwhelming odds. Sherman had seen to it that only a conventional attack would pose any threat to his mission, and the Confederates were incapable of launching one.[33]

The even bigger question was, just who was commanding the Confederate army? Loring wrote Polk of his and French's decision: "This force being so much larger than ours I determined to fall back in the direction of Newton." He furthermore insisted that the enemy's objective was Meridian. The wording "I determined to fall back" that Loring used in his telegraph to Polk was particularly significant. Loring, not Polk, had decided to fall back to the east. Loring's decision, however, fit into Polk's long-held thoughts. Polk remained convinced that Sherman had his eyes on Mobile, so he did not dispute Loring's decision but made preparations to move his army into Alabama. After all, he had sent the reinforcements back to Mobile, and his army was scattered between Morton and Newton. If Sherman went to Mobile, Polk could flank him from central Alabama as he marched toward the southern port city.[34]

Just before daylight on February 9, Winslow's cavalrymen rode toward the previous day's enemy line. They found half-finished earthworks but no soldiers, the Confederate infantry having completed most of their withdrawal during the night. As they neared Morton, the Federal cavalry came upon the rear guard of the retreating army. The two forces fought into and through the town, continuing to skirmish intermittently throughout the remainder of the day. The Union horsemen captured several prisoners as well as securing nearly sixty Confederate deserters.[35]

Orders to withdraw had reached French's division two miles west of Morton around ten o'clock on the evening of February 8. Many of the Confederate soldiers were disappointed about the decision to retreat, especially those from Mississippi. "I do not know why Gen. Loring did not fight," a member of the Fourth Mississippi wrote home. "It seems to me they ou[gh]t to have kept the Yankees back. I am afraid our state will be given up. I am at a loss to know what to do. It is an awful thing." The rear guard built large fires along the line to cover their retreat and to deceive the Federals into thinking that they had not left their defensive positions. The Confederate infantry retreated along the road toward Hillsboro around midnight.[36]

McPherson's Seventeenth Corps followed its cavalry toward Morton ready for a fight. Nighttime rumors had insisted that the Confederate army was waiting for it, and a heavy battle seemed probable. By morning, however, news arrived that the enemy had departed. "Several places show the marks of Rebel guns bro[ugh]t in position to be moved again," one marcher observed as he traveled the road eastward. "Broken wagons, dead horses and mules, and the thousand things that soldiers throw away when hard pressed were to be found strewed along the road." The Federals reached Morton around midday without seeing any enemy soldiers other than deserters. They camped there, waiting for Hurlbut's Sixteenth Corps to take the lead, a position they would keep until the army reached Meridian.[37]

Several of the bluecoats welcomed the reprieve from marching. "Many of the men are suffering from blistered feet," one soldier remarked. Some troopers also complained of sunburn. The long walk also shortened tempers. While the men prepared their dinner with ample portions of hams and chickens from the Morton citizens' pantries, they continued to watch as Hurlbut's corps marched by.[38]

The Seventeenth New York Infantry came through Hurlbut's men late that afternoon, dressed in their colorful Zouave uniforms. "They turned out and lined the roadside to see us pass we being the first Zouaves they had ever seen. They being a rather low ignorant set mostly made up of western troops were not satisfied with looking at us but greeted us with insults," creating a "bitter feeling between us that was never effaced." General Hurlbut passed through the Fifteenth Iowa camp near sundown. "He was so intoxicated he could hardly sit on his horse," one Iowan observed. Hurlbut was well known for imbibing from time to time, so the march, it seemed, had apparently taken its toll on officer and man alike.[39]

In both armies throughout the war, soldiers and commanders often argued and fought among themselves. Eastern troops thought the western soldiers were ignorant, unkempt, and uncouth. Westerners viewed the easterners as dandified softies who could not fight for fear that they might soil their clothes. Infantrymen growled that they had never seen a dead cavalryman and that horsemen had it much easier in the field because their horses did the walking for them. Horse soldiers argued that they were the first in the action and the last to leave the field during hostilities. These conflicts were part of everyday military life, and most of the time they proved harmless to all involved. Such was the case in Sherman's army during this march.

That afternoon and early evening, Sherman detailed men to destroy the railroads and bridges near Morton, which they did before nightfall. The railroad was not the only thing destroyed in the little station town. "The principle [*sic*] houses in town were being burned," one fellow commented. An

Ohio soldier summed up the damage when he wrote in his diary: "Town all burned." Foraging parties had also cleaned the town out of most of its victuals, and Sherman's officers did little to stem the rampant pillaging and robbery. "Well this rebellion must be put down if it takes every chicken in the confederacy," remarked one officer to his men. "Of course the boys take this as a permission to . . . 'jayhawk' everything," a soldier commented. Sherman's army continued to take or destroy Confederate property, public and private.[40]

While Sherman's army had continued its advance, Polk had finally caught up with his retreating army near Morton on the morning of the ninth. He called an officers' meeting and announced his decision to split his force. He sent French's division to Newton Station and sent the regiments that had arrived from Mobile to catch the train back to the port city. French, since he outranked Dabney Maury, would take command and defend Mobile. Polk ordered Loring to continue falling back to the east toward Meridian and into Alabama.[41]

Polk telegraphed Richmond to inform President Davis that Sherman's force was "so much larger than anticipated" that all signs indicated "a combined attack on Mobile" and that Polk had ordered the return of all garrisoning forces to that port city. He planned to remain in the field with his cavalry and Loring's division, moving into Alabama via Meridian. Polk also sent a message to Maury at Mobile, informing him of the plan and insisting that the commander "urge the non-combatants to leave at once." "The fewer mouths [to feed] the better," he said, concerned about a long siege. Maury also wrote a letter to the editor of the *Mobile Tribune* and requested the departure of "all persons who cannot take part in the defense of the city."[42]

Winslow's cavalry left their position a little east of Shockaloo Creek on the morning of February 10 and soon met W. L. Maxwell's cavalry brigades acting as Loring's rear guard about two miles from Hillsboro. They continued skirmishing with the Confederates sporadically throughout the day. Hurlbut's Sixteenth Corps, traveling behind Winslow toward Hillsboro, soon heard the sound of the cavalry battle, but they were too far in the rear to support their comrades. A short distance from Hillsboro they saw three dead Confederates lying along the roadside, casualties from the earlier fight. They arrived at Hillsboro, the seat of Scott County, without firing a shot.[43]

The road between Brandon and Hillsboro contained few dwellings, the soil sandy and covered with tall pine trees. "The inhabitants were scattered and belonged to the poorer class," a marching Federal trooper observed. The town contained only twenty houses in all. As Hurlbut's corps marched through town, sniper fire came from one of the unburned buildings, and the blue-clad soldiers quickly moved to secure the area. Not able to discover the perpetrators, they set fire to the remaining buildings. "Most of the town was burned up," a fellow commented. "I could not help pitying many women and children who were thrown outdoors." "The town is in flames," a member of the Ninth Indiana noted in his diary.[44]

Just as the Sixteenth Corps cleared town across a small bridge, and before McPherson's Seventeenth Corps could arrive, a group of Confederate cavalry dashed in and fired the bridge. When the Seventeenth Corps passed through, the town looked like a scene from Dante's *Inferno.* "Scarcely a house remained," remarked a member of McPherson's corps. "The jail, too, where Sambo once waited for his kind and indulgent master, vanished in smoke and ashes," one sarcastic trooper wrote. Crops from local farmers and planters for the Confederate army filled warehouses throughout town. The retreating forces had carried as much as they could away with them, but the Union troopers discovered that some corncribs and warehouses still contained provisions. "The residue is consigned to flames," one Federal soldier said, "which sometimes spread to buildings not ordered to be burned." Some of the pine trees caught fire from the flaming buildings, and blazing trees fell across the road, making it hazardous to move wagons filled with supplies and ammunition. The flaming but still standing bridge was difficult for the wagon trains to cross. Despite all the hazards, however, the Seventeenth finally managed to reach the other bank. Both corps camped a short distance east of the burning town, McPherson's at Tallabogue Creek and Hurlbut's just east of there. That night Sherman issued orders to Hurlbut to start early the next morning and "be prepared to make a march in the direction of Decatur." The main Federal column was leaving the Southern Railroad.[45]

French had pushed his men the entire night of the ninth, and they reached Newton Station the following morning at daybreak. He learned that the War Department had placed Maury in command of Mobile, so it did not matter what Polk said about who should command there, the War Department's orders taking precedence over Polk's. To avoid confusion, Polk changed his orders and instructed French to turn his troops over to Maury when he reached Mobile. He was then to return in person to the Meridian area.[46]

Lee had informed Polk that he had ordered all of his cavalry forces away from the rear of the enemy and ended his offensive against the Union army. He had moved them closer to Meridian so they could be sent to important defensive locations. "I think a large column of infantry is coming down the Mobile and Ohio Railroad, which will unite with Sherman at Meridian," Lee insisted. He believed that even if the enemy's objective was Mobile, they would go to Meridian first. "There is little opportunity to do much with the enemy on the march. He moves in perfect order," Lee complained.[47]

This information turned Polk's attention toward the Federal cavalry column in Collierville. Spies had informed the Confederates that about ten thousand enemy cavalry were preparing to move eastward across the state, strike the Mobile and Ohio Railroad north of Columbus, Mississippi, and travel southward. Polk guessed that Sherman intended to join with the cavalry somewhere along the railroad on the eastern side of the state along the Alabama border. After the two Union forces had joined, Polk believed, they would march on Mobile. He decided to focus his attention on keeping the cavalry from linking with Sherman's army and headed to Meridian to direct operations from there. He sent word to B. G. Bidwell at Enterprise to ready the public stores for shipment to Meridian; if he could not find enough transportation, Bidwell should burn the supplies.[48]

Lee sent Adams to the south of Meridian to watch the Mobile and Ohio Railroad for enemy troop movement there. He told Lawrence Sullivan Ross's brigade, recently arrived from Yazoo City and located too far west to go on the defensive, to harass the enemy by driving in foraging parties and attacking vulnerable supply wagons. Lee remained near Decatur, directing his cavalrymen from there.[49]

On February 10, Jefferson Davis issued a public letter to "Soldiers of the Armies of the Confederate States," and many newspapers quickly carried his statement. He congratulated the soldiers for their "glorious victories over vastly more numerous hosts" during the "long and bloody war." The commander in chief then thanked the men for enduring the hardships that came with soldierly duty and the "restraints upon [their] individual will," extending special thanks to those who had reenlisted. Looking toward the future, Davis expressed his belief that the Confederate army could defeat the foe because the enemy had become "overstrained" over the last three years of service. He closed by promising the men that "assured success awaits us in our holy struggle for liberty and independence, and for the preservation of all that renders life desirable to honorable men." Although the message was intended to uplift the spirits and rejuvenate the hearts of the Confederate army, those who faced Sherman in Mississippi probably did not receive the message until much later. Even if they had, the Confederates were in full flight before a superior force and could do nothing to stop the Federal advance straight into the heart of the Confederacy. A "pep talk" would have done little to change their hardening attitude toward the Confederate high command.[50]

The Army of Mississippi had, indeed, witnessed the march of Sherman's army across the Mississippi bottomlands virtually unchallenged during the past six months. Now it seemed as if the Federals could go anywhere in the Magnolia State, and Polk could not or would not do anything to prevent it. The Army of Mississippi contained several Mississippi regiments, and it was their homes that the Confederacy was now abandoning. This retreat would have a significant impact on the Mississippi soldiers' actions after Sherman returned to Vicksburg. Hundreds of Mississippians deserted before the spring campaigns began, returning to their farms and homes to protect their families. If the Confederacy could not defend them, then the men would leave the army and take care of their homes themselves.

On February 11, Winslow's cavalry continued to screen the infantry's line of march. Confederate cavalryman W. L. Maxwell's regiment, heavily outnumbered four regiments to one, battled stubbornly against Winslow's cavalry brigade and burned bridge after bridge before the Union cavalry. The armies had moved into an area of low river bottoms with crisscrossing creeks and swamp-bottom lowlands that made traveling off the road impossible. The Federal cavalry spent most of their day repairing bridges rather than fighting the enemy.[51]

Hickenlooper's Pioneer Corps worked to corduroy more than three thousand feet of road across the Tuscalemeta Swamp. The march had become slow because of the bridges burned the day before, and now poor roads further hindered movement. The swampy conditions had an even worse effect on the Federal infantrymen. They slogged and sloshed their way through ankle-deep mud for ten to fifteen miles a day. Mule and horse teams became exhausted from pulling wagons and guns through the thick muck. A member of the Fifty-third Indiana described the scene: "The wagons and mules were stuck and mired and drivers were cursing and hollowing [*sic*] until they became hoarse."[52]

Throughout the expedition, the Pioneer Corps served two main purposes: they repaired roads and bridges to allow the Union army to continue its advance, and they assisted in the destruction of railroads and other property. The proficient work of the Pioneer Corps, like the lack of a cumbersome supply line, allowed Sherman's army to move quickly across Mississippi. Although the Confederates attempted to slow the Federal advance with burned bridges, the workmen's excellent efforts permitted Sherman to continue the march with little interruption. Mississippi's vast, impenetrable swamps also compelled the Federals to repair miles of bad roads. Hickenlooper's men had built bridge after bridge since leaving Jackson, and they had corduroyed thousands of feet of road, continuing to provide valuable service to the Union army.

Sherman also depended upon his Pioneer Corps to point out the best locations to obtain maximum results from his army's destructive effort. On numerous occasions, Hickenlooper and other engineering officers traveled with Federal cavalry and infantry to other towns to oversee the demolition of an important rail junction or bridge while the Pioneer Corps continued its work in front of the marching Union army, repairing and corduroying. As he neared Meridian, Sherman looked to Hickenlooper and his men for results. The commanding general recognized the importance of an efficient Pioneer Corps in his later campaigns, a lesson he learned on his long march across Mississippi.

When men of Hurlbut's Sixteenth Corps halted to wait for a bridge repair, they often set fire to the tall pine trees that lined the road in order to warm themselves. The sap from an injured pine "burns like oil," one fellow remembered, as did "the leaves which covered the ground thickly," creating a perfect environment for a fertile blaze.[53] The fires soon got out of hand. The Sixteenth Corps moved out, but the Seventeenth still had to pass. When they reached these blazes, "the fires had gotten under good headway." Dead trees "were burning rapidly [and] falling in every direction, across the road and elsewhere." The teamsters screamed at their horses and cracked their whips to induce the animals to rush through the fires. "We had several very narrow escapes from falling trees," an Illinoisan commented. The cold weather, the deep quagmires of swamp, enemy soldiers, and fires started by their own army all caused a slower march.[54]

Hickenlooper had received orders that morning to travel with John S. Foster's reconnaissance force of about one hundred cavalrymen down to

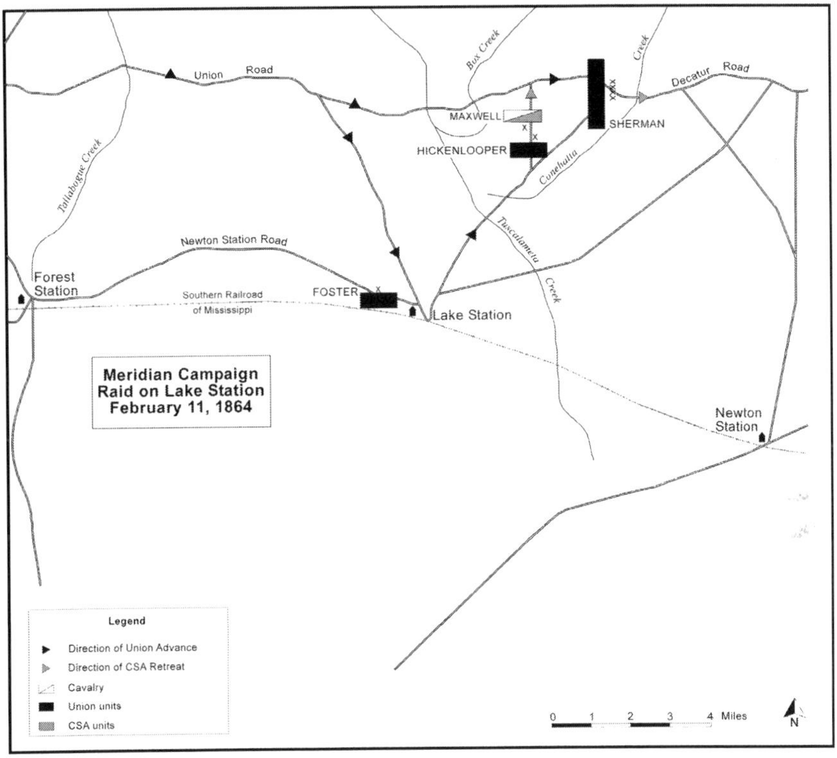

Lake Station, the site of Polk's headquarters a few days before. He met no resistance along the way and rode straight into the town, catching the citizens unaware. His force destroyed two locomotives, the engine house, thirty-five cars, a railroad turntable, and about half a mile of track. In addition, the men fired the depot, two livery stables, several machine shops, a warehouse, two sawmills, a large stand of milled lumber, several hundred gallons of turpentine, and the water tank. Hearing all the commotion, a few Confederate cavalrymen rode into town and, briefly and ineffectively, confronted the enemy raiders. Captain Lucius M. Rose, commander of the Signal Corps, noted in his report: "While the cavalry were fighting the rebels the Signal Corps went through the town like a dose of salts, and just as we were leaving I noticed a man hunting around to get some one to make an affidavit that there had been a town there." He estimated the damage to the equipment and buildings at a million dollars, a tremendous amount in 1864.[55]

Lake Station contained a large amount of Confederate government equipment and supplies. Serving as an important railroad repair center, the town contained machinery for locomotive repair. Sherman's objective in Mississippi was to leave the rail lines destroyed and unusable for the Confederacy, and the Federal destruction at the important little settlement served that purpose well. Railroad engines in particular were becoming increasingly difficult for the Confederate government to obtain.

While Foster's cavalry was busy in Lake Station, the Federal infantry settled wearily into camp four miles west of Decatur. Near dark, Sherman penned an order to his officers. He had decided to combine the bulk of his supply wagons, along with all the ill soldiers, in one "general train under the escort of one regiment to a division and one battery." Only two wagons would travel close up with each regiment now, one for bread and one for ammunition. The general train would stay with the army until it reached Tallahatta Creek, and then it would halt and await further instructions. Once the army had reached Decatur, it would move directly upon Meridian with great haste. Sherman did not want a great many wagons to slow the advance. He also ordered McPherson to detail a regiment to strike the Southern Railroad south of Decatur and move parallel along its tracks as the army traveled eastward. As it advanced, the regiment was to demolish the rails, bridges, and culverts along the railroad. Sherman told Hickenlooper that he was relying on him to keep his Pioneer Corps close to the front in order to work constantly on the bridges and roads as needed. He wanted the final rush into Meridian to go smoothly and swiftly.[56]

Meanwhile, Lee met with Samuel Ferguson, who had been at Newton Station covering French's withdrawal. He ordered Ferguson to join Maxwell in screening Loring's retreat near Morton. He hoped that the combined cavalry forces could hamper the enemy's march toward Meridian. "It was then evident he [Sherman] was moving on Meridian and not Mobile," Lee noted. Ferguson immediately began the difficult cross-country ride through the swamps and bottomlands and met the enemy the following day near Chunky River. Polk needed more time to maneuver his troops.[57]

Polk had finally realized that Sherman was heading to Meridian, but he still believed that the Union army would then move on Mobile. He continued to fall for feints and false reports just as Sherman had hoped. Polk sent a message to Loring informing him that reports indicated that the enemy army was following his retreat to Decatur. Additional reports confirmed that

Sherman was indeed moving his entire force toward Meridian. Polk decided to act.[58]

On February 11 the bishop ordered Lee to send his cavalry, now near Chunky Station, to intercept Sherman's vanguard, placing the Confederate horsemen between the Union army and Loring's retreating division. In his message to Lee, Polk blamed the cavalry commander for causing him to believe that the Union army was moving straight to Mobile. Polk indicated that he had come to his conclusion "in support of your [Lee's] dispatch to General Loring at Morton that the enemy was moving south of [the] railroad, bearing down on Mobile." Because of his belief that Sherman was marching to the Alabama town south of the railroad before he reached Meridian, Polk had maneuvered his troops accordingly and incorrectly. Lee replied curtly in two separate messages that he had "never reported them bearing down on Mobile to General Loring." He had "examined [his] letters" and found that he had only suggested the possibility of Sherman's army moving to Mobile, but only after they had visited Meridian. Indeed, Lee had argued since the expedition's start that Sherman was going to Meridian. Polk was either too far away from the action or lacked the ability to determine his enemy's intentions in Mississippi. Lee was on the battlefield, and he knew what was important to Sherman—Meridian railroads. True, Lee considered the possibility that the Federals might march on Mobile, but he was convinced from the earliest days of the expedition that Sherman would hit Meridian first.[59]

Feints had always been a part of conventional military strategy, Grant brilliantly demonstrating their effectiveness in the recent Vicksburg campaign. They served to divert attention away from an army's main objective. Sherman's successful use of feints in the Meridian campaign illustrated a key component in the new strategy of raiding. As previously discussed, it is important to keep the enemy forces separated so that they cannot combine together in a large force to meet the raiding army. In this case, Sherman wanted to keep the Confederacy from reinforcing Polk with troops from Georgia or Alabama. Therefore, Federal feints from Tennessee into Georgia and from the Gulf coast on Mobile kept Polk, Johnston, and Richmond guessing wrongly about Sherman's main intention of attacking Meridian. By the time Sherman reached Jackson, he knew that his feint had worked up to that point, saying that he had completely confused his enemy. Sherman had believed that the Confederates could not move fast enough to stop him from taking Jackson. In fact, he had counted on it. But when he arrived a few miles from Meridian and understood that his feints continued to keep Polk guessing, he was astounded at their success.[60]

Feints would continue to be a significant part of Sherman's new war. Traveling without immediate support deep into Confederate territory meant that he had to take measures to offset his chance of meeting superior numbers. Feints and rumors served that purpose, and his success with them during the Meridian expedition convinced Sherman that this tactic should remain a part of all his future campaigns. Sherman biographer Basil Liddell Hart believed that what he called Sherman's "indirect approach," or the use of feints, was the key to his successes on the battlefield. In *Sherman: Soldier, Realist, American,* Liddell Hart focuses mainly on the general's use of this tactic in Georgia and in the Carolinas. It was during the Meridian expedition, however, that Sherman had his best results with the maneuver. Sherman's plan had worked, and now Polk could only try to salvage what he could.[61]

Polk sent word to T. F. Sevier at Meridian to halt Matthew Ector's and Francis Cockrell's brigades there. Because of the lack of transportation from Newton, they were not allowed to entrain until that afternoon. The other brigades had already reached and passed through Meridian on their way to Mobile. At the moment, it was too late to recall them. Polk further instructed Sevier to "ship all public property to Demopolis as soon as possible." He should also evacuate the sick from the Meridian and Enterprise hospitals to a location further east.[62]

Polk received word from Forrest in northern Mississippi that a Union force of approximately ten thousand cavalry and mounted infantry was moving out of Collierville on its way east. Forrest believed that the enemy intended to cross Mississippi and strike the Mobile and Ohio Railroad on the eastern side of the state. Polk telegraphed Lee to gather his cavalry together and ready them to join Forrest in northern Mississippi to assist in halting the enemy movement from Collierville. Polk hoped that, if he could stop this force, it might end Sherman's expedition. Knowing that he would not receive assistance from Johnston, and concluding already that he did not have the strength to fight Sherman, he saw no other option.[63]

Polk ordered Loring to fight a delaying action so that the Confederates at Meridian could remove all the public stores and send them safely beyond the reach of Sherman's army. He informed the general that Ferguson's cavalry would assist in the slowing of the Union army's advance. If Loring could stall Sherman, the public stores could be removed from Meridian, and Polk would have time to deal with the enemy cavalry force now bearing down on him from the northwest.[64]

Davis, in Richmond, had received word from Polk about the bleak situation in Mississippi. He decided it was time for Johnston, at Dalton, to aid the floundering bishop. "Do whatever you can to assist him, either by sending him re-enforcements or joining him with what force you can," Davis wrote Johnston. Still stinging from their earlier disagreement over helping Polk, Johnston replied tersely that the enemy had thirty-five thousand troops and sixty cannon moving toward Mobile and that "General Polk's cavalry ought to prevent such a march."

Because of his prior experience, Johnston knew that Davis would side with Polk if the president deemed the bishop endangered in Mississippi. The Dalton commander, however, thought that the Union army threatened his position in Georgia as severely as it did Polk's in Mississippi. Johnston wanted to know more about the situation in Mississippi before he freely sent reinforcements. By the time Polk received the message of inquiry, however, it was too late to save Meridian.[65]

While Davis and Johnston battled over the wires, Grant was having problems with one of his subordinates. On February 12 he ordered George H. Thomas to "take Dalton and hold it, if possible." He wanted Thomas to make a strong attack on Dalton so that Johnston could not send reinforcements to Polk. Grant also thought that if Thomas could hold the position, it would serve nicely as a base for spring campaigns. Thomas, however, delayed in getting under way. He did not head toward Dalton until February 22, too late to assist Sherman's expedition, which, by that time, had already begun its return to Vicksburg. Sherman's army continued its march toward Meridian, oblivious to Grant's difficulty in getting Thomas started in Tennessee.[66]

On February 12, Winslow's cavalry, riding in front of the army toward Decatur, met a dismounted brigade of enemy troops scattered along a crossroads. It was Ferguson. He had ridden all night from Newton Station, relieved Maxwell, and taken the position awaiting the Union advance. After a short fight, Winslow flanked Ferguson and forced him to withdraw eastward. Twelve Federal soldiers were killed in the fight, while the Confederates lost eighteen to death and capture. "From the confidence with which he advances," Ferguson wrote Loring, "I judge there is a large force of infantry moving in this direction." This confirmed Loring's fears. The entire Union army was bearing down on him, just as Polk had predicted. How could he face such tremendous odds? He did not know. Polk had given Loring discretionary powers to withdraw when he deemed it necessary. The Confederate division left Decatur and headed for Meridian. Lee rode hard for Decatur from Chunky Station. He would assist the heavily outnumbered Loring as best he could.[67]

Near midmorning, Hurlbut's corps moved toward Decatur, the seat of Newton County with over five hundred households and an 1860 population of thirty-two hundred white residents. The corps' vanguard tramped into the "dilapidated old town" that afternoon with ragged feet and weary bones. Their fight with the swamp had drained their strength, and they were ready for a rest. Many collapsed beside buildings or lay down at the edge of the street. Fires flickered in some of the buildings not long after their arrival, and the division commander placed his cavalry escort as guard over the town. "While waiting [to move] we cooked coffee on the ruins of one of the buildings," an exhausted Zouave reported in his diary. The commander gathered his men together and marched them beyond town to keep them from causing any further damage. By the time the Federals left, however, thirty of Decatur's buildings were afire.[68]

Sherman sent a message to Hurlbut ordering him to take his corps beyond Decatur and camp near a good water source. He wanted the army out of Decatur as soon as possible. Lingering meant damage, and there was no railroad there to destroy. Soon, however, Sherman became highly agitated. All the commotion in town, with the burning buildings, the placing of guards, and the weariness of the soldiers, had slowed Hurlbut's corps to a crawl. "Your train has been standing here for the last four hours," Sherman wrote hotly, "and does not move a bit." It was not until after dark that the Union army finally moved out of Decatur and into camp beyond town.[69]

Tired from the day's events, Sherman decided to take shelter in a small "double-log house," where he arranged for supper. His staff unsaddled their horses and made preparations for the night, Sherman deciding to lie down in the back room to sleep. Shouts and gunfire awoke the sleeping commander; as he sprang from his bed, one of his aides shouted that enemy cavalry was attacking. When Sherman asked about the whereabouts of the regiment of infantry that he had assigned as guard, the answer came back that they were nowhere to be found. Someone mentioned seeing them marching east behind Hurlbut's corps. The aide bolted out the door and dashed down the road to overtake the troops to bring them back to defend their commander.

Sherman ran into the backyard to see teamsters driving their wagons wildly in all directions as Confederate cavalrymen dashed to and fro, screaming Rebel yells and firing into the mules and at the men. The commanding general gathered what men he had and prepared to use a corncrib for protection. Just then, however, he saw the lost brigade coming back to his defense at a full run. They promptly drove the Confederate cavalry away.

It turned out that the regimental commander guarding Sherman had mistaken some of McPherson's staff for the head of his infantry column and had moved down the road prematurely. This left a gap between the two columns of infantry. With Hurlbut's wagons scattered along the road, Adams had noticed that several were vulnerable for attack. The assault came, coincidentally, when the Union wagons were close to Sherman's location. The result of the attack was seventeen mules killed and some wagons disabled, but no human lives lost on the Federal side. The Confederate attackers lost eight, five killed and three captured. Adams reported later that up to that day he had sustained 129 men killed, wounded, or missing with nearly 150 horses dead.[70]

Sherman's quick thinking and the promptness of the Union infantry had thwarted any chance of Confederate success, and the enemy was not able to escape with any of the wagons. "I jumped on a six mule Yankee team," one Mississippian wrote, and "our own men . . . rushed past me and killed every mule on the wagon before I could explain." His comrades, in their excitement, could not identify who was the enemy and who was not, so they shot even the single mule that the unlucky Confederate rode. The only prize he got away with was his life. The near disaster was the only mistake Sherman made during the entire march. Although the Confederate cavalry made several attempts to attack wagon trains, the Federal infantry escorts defended each attempt effectively.[71]

Sherman later noted in his memoir that if the wagon escorts had not kept the attention of the attackers, "I would surely have been captured." The loss of Sherman would have taken a heavy toll not only on the expedition but, more importantly, on the Union war effort. Grant would have lost his most trusted and favored general and friend. McPherson, as next senior officer, would have taken command, and most likely he would have completed the march on Meridian. A competent permanent replacement for Sherman might have been more difficult to obtain, however. Grant liked McPherson, as Sherman did, but Thomas was senior to McPherson. Would Grant have ignored seniority and appointed McPherson over Thomas? If so, did McPherson have the talent to complete the Atlanta campaign? Would there even have been a March to the Sea? Since the 1864–65 Federal offensive strategy primarily consisted of a two-pronged Grant/Sherman attack, the war might have lasted much longer without Sherman.[72]

What of Sherman's postwar image? If the Confederate cavalry had killed Sherman at Decatur in February 1864, historians would have labeled him a mediocre commander at best, having been accused of insanity in Kentucky and Missouri, having endured disaster at Chickasaw Bluffs, and having mounted a failed attack at Chattanooga. He certainly would not have become the icon for murder and destruction to Lost Cause advocates. Because of Sherman's near death or capture, the importance of the Meridian campaign for Sherman's meteoric rise to fame during the last two years of the war becomes even more obvious. The Meridian expedition served as the beginning of his success (and infamy), because it was the first major implementation of his new philosophy of warfare.

The death or capture of the Union general would have influenced Polk's Confederate army as well. It had witnessed Sherman take mile after mile of Mississippi ground since summer 1863. They retreated in front of his army, and their army commander had few plans to stop the Federal movement. Sherman's capture or death would have given the Army of Mississippi a new, invigorating outlook on their possibilities. Even if they had continued to retreat, they would have achieved a major triumph by eliminating Sherman, the leader of the advancing Federals. Sherman did not die, however, and the march continued with few Federal soldiers appreciating the profound possibilities of the incident. One Union soldier summed up the occurrence when word about the failed capture of his commander came through camp: "A miss is good as a mile."[73]

It was soon discovered that a resident of Decatur had taken part in the raid, so "his splendid residence and the principle [*sic*] part of the town were burned in retaliation," a member of the Fifteenth Illinois wrote. Most of the town burned during the night, causing some of the Union division commanders to order their men to cease such excessive actions. "[Our commander told us] that he would hang the first man who fired his gun at anything except a rebel," one soldier remarked. Although the officers issued warnings, the men continued pillaging, robbing, burning, and shooting. "I heard of none being even arrested for it," the same fellow concluded.[74]

While one Mississippi town went up in smoke, the Confederates attempted to save as many goods as they could from another. At Meridian on February 12, Polk scrambled to get the public property loaded and sent to Demopolis. He estimated that "all the stores [would be] removed by the afternoon of tomorrow or earlier." With any luck, he would leave few supplies for the Union army's use.[75]

It was, however, Sherman's ability to cut loose from vulnerable supply and communication lines and the resourcefulness of the Pioneer Corps that gave him the freedom to move freely and quickly. Sherman understood that the absence of rear lines allowed his army to move quickly and not drain itself of manpower. Because the vulnerable lines were not available for Confederate attack, the enemy's cavalry had great difficulty disrupting the march. His feints kept the enemy off balance, and the Pioneer Corps allowed his troops to keep moving no matter the conditions. Sherman was on the verge of taking Meridian and breaking the Confederate rail link there. If William Sooy Smith's cavalry force reached him at Meridian, he could continue into Alabama and break the railroad at Demopolis or Selma. First, though, he had to take Meridian, and he made preparations for a final dash to capture the important rail hub. His destructive war strategy continued to evolve as he marched to take the Mississippi town.

5 / Meridian Falls

William T. Sherman's army had traveled nearly 150 miles in less than two weeks to reach the eastern edge of Mississippi. By the time he reached Meridian, near the Alabama border, Sherman realized that a key to his success had been his careful planning and preparation. Mississippi, although appearing to be under Confederate control, was nothing more than an empty shell, and he had been able to march into areas previously believed to be well defended. In Meridian, Sherman intensified his destruction of the region on a massive scale, burning, confiscating, and smashing anything deemed of military value. He continued to send out foragers, searching for provisions for his hungry army. These troopers, isolated from the main column, often found themselves in a dangerous position, and some fell to enemy bullets or were captured.

Even as Sherman reached Meridian, the Confederates continued to fall back eastward in front of his larger Union army, trying to save all the supplies and equipment they could before it fell into his hands. And the stubborn Leonidas Polk remained convinced that Sherman's objective was Mobile. The beleaguered Confederate army, therefore, moved toward Demopolis, waiting for an opportunity to strike at Sherman when he passed there to make his attack on the port city. Polk placed great emphasis on the importance of halting the enemy cavalry advance, then on stopping Sherman's infantry. Without his main cavalry force, Polk believed, Sherman could not continue his movement toward Mobile.

In 1860, Meridian's population stood at 400, out of Lauderdale County's 13,500 white residents, 5,088 slaves, and one free black. The small settlement, earlier known as Sawashee Creek, had been incorporated into a town just a year before the outbreak of hostilities. Nestled about fifteen miles from the Alabama state line, the beautiful surrounding countryside of pine timber and rolling hills and the burgeoning opportunities that a newly created town offered made Meridian an attractive place to migrants.[1]

By the time the war started, the settlement contained nearly one hundred homes and a number of hotels and boardinghouses, including the Ragsdale Hotel, Terrill's Inn, Meridian House, and the Burton House; three or four small stores, with the two largest being John Ball's grocery store and W. E. Brown's; a boarding school under the direction of Rev. W. C. Emerson; and two churches, one Methodist, the other Baptist. The Baptist church became an arsenal in 1861 and, by war's end, a hospital. The Methodist church was a one-room log cabin located on the side of the railroad tracks where, each month, eight or ten families would gather to hear the itinerant preacher's sermon. The cobbler William Massengale had a shop in town, as did W. J. Berry, the town's doctor, and T. S. James, a marble craftsman who made beautiful mantels. I. S. O. Greer, one of the wealthiest citizens of Meridian, had started a shingle mill, and it did excellent business meeting demands. In 1863 the Pioneer Manufacturing Cotton Mill started operation, taking advantage of the perfect location to ship processed cotton out of Mississippi.[2]

Eighty of Meridian's male inhabitants had answered the Confederacy's call, forming the "Meridian Invincibles" in May 1861. Samuel J. Randell, captain of the Pettus Guards of the Eighth Regiment of Mississippi Volunteers, led the group. The troops had hurried off to Corinth to complete training, and subsequently they fought in the battles of Forts Henry and Donelson. In total, Lauderdale County furnished fifteen companies to the Confederacy.[3]

Lauderdale County was not as large an agricultural area as Hinds, Rankin, or Warren county, although it did produce nearly five hundred thousand bushels of corn and twelve thousand bales of cotton in 1860. Most of the farms contained less than fifty acres, but the county did have seventeen farms of over five hundred acres; and it had a slave population of five thousand countywide. Because of the acres of pine forest covering its landscape, timber was one of the county's major industries. Sawmills dotted the countryside, and the railroads shipped thousands of yards of lumber to locations across the South.[4]

While the Mobile and Ohio Railroad had a stop at Meridian by 1855, it was not until May 1861 that the first locomotive, the *Mazeppa,* steamed down the Southern Railroad on the completed link from Jackson, reaching Meridian loaded with the "Vicksburg Southrons," a volunteer company from the river city. The Confederate government completed a rail line from Meridian to Selma in December 1862. When the workers hammered the final spike into the tie, they had completed an all-rail link between Vicksburg and Richmond, with the exception of a section across the Tombigbee River west of Selma and a steamboat connection between Montgomery and Selma. Telegraph wires were installed later that same year.[5]

Because of its location at the junction of the Mobile and Ohio Railroad and the Southern Railroad, the little hamlet became a Confederate transportation hub for goods and men. The Confederates constructed new buildings there to service locomotives, store goods, manufacture arms, and house soldiers. A Federal soldier remarked on this construction when he entered Meridian for the first time: "The town looks as though it had been built within six months." Because the Federal advances in Tennessee and northern Mississippi had cut off alternate shipping routes, Meridian had gained an even greater importance as a rail hub. A hospital on the edge of town treated injured soldiers from the battles of Corinth, Iuka, Chattanooga, and Vicksburg, while a large prison stockade served as a point of parole and exchange of prisoners of war. After the fall of Jackson in 1863, the town even briefly served as Mississippi's capital. Because of a lack of suitable buildings to house state officials and records, however, Governor John Pettus soon moved his entourage to Macon in Noxubee County.[6]

By 1863 Meridian served as the headquarters of the state of Mississippi chief of ordinance and of the Confederate pay quartermaster and department quartermaster. Each of these offices brought a great amount of military business to the town. For example, in August, Mississippi's chief quartermaster placed an advertisement in the local paper announcing that his department would purchase all the wool in the state to make winter clothing for the soldiers. Meridian's ever-growing importance to the cause, therefore, had convinced Sherman to place it high on his destruction list.[7]

On February 13, as he prepared to make his final rush toward Meridian, Sherman left most of his supply wagons between Chunky River and Tallahatta Creek. He placed the Confederate prisoners and the Union sick and wounded near the wagons with a strong infantry force of four regiments to guard against an enemy attack. He did not want anything to slow his final advance toward his objective. The wagon trains covered nearly forty acres—some six hundred vehicles and three to four thousand mules and horses in all. The Union soldiers carried five days' rations in their haversacks and were under orders to drop baggage "to the smallest possible limit."[8]

As the Confederate forces withdrew before the Union army, they dropped trees across the road. They also burned all the bridges in Sherman's path. The Pioneer Corps, therefore, had to engage continually in removing timber and constructing new bridges. The work proved so exhausting that the regular infantry had to help in clearing the roadways. "Some of the poor fellows could hardly drag themselves along," an Iowan observed. Fortunately, the Union army reached better roads, with fewer obstructions, just at dusk that February 13 and covered six or seven miles before settling into camp.[9]

Rumors circulated around the campfires that the Confederates were sure to make a stand at Meridian. Late that evening, Federal soldiers had found a board nailed to a tree that read: "13 Miles to Hell." Many of the men were convinced that this meant the Confederates would not give up Meridian without a fierce fight. The Union marchers wondered if now, nearly two weeks after leaving Vicksburg, they would finally meet the Confederate infantry in battle. Just outside Decatur, a soldier had discovered some old issues of the *Daily Clarion,* a newspaper from Meridian. "It seems to doubt our force and thought we would be repulsed at Pearl River," one soldier noted. Many of the officers carefully prepared their men for a severe fight. Colonel John Scott, commander of the Thirty-Second Iowa in Hurlbut's corps, made a moving speech concerning the hard march, the possible lack of provisions, and the high probability of a battle at Meridian: "Men, you have now been in the service over a year, and have had comparative ease and sufficient food, but now, as it seems, the Government will soon have urgent need of us. I ask you, man to man, to set your faces sternly to the performance of every duty, and be prepared to make the great sacrifice, if need be." The men cheered their commander's words, expressing their readiness to perform their soldierly duty.[10]

The Sixteenth Corps left camp at sunrise the morning of February 14, with the Seventeenth behind it. After a few miles of battling fallen timber, it made its way to Tallahatta Creek, about nine miles west of Meridian. Confederate cavalry was in position just west of the river on a small hill, watching the advancing Federals as they prepared to cross the river. The lead elements of the Federal column halted on the west side of the creek and considered their options.[11]

The Union army had bivouacked in a rough, hilly section of Mississippi that had few inhabitants and little sustenance. Hurlbut and Sherman agreed that the army needed to pass through this area and get to the city as quickly as possible, first, to capture Meridian before the Confederates could concentrate, and second, so that the city's rich stores could supply them. Hurlbut ordered his lead division, A. J. Smith's Third, to keep a "strong pioneer force at work clearing the road of any obstacles, and push rapidly and steadily on."[12]

In this vein, Sherman decided to continue on toward Meridian through the early hours of darkness. He ordered Edward Winslow to take his cavalry force, with Hurlbut's corps supporting, and attack the enemy's defenses. When Winslow's four cavalry brigades reached the Confederate position, they found nearly five hundred men engaged in chopping down trees. The Union cavalryman quickly dismounted his advance regiment, drew it up into a line, and advanced, filling the air with carbine fire. The butternuts recoiled in surprise but quickly composed themselves and began to return fire. They withdrew slowly as Winslow's cavalry advanced on foot. Because of the rugged terrain, the Union soldiers had great difficulty keeping a battle line, but they were able to push the Confederates off the hill and into the low meadows below. There the Confederate soldiers formed in two defensive lines with their right flank anchored in a strip of woods. Winslow's men moved forward, attacking the enemy's advance line, and because of the darkness and confusion, the second line fired into the first. Soon after, both Confederate lines collapsed and melted into the woods. Winslow's cavalry withdrew a short distance and bivouacked for the remainder of the night. They had achieved a success, securing the west side of Tallahatta Creek for Sherman's army.[13]

Meanwhile, Polk continued to rush around trying to save supplies and equipment in Meridian before the arrival of the Union army. He wrote to Dabney Maury at Mobile that Sherman was not heading to that port city until he first went to Meridian, as "all information received led" him to believe. Polk informed the garrison commander that he intended to hold Sherman "in check" until he could evacuate Meridian. After that he planned to send another infantry regiment and some more supplies to Mobile, but he reserved the remainder for Selma and Demopolis.[14]

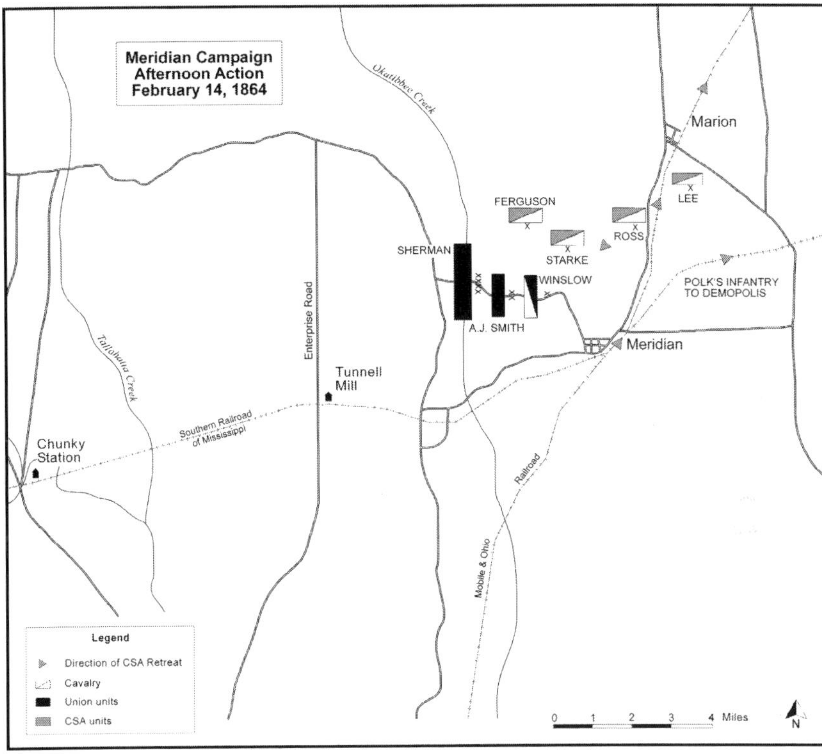

Polk ordered Stephen D. Lee and his cavalry, early that morning of February 14, to get between Sherman and the Mobile and Ohio Railroad north of Meridian and slow him down. Lee could not do it, however, because he was too far south. He decided, therefore, to move his two brigades (Wirt Adams's and Peter B. Starke's) to a location north of Chunky Station and there monitor Sherman's progress. Lee told Polk that he did not know what to do, because he did not have enough troops to meet the enemy in the field. His horses were tired, and many of them were lame. Polk still insisted that Lee make an attempt to get into position, but Lee replied, "I fear it is too late."[15]

When Lee informed Polk of his whereabouts late that afternoon, the bishop insisted that Lee come to Meridian that night. Polk wanted Lee's two cavalry brigades to cover William Loring's retreat eastward out of Meridian. Loring was only five miles from Meridian, and he would arrive early the following morning. For Lee's cavalry to be in position, they had to ride through the night. Lee sent Starke's brigade toward Meridian, with Adams's to follow in the morning.[16]

Loring had been falling back toward Meridian throughout the day. His division, along with his cavalry screeners under S. W. Ferguson, had cut countless trees and burned numerous bridges to slow the Union advance. Late in the afternoon, Polk told Loring that it was his intention to keep Sherman's army from getting to the Mobile and Ohio Railroad until the night of February 14. He ordered Loring to search for a position tenable for defense and to fight a delaying action against the Union army. Polk insisted that he needed more time to evacuate Meridian. "French is held [at Meridian] to support you should it be necessary," Polk said reassuringly.[17]

Loring replied that Sherman was advancing at that very moment on his immediate location and that he did not have time to establish a defensible position. Polk retorted: "I am inclined to doubt the correctness of the report as to the near approach of the enemy tonight." Nevertheless, he agreed that Loring could continue his retreat toward Meridian. A demolition team was about to burn a bridge over Okatibbee Creek, and Polk believed that the Union army would need at least a day to repair it. This delay would provide Loring and the rest of the army plenty of time to move eastward out of Meridian transporting the rest of the town's supplies and equipment.[18]

Valentine's Day 1864 opened warm but cloudy. Hints of rain filled the air. Many of the fruit trees along the roads were in full bloom. The expedition, thus far, had not met with any poor weather other than a cold night now and then. No significant precipitation had fallen since Sherman's departure from Vicksburg, and the roads for most of the trip had been good, allowing the Union army to travel at a fast pace.[19]

Confederate wagons and men scurried frantically through the streets of Meridian, trying to save the last supplies there. Massive bonfires had burned through the night, lighting the streets and warehouses and warming the workers against the night air. While loaded trains pulled out of the depot bound for Mobile and Demopolis, empty trains took their place in an ever-revolving effort that had been going on for three days. Polk worried that he would not save all the supplies before Sherman reached him.

Unlike his men, Sherman did not expect Polk to make a stand at Meridian, since the Confederate general had already ignored several earlier chances to meet him on the battlefield. Considering the Confederates' persistence in felling trees and obstructing the roadway, Sherman correctly believed that the bishop wished only to gain more time to remove all the goods from Meridian. The Confederate army, Sherman assumed, would withdraw into Alabama before the Union army could reach the town.[20]

Later on the thirteenth, James B. McPherson ordered Mortimer Leggett, commander of the Third Division, to send one of his regiments under Manning Force, along with a few cavalry, to Chunky Station, about eight miles south of camp, for the purpose of performing "all the damage to the railroad [they] possibly can." Force's First Brigade left at first light on the fourteenth, planning to complete the work at Chunky Station during the day and meet the main column further eastward near nightfall.[21]

While the Confederates moved back slowly, Force's raiding party headed toward Chunky Station that morning to destroy the railroad and bridges there. Around 9 A.M., about a mile from the rail station, Force met skirmishers from Lee's cavalry. The Union troopers pushed forward immediately, driving the butternuts into town at a run. When they reached the station, the Federal troops surprised the rear guard of Adams's cavalry brigade and captured three artillery pieces, losing twelve men in the scrape. The Confederate cavalry, shocked at the appearance of Federal troops (four infantry brigades and two companies of cavalry), fell back across Chunky River eastward in confusion. "When we came near the station, they were eating their breakfast and we came upon them so unexpectedly that they left some butter and cornbread ready buttered," an Illinoisan said cheerfully. As they retreated, the Confederates abandoned seven wagons full of provisions, which the Federals quickly torched.[22]

While half of his soldiers pursued the retreating Confederates, Force had the other half destroy the trestle railroad bridge, railroad, depot, public buildings, and Confederate stores. They discovered a hundred cotton bales in a warehouse and set the building afire, along with six unoccupied homes and a house that Lee had used for his headquarters. The troopers tore apart half a mile of track, burning the ties and twisting the iron. Having accomplished the task with few casualties and no deaths, Force began his return at 10:30 A.M. and rejoined the main column at the Okatibbee Creek camp near dark.[23]

Before dawn that morning, Hickenlooper's Pioneer Corps rebuilt the bridge across Tallahatta Creek and corduroyed the swamp just east of the waterway. Large pine timber made it easy for the men to find logs for their task, but the trees also worked against the Pioneer Corps. The retreating

Confederates had continued to cut the large trees lining the road to obstruct the Federal march. The road also passed over several ridges, making it difficult for the mules and horses to pull their loads. Sherman's army had made progress rapidly toward Meridian during the first two weeks of their march. As it moved closer to its prize, however, the army found it becoming much more difficult to march.[24]

With the Pioneers having completed the bridge, Winslow's cavalry rode east of their camp at Tallahatta Creek toward the bridge at Okatibbee Creek, about two and a half miles west of Meridian. They found the last embers of the destroyed bridge dying out. Because he understood that Sherman wanted the town captured as early as possible, Winslow decided to splash across the river and not wait for the Pioneer Corps to repair the bridge. Some soldiers swam with their horses while others created a makeshift bridge from a shattered cotton press. The Union cavalrymen had earlier promised the infantry that they would reach Meridian first. The foot soldiers, laughing at the notion, had replied that it was the infantrymen who would "be the first to enter the Rebel Rendezvous and Stronghold."[25]

Upon reaching a small strip of woods where the road turned eastward, Winslow noticed a dismounted line of Ferguson's and Starke's cavalry with another line of mounted troops in support. Starke had pushed forward most of the night from Chunky Station attempting to reach Meridian before the enemy and had found Ferguson near Meridian. Winslow dismounted the Fifth Illinois and ordered a charge. The blue-clad soldiers rushed forward with their artillery firing overhead, "driving them [the Confederates] from every stump and fence and tree," taking several prisoners. The Third Infantry Division from Hurlbut's Sixteenth Corps arrived just as the two cavalry forces began fighting.[26]

As Winslow rode forward to order another charge, Brigadier General A. J. Smith, the infantry division's commander, confronted him. He wanted the honor of taking Meridian for the infantry: "Colonel, you had better halt your men and let my Indianans and Iowans charge at them." Winslow sharply replied, "I believe this cavalry would charge the Gates of Hell if I tell them." With that, he spurred his horse and rode into the fray, shouting for his men to keep attacking.[27]

The Confederate cavalrymen withdrew, but they soon redeployed in a line west of the Mobile and Ohio Railroad tracks. Because of Starke's rapid move from Chunky Station to near Meridian, the artillery was not able to keep up and had received orders to march to Enterprise. With no artillery and faced with both Federal infantry and cavalry, the Confederate commander ordered a withdrawal, moving his force through town northward toward Lauderdale Springs. Winslow's cavalry pursued closely. Meridian had fallen, and the Federal cavalry had won the race to the prize.[28]

A pelting rain began to fall as the Third Division moved into town around 3 P.M. and discovered that the enemy had withdrawn. "With music playing and banners flying," the infantrymen entered Meridian, many of them shouting out "with a perfect yell." Retreating forces had set fire to the commissary on their way out of town, and the building was engulfed in flames. They had also burned a disabled locomotive, some cars, and the depot. A trail of clothing, empty boxes, and broken wagons left from the Confederate withdrawal littered the ground. The Union infantry wasted little time in adding to the already existing inferno, firing "some public workshops, a rebel gun shop and barracks." Except for the Union soldiers' commotion, the streets were deserted. Meridian citizens remained indoors and out of sight, wondering what the "Yankee Devils" would do to them and their homes. Smith sent brigades to all four corners of the town with orders to protect the roadways against any Confederate counterattack.[29]

As Smith's Third Division marched into town, Confederate cavalry struck the wagon trains at Tallahatta Creek, fifteen miles away, searching for an opening. The Union defenders quickly fell into line and repelled the lackluster attempt. About an hour later the horsemen attempted another attack farther down the picket line, and once again the Federals easily swatted them away. The Confederate cavalry attempted several more strikes on the Federal trains, each attack ending in the same disappointing result for the Southerners.[30]

The main column of Sherman's infantry had, meanwhile, continued eastward throughout the morning, crossed Tallahatta Creek, and reached Okatibbee Creek around midday. The Pioneer Corps worked for about three hours repairing the bridge. Sherman appeared, on foot, with two staff officers accompanying him. He wanted to know what was delaying the advance. Happy with the Pioneer Corps' work, Sherman ordered one of his officers to send a message to McPherson, who was down the road to the west with his Seventeenth Corps. Sherman had interrogated a prisoner, who had insisted that the Confederates had deserted Meridian. Sherman had heard nothing from Winslow, but he felt sure that the Federals held the town. He discovered the truth of the report when he rode into Meridian himself later that morning.[31]

In the evening McPherson met with Sherman at his new headquarters in Meridian. After a brief consultation, McPherson ordered Alexander Chambers's brigade to protect the train at Tallahatta Creek "beyond all hazard." Force's brigade was to join the guard later that night. Confederate cavalry might attack the train at any moment, and McPherson wanted the supplies and prisoners well guarded. Provisions were extremely important to the Union army. The expedition would be in great peril if the wagon train were lost while the main command was destroying Meridian. McPherson ordered two brigades from Leggett's Third Division into town and sent another to Marcellus Crocker's position near Okatibbee Creek to assist in guarding the bridge.[32]

That night near the Okatibbee Creek bridge, after the weary men had gathered grass and pine straw for their beds and curled up for the night, gunfire shocked them from their sleep. "For the instant," a member of Crocker's Fourth Division remembered, "we supposed we were completely surrounded and were in for a hard fight," The stunned men jumped to their feet, frantically searching for their weapons. Just as they began to form a line to repel "the enemy" attack, the true source of the noise became apparent. "It appeared that some soldier on the outskirts of the town had taken a notion to try his wet gun to see if he could discharge it," reported the same fellow, and "the old musket performed all right." This "contagion" to fire rifles spread from brigade to brigade "until pop, bang, rattle, and roar sounded all over the camp, and probably some fifteen or twenty thousand muskets were discharged within a space of five minutes." Whether from boredom or celebration, the Union soldiers had great fun in letting out pent-up anxiety over a fight that had never occurred. While the Federal soldiers fired their weapons, the town's inhabitants and Confederate cavalry must have thought that a great battle had begun.[33]

When Polk had issued retreat orders at Meridian early on February 14, he had sent Loring and French east toward Moscow, Alabama, across the Tombigbee River. Lee "assume[d] control of all the cavalry west of Alabama," with the authority to "impress all horses, mules, and other property that may be necessary for the efficient conduct of his campaign." The Confederate cavalry was to cover the infantry withdrawal.[34]

By the time the stores from Meridian reached Demopolis, the Confederates thought they had performed a Herculean feat. "By very hard work, we saved all stores at Meridian; all at Enterprise, including all Government cotton in shipping order, except the corn in the shuck," the Mobile and Ohio Railroad's general superintendent, L. J. Fleming, reported happily to Polk. All the rolling stock "except eight or ten cars have been saved," he added. "The whole movement was conducted with the utmost coolness and deliberation, and was entirely successful." The Confederates had saved a large amount of the goods from Meridian but not the town itself. Over the next six days, Sherman's army made every effort to render the town and its railroads unusable to the Confederacy. As his troopers systematically destroyed property and supplies around Meridian, Enterprise, Marion Station, and Quitman, it became clear that Fleming had misinformed Polk about removing all of Meridian's supplies. Sherman's soldiers found thousands of bales of cotton, hundreds of weapons, thousands of bushels of corn, and yards of lumber over the next week, consuming or destroying all they discovered. Sherman's war of destruction had gained another huge success.[35]

Sherman issued orders on Valentine's night for the destruction to continue, this time against the railroad in every direction. "The destruction of the railroads intersecting at Meridian is of great importance," he said. He ordered Hurlbut's Sixteenth Corps to destroy the railroad north and east of town, while McPherson's Seventeenth took the south and west. "Every tie for many miles in each direction should be absolutely destroyed or injured, and every bridge and culvert completely destroyed," Sherman commanded. Half of each corps was to work at demolishing the rails while the other half stood ready for possible Confederate attack. Winslow's cavalry was to screen Hurlbut's troops working to the east to give the illusion that the Union army was pursuing the retreating Confederate army. Foraging parties were to scour the countryside to search for meat, meal, and other necessities. Sherman decided that the "destruction of the buildings must be deferred until the last moment," when a special detail would perform the task. He did not know how long his army might stay in Meridian, and he wanted to reserve abandoned buildings for soldiers' quarters.[36]

Sherman dictated a special field order to his aide L. M. Dayton for release the following day. "The general commanding conveys his congratulations and thanks to the officers and men composing this command for their most successful accomplishment of one of the great problems of the war," he began. The Union army had Meridian, "the great railway center of the Southwest," in its possession and could now render it useless to the Confederates. Destroying the railroads there would "deprive him [the enemy] of the chief source of supply to his armies." Sherman attributed the operational success to his ability to keep the enemy unaware of his carefully laid plans and to the speediness of the Union army's movement across Mississippi. If his soldiers would continue to follow their officers "with confidence," they would help secure "a peace that will never again be disturbed in our country by a discontented minority," he concluded. Sherman believed that the success of the Meridian expedition moved the Union one step closer to victory over the Confederacy. He had removed Mississippi from the war by cutting the state off from the rest of the Confederacy. He still wanted to destroy entirely the rail lines, bridges, and culverts, leaving them unrepairable and thus unusable to the Confederacy. At that point, Sherman was particularly determined to compel Meridian citizens to give up the Southern cause, and he sent his army to lay waste to the region.[37]

The Federal soldiers in Meridian found shelter from the cold rain that night in some of the town's newly constructed homes, barns, stables, and warehouses. The brigades still in the field suffered from the lack of tents and no cover except for a few rubber blankets. A member of Leggett's Third Division described how the soldiers dealt with their predicament: "It became necessary that the inhabitants should contribute their share towards the comfort of the weary soldiers . . . and every cabin along the road would be visited by from ten to twenty different soldiers, and every blanket, quilt, or carpet would disappear from the house; they would be carried to where the army camped, used for the night, and in the morning the camp would be full of women looking for their bedding."[38]

On the morning of February 15, the rain still poured steadily. Officers in Meridian allowed their men to stay indoors until that afternoon when the rest of the army, except the wagon trains, arrived. The soldiers slept, played cards, made coffee, wrote letters, and read books to pass the time. Luckily for the chilled men, the heavy rain stopped around noon. The coldness and wetness, however, still made conditions miserable for the work and foraging parties, the rain having turned the roads to mud. Small bands of Confederate cavalry added danger to the foraging task. A member of the Thirteenth Iowa, for example, was captured together with five of his comrades. "Robbed of hat, coat, and boots, shot twice and left for dead," the determined survivor limped his way back to camp. He informed his fellow Union soldiers that he believed that the Confederates had killed his friends after their capture. During the expedition, because Confederate forces were unable to halt Sherman's main column, the Confederate cavalry particularly focused its attention on foragers and supply wagons, the most vulnerable part of the Union army. Most foraging parties contained fifty to a hundred men, but sometimes as few as two or three traveled together. The army consumed huge amounts of forage and food daily, forcing Sherman to continue to send foragers out no matter the danger.[39]

During a typical day more than a thousand foragers tramped across the Mississippi countryside, bringing back meat, corn, and other provisions. Some of them, however, never returned. During the Meridian campaign, more soldiers were lost from foraging than in combat. As the expedition continued, Sherman understood that these units were the most exposed of his army, and he took measures to halt the loss of men by placing heavy guards on wagon trains, sending out larger foraging units, and limiting straggling.

While the foraging continued, Crocker's and Leggett's divisions moved toward Meridian, beginning their cold and miserable march at first light on the fifteenth. They joined the rest of McPherson's Seventeenth Corps on the south and west sides of town around 10 A.M. That afternoon they began destroying the railroads, bridges, and culverts at the edge of the municipality while also burning most of the government buildings, including the six large structures of the half-finished Confederate hospital.[40]

Hurlbut sent Smith's Third Division east of town toward Selma to destroy twelve miles of track while Winslow's cavalry covered the movement. After Smith had completed his destruction, he fell back toward Meridian for the night. Hurlbut ordered Winslow to report immediately any word of William Sooy Smith's whereabouts. James Veatch's Fourth Division moved out to break up the ten miles of track around Marion Station, six miles to the north of Meridian.[41]

When Veatch's six thousand soldiers neared Marion Station late that evening, Lawrence Sullivan Ross's Confederate cavalry brigade fired on them. The Federal commander summoned his artillery battery, which sent several shots into the enemy, and the Confederate horsemen withdrew after taking a dozen casualties and losing about thirty prisoners. The Fourth Division captured Marion Station and camped there for the next four days, continuing its destruction of the railroad in all directions.[42]

A lively town located on the tracks of the Mobile and Ohio Railroad just north of Meridian, Marion Station was actually larger than Meridian, with nearly a thousand citizens. With H. R. Wilson's and D. M. Ford's doctor's offices, A. Boatswell's dentistry, W. L. Patton's inn, A. Threefoot's prosperous drugstore, and several cotton merchant and shipping offices, Marion Station had grown to over 150 houses by 1860. The most populous settlement in Lauderdale County, it sported a beautiful, newly constructed courthouse. The Federal cavalry burned the Bains Hotel, the Temperance Saloon, the courthouse, and other structures ringing the town square.[43]

The Confederate cavalry attempted several times over the next four days to halt the Federal demolition of the rail lines, but the horsemen had little success. Too greatly outnumbered to make any headway, they could only continue capturing isolated foraging parties or sniping at unwary Union marchers. Lee, with Ferguson, Starke, Adams, and Ross, remained north of Marion Station, waiting to see where the Federals would move next.[44]

On the night of the fifteenth, McPherson issued orders to his two divisions. He told Leggett to send Benjamin Potts's Second Brigade westward down the Southern Railroad toward Chunky Station to burn and destroy bridges, culverts, and rails. Potts should pay special attention to keeping his men from straggling, as enemy cavalry was reported in that area. After reaching Chunky Station, Potts should march his brigade northward to relieve Chambers's brigade guarding the wagon trains. Chambers should then join the army at Meridian.[45]

McPherson also ordered Crocker's Fourth Division to move south toward Enterprise the following morning, while Winslow detailed the Eleventh Illinois cavalry regiment to accompany the infantry division. When Crocker came near Enterprise, he received orders to send the cavalry, with a brigade of infantry supporting, down to Quitman to destroy the railroad bridge across Chickasawhay Creek. McPherson ordered Crocker to destroy the bridge over Okatibbee Creek near Enterprise as well and cautioned Crocker to keep his "command under control" at Enterprise because the town was not a "place as purely military as [Meridian]." Private property should remain unmolested, but "the railroad and any building connected with it will . . . be destroyed," damaging it as "far as practicable and . . . beyond the possibility of being repaired in months."[46]

The Union army had captured Meridian easily. No large pitched fight, no great fanfare, not even a sign of the Confederate infantry marked the Federal capture of the Mississippi railroad junctions. The Federal soldiers expected a battle at Meridian that never came. The danger to foragers and supply wagons remained the only real hazard facing the Union army. Sherman faced no opposition as he began his attempt to destroy utterly all he could in order to leave the region barren for future Confederate use.

With the ease of his march to Meridian, Sherman realized just how vulnerable the South was to this type of expedition. The speed of march and his careful planning had prevented the Confederates from fielding an army large enough to stop him. Sherman's extensive preparation and calculating movements during the Meridian campaign negates much of the criticism and postwar image of him as an indiscriminate destroyer. While Sherman knew exactly how he intended to take Meridian, Polk, on the other hand, continued his indecisiveness until it was too late to save the Mississippi railroad town from Federal capture. Sherman's expedition was successful largely because of the continued incompetence of Polk. The Meridian campaign convinced Sherman that he could travel deeper into the Confederacy, wreaking havoc on the interior, and thereby compelling the populace to end their fruitless support of a dying cause. First, however, he would complete his mission in Meridian, destroying the tracks, equipment, and supplies of the important Confederate railroad junction.

6 / "One of the Most Pestiferous Nests . . . in All the Limits of Dixie"

While the Union army destroyed the railroad and property in Meridian and the surrounding area, attempting to leave the region unusable to the Confederacy, several incidents occurred that illustrate the Federal soldiers' attitude toward Southern civilians and how much it had changed under William T. Sherman's destructive war strategy. Pillaging and looting of private property remained a problem for Federal officers, but the growing crisis of an ever-shrinking food supply proved even more worrisome. With the continued absence of William Sooy Smith's cavalry, the Union army was forced to delay its departure, consuming all of the resources around Meridian, forcing Sherman into a decision about whether to continue into Alabama without the cavalrymen or to return to Vicksburg. While Mississippi burned, officials in Richmond and Dalton continued to argue over sending reinforcements to Leonidas Polk. By the time they decided to assist him, Sherman had already made up his mind and begun his return to Vicksburg. Once again, Sherman outplanned the Confederates.

February 16 dawned warm and sunny. The pall of smoke from burning buildings and rail ties cast a dark cloud across Meridian and its surrounding farmlands. Stephen A. Hurlbut's Sixteenth Corps continued its destruction around Marion Station to the north and on the railway east to Selma. The battle with Lawrence Sullivan Ross's Confederate cavalry had kept some of Hurlbut's command from reaching Marion Station until late that afternoon. Andrew Hickenlooper's Pioneer Corps assisted the infantry details in their effort and provided valuable advice on how to destroy the rail lines most efficiently. The men burned the ties, heating the rails until they grew red. The soldiers then took the hot iron and wound it around a tree, creating what many troopers referred to as "Sherman neckties." "Sometimes we would ring a tree for eight feet above the ground," a member of the Twenty-fifth Wisconsin boasted. The Federal soldiers also discovered stores of cotton and several cotton gins, which the men burned as an "offering to the demon of treason."[1]

Edward Winslow's cavalrymen, still covering A. J. Smith's division west of Meridian, rode toward Lauderdale Springs, eleven miles northeast of Marion Station, searching for Stephen D. Lee's cavalry and any sign of Sooy Smith. The Federal cavalrymen ran into Lee's cavalry near Old Marion, between Marion Station and Lauderdale Springs, and briefly skirmished. With Peter B. Starke on his left, S. W. Ferguson in his front, and Ross to his right, Winslow decided not to bring about a full engagement without gaining additional cavalry or infantry support. Earlier in the day, A. J. Smith had ordered Winslow not to put himself in a position where the enemy could cut him off from infantry support, so Winslow withdrew to a position nearer to Marion Station and camped for the night. The Federal cavalrymen questioned several citizens about Sooy Smith, but none had any information. They did ascertain, however, that the telegraph wires were cut north of Macon, making it difficult for any news from northern Mississippi to reach them.[2]

Marcellus Crocker's Fourth Division started around 6 A.M. for Enterprise, about sixteen miles below Meridian. Because of the previous day's heavy rains, the roads were filled with muck, and the infantry had a difficult time traversing swollen streams and standing water. The cool February temperatures combined with water-soaked shoes and trousers to make for a miserable march. Meeting no Confederate opposition, Crocker arrived at Enterprise around 3:30 P.M. and found the place bare of any Confederate supplies and equipment and most private property. The 1860 census showed a thousand people residing in Enterprise, but many had fled before the Union army. Crocker sent a message back to McPherson in Meridian that Walter Q. Gresham's Third Brigade and the Eleventh Illinois cavalry would go that afternoon to Quitman, a small town of less than four hundred people about six miles further south, to burn the bridge across the Chickasawhay and would return the following morning. The rest of the Fourth Division would commence the destruction of the railroads and bridges around Enterprise on February 17.[3]

Gresham reached the 210-foot-long covered railroad bridge across the Chickasawhay before dark and quickly burned it. Before his men bivouacked for the night near Alligator Swamp, the Federal troopers also destroyed six hundred feet of trestle near the burning bridge. On its return to Enterprise the next day, Gresham's brigade ripped down the trestle over Alligator Swamp and also tore up two and a half miles of track.[4]

Benjamin Potts's Second Brigade of Mortimer Leggett's Third Division also moved out that morning, heading west of Meridian to Chunky Station. Realizing that the brigade could not destroy all twenty-eight miles of track between Meridian and Chunky Station, McPherson had decided that Potts should concentrate on bridges, culverts, and trestles. That afternoon the Second Brigade came upon the two-hundred-foot-long Chunky River bridge across the Southern Railroad and torched it. The flames spread quickly to engulf the entire structure. One Union soldier remarked: "It was a sight worth seeing." The Federal troopers discovered five railroad cars parked on a sidetrack and burned them, together with a water tank.[5]

Potts's brigade staggered into Chunky Station around ten o'clock that night, weary from their march. "Scars from the Union raid a few days before showed . . . a stark chimney here . . . uncharred rubble there," a Union foot soldier said. Growing increasingly hungry from their long walk and hard work, some of the infantrymen "ransacked the dwellings [along their route], then made for the ranks loaded down with hams, shoulders, bacon, and chickens." Potts camped that night near Chunky River, not far from the station, having torn up several miles of track and bridges.[6]

While Sherman's army wrecked Meridian, Enterprise, Marion Station, and Chunky Station, Polk's infantry was nowhere in sight, continuing its retreat eastward toward Demopolis. By midday they had reached Lewis's Ferry on the Tombigbee River, where they had some difficulty procuring a pontoon bridge. Lashing together some Confederate vessels as a makeshift bridge, the infantry crossed the waterway before nightfall. Polk decided to rest the troops after the crossing and issued orders to William Loring and Samuel French to bivouac on the eastern side of the river. The Confederate army remained camped there all the following day awaiting further orders. Polk wanted first to inquire about reinforcements and to obtain word from Forrest about his situation in northern Mississippi.[7]

Lee, still in the field between Marion Station and Lauderdale Springs, had already telegraphed Nathan Bedford Forrest and apprised him of the situation at Meridian. He told Forrest to follow any "large raiding party" coming down from the northwest to the point where Lee could join him. Together they would then defeat the raiders. Unknown to Lee, Forrest, at that very moment, was maneuvering his command near West Point to stop Sooy Smith's "large raiding party" from linking with Sherman at Meridian.[8]

The temperature dropped precipitously that February 16 night, freezing the ground and covering it with a coating of frost. "Water froze about one inch thick in the water bucket," one cold Illinoisan observed as he went to dip a drink the next morning. He vowed to sleep in the wagon with his friends that night to avoid the chill. Some of the men nearer town had earlier confiscated some feather beds and had slept warmly. Federal troops in Meridian, after they had cooked breakfast and eaten, continued to demolish the railroad and the town.[9]

Federal soldiers burned all of Meridian's unoccupied residences along with the public buildings. There were some rare instances, however, of troopers setting fires to dwellings that contained civilians. "A soldier was seen to deliberately set fire to an occupied residence," observed a member of Leggett's Third Division, "and when the family took refuge in another house, he followed and wantonly applied the torch to that." Officers ordered the man arrested. After the soldier was in custody, he explained why he had burned the houses. After the fall of Vicksburg, the individual, then a prisoner of war, had been transported to Meridian to transfer trains. As he had waited, he said, a Southern woman had stepped out of the crowd and "deliberately spit in his face." He swore vengeance if he ever returned to the town. When the soldier had marched into Meridian with Sherman, he had searched for the woman. Finding her, he burned her house and the dwelling she ran into for refuge. "All who witnessed the burning building can testify that he kept his word, and it is almost useless to ask that he was not punished," the observer noted. The Union army torched only a few private homes during their stay at Meridian, with even fewer arrests of any perpetrators. One Ohioan put it very simply: "[We] had orders to burn all unoccupied houses, but [the soldiers] were not very particular whether the houses were occupied or not."[10]

Some of the ladies in Meridian fared better than others because they were able to appeal to Union officers, who would sometimes grant protection. A Mrs. Ball wrote to her mother about her experiences during the Federal occupation of her home. "The mob [of Union soldiers] ran around going into the house, breaking doors, trunks, locks, etc; tearing up and destroying everything they could," she said. While five men ransacked her house, she sent her mother-in-law to search for a Federal officer. Hurlbut sent a guard detail, but by the time they arrived the thieves had gathered her blankets and all the flour and were headed out the door. The guard ordered the flour returned, which the sackers did; but he allowed them to keep the blankets. A few days later, Leggett made the woman's house his headquarters, his staff living in a portion of the house while the two ladies and three children lived in three rooms. Mrs. Ball approached Leggett and asked that he protect her family. He replied: "I will take care of you, madam, as long as I am here."[11]

After a neighbor, Mrs. McElroy, had her house looted, she insulted a junior Union officer and his men. The soldiers then set fire to her home. When Mrs. McElroy tried to take refuge with Mrs. Ball in Leggett's headquarters, the general turned to the mistress of the house and said: "If you [let the woman in], your house will be burned in an hour, for I cannot prevent it." The refugee was turned away. By appealing to the enemy officer, Mrs. Ball contended proudly, "I got on better than any other lady in Meridian." These two cases illustrate the range of experiences that women endured during Sherman's occupation of Meridian. Mrs. McElroy openly scorned the Federal presence in her town and received harsh treatment. By using the opposite tactic, welcoming the enemy officers into her home, Mrs. Ball protected her property and home from destruction.[12]

The stories of the prisoner of war's experience and the destruction of Mrs. McElroy's house for cursing Federal troops are excellent examples of how a few Federal soldiers sometimes sought vengeance upon the white Southern civilian population. By 1864, patience for the disrespectful actions of some secessionist civilians had reached its limit among the Union soldiers and officers, causing some of the troopers to lash out. These were isolated incidents, however, and were certainly not condoned by Sherman.[13]

At Meridian, some of the soldiers showed their contempt of Mississippi slave owners. An "intelligent contraband" had informed the men of the Thirty-second Iowa of a "brutal slave driver" who had mutilated and even murdered some of his charges. The Union troopers captured the accused man and brought him before the brigade commander, William T. Shaw. The officer ordered his soldiers to "take him into the woods and hang him." The sergeant, not realizing that his commander was jesting, marched the condemned man out of camp, searching for an appropriate tree. Before the sentence could be carried out, however, word reached the division commander, A. J. Smith, who confronted Shaw. The brigade commander explained that he was merely joking and that he meant only to frighten the slave driver. He ordered the man released, much to the dissatisfaction of the contrabands.[14]

Another band of Union soldiers went north of Meridian about ten miles in search of a "notorious rebel by the name Davis." They caught the man, burned his mill, and carried away enough "corn, meat, and forage to load" a large assemblage of wagons. Most Federal soldiers did not go this far in capturing civilians and bringing them in for disposition; they only looted private homes or burned structures out of disdain for Southern citizens. The majority of Federal soldiers, however, merely carried out their assigned duties of destruction, waiting for their next assignment.[15]

Unquestionably, Federal soldiers' attitudes toward Southern civilians had changed. In the case of the possible hanging of the slave driver, Union troopers were ready to carry out the execution of a man on the basis of a slave's accusations. Most other times, white men would have dismissed the testimony of a black man. The philosophy of hard war had conditioned some of the men to accept any destructive measure against Southerners as permissible. They stole and burned private property to punish the owner for his or her support of the Confederacy. It was a small step to consider executing those individuals deemed most responsible for the war, and many Federal soldiers believed that those people were the slave owners.

Meridian citizens did their best to hide their valuable personal items from the Union army. When he heard word of the approaching enemy troops, I. S. O. Greer, a plantation owner, tossed his silver into the garden pond, hid his horses and cattle in a canebrake, and stuffed other items into the attic. His daughter described what happened next: "The Yankees found the fine horses and fine cows. They fished out the pond for the hidden silver. They emptied the smoke house of the plantation's winter supply of lard, bacon, [and] sugar. They burned the barn . . . but the house was left intact. Only two of our slaves left with them. The darkies were loyal to the 'Massa' and with a will set about trying to repair the damage."[16]

If what Ms. Greer said is true about the majority of her family's slaves, such loyalty was uncommon. The majority of slaves seized upon the opportunity of Sherman's arrival to leave their masters and follow the Union army. Mrs. Ball, writing to her mother at Mobile, commented that she felt lucky that her house servant had not left: "So many negroes went from about here; all of Mr. McElmore's, Semmes's, and Dr. Johnsons." Many of them had no idea where they were going or how they could provide for themselves, but contrabands believed it was better to travel down the road of uncertainty than to remain in the reality of slavery. Thousands of slaves joined Sherman's column as it crisscrossed Mississippi. A long-believed misconception, propelled by plantation owners' stories, was that the majority of slaves stayed on their plantations. The slaves remained loyal, the story goes, because of the excellent treatment and care they received from their masters. As later studies have shown, this was simply not the case.[17]

Indeed, during Sherman's expedition, runaway slaves frequently guided the Federal soldiers to the hiding places of their masters' goods. The discovery of Greer's silver came because of a tip from one of his slaves. In Decatur, contrabands had led the way to a cache of concealed cotton. "Repeatedly were our men advised of the hiding places of hoards of bacon, pork, ham, stock, carriages, etc., the movements of the rebel military and the whereabouts of citizens fighting in the rebel army," a Federal soldier noted happily. While contraband-led search parties scoured the countryside for hidden goods, the Union army continued its demolition of Confederate property.[18]

Crocker's Fourth Division began its destructive work at Enterprise just after dawn on February 17. Early risers rekindled campfires that had died out during the night in an effort to ward off the morning cold and to make coffee to warm their shivering bodies. They had arrived late the previous afternoon and, tired from the long march, had done little work before going into camp for the night. Now, Crocker sent Cyrus Howe's Second Brigade north of town to tear up the rails, "which was done in a most thorough manner, every tie being burned and every rail bent for a distance of six miles." The Federal soldiers set fire to the depot, two flour mills, two military hospitals, and several new Confederate buildings connected to the parole camp. They also searched for provisions in the locked fruit cellars, smokehouses, and pantries of the town's inhabitants. The Federal troopers ground three hundred bushels of meal before they torched the mills.[19]

Enterprise brought forth deep resentment from Crocker's men when they explored the town. One of the troopers later called it "one of the most pestiferous nests that the sun shone on in all the limits of Dixie." Federal soldiers discovered a camp filled with paroled Confederate prisoners from the Vicksburg garrison. When questioned, they informed the Federals that the

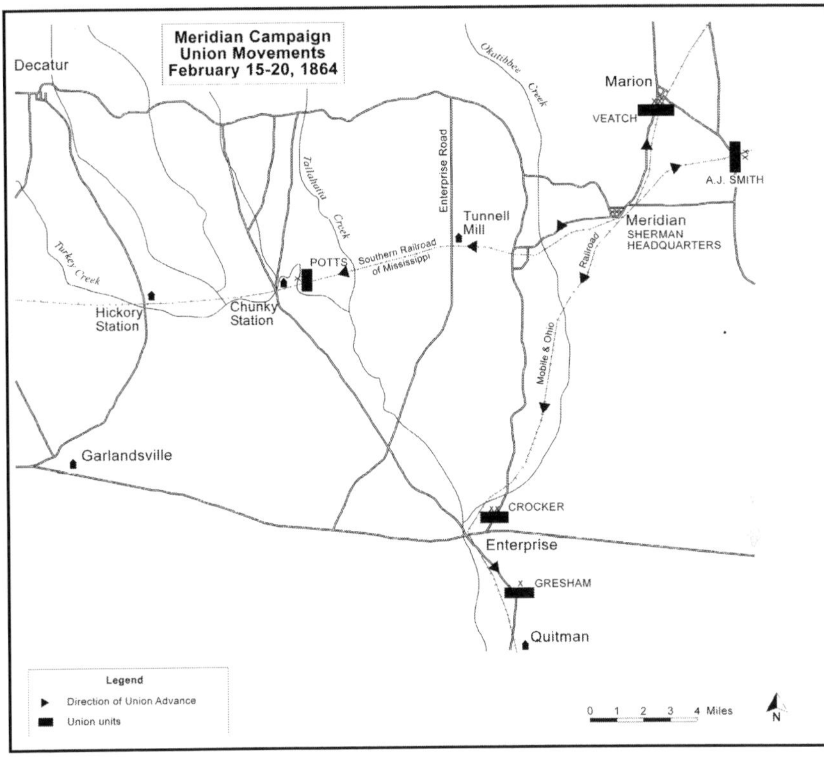

"Confederate authorities had been forcing many of their number into the army again, telling them they had been exchanged." They did not want to fight any longer, so they wanted to honor their parole.[20]

Many of the Federals were also tired of the war, and the Confederate officials' attempt to force paroled soldiers not yet exchanged back into the war angered them. The blue-clad soldiers decided to take it out on the town. One of the angry Federal soldiers commented: "Enterprise, all and singular with its improvements, public and private, its parole camp, and its conscript camp, with its associations, historic, poetic, and secesh has been—according to compliance—wiped out." A citizen described what he saw: "No place or house escaped them. Locks and bars availed nothing. Every room, trunk, wardrobe, and the beds and bedding were plundered, and torn up, nor did the poor negroes, whom they came to set free, as they said, escape those low-down pilfering rascals. Everything they could carry off was taken, and what they could not, was torn and destroyed, even to servants' underclothes." This behavior is significant because it indicates just how bitter soldiers' feelings toward Southern civilians had become. At Enterprise these Federal troopers sought retribution from a Southern town, punishing a populace for the Confederate government's treatment of its own men. The Union soldiers wanted the war to end, while Confederate officials were working to continue it.[21]

There were, of course, other reasons why Federal soldiers lashed out at the civilian populace. Physical discomfort was a motivation for soldiers to search through houses for blankets and food. Sherman's troops were tired, cold, dirty, and sometimes wet. They justified breaking into homes to search for clean clothing or breaking apart buildings to build fires from their wood because they saw it as a necessity. Psychological stress most likely drove Union soldiers to strike at private property together with the public buildings. Guerrilla units and fast-moving Confederate cavalry sniped and captured unwary Federal soldiers during the entire march, creating great anxiety among many of the bluecoats. Emotional strain, therefore, also played an important role in helping cause Federal soldiers to act as they did toward Mississippi civilians.

Early on the morning of February 18, Gresham's soldiers marched triumphantly into Enterprise, deeming their mission to Quitman a success. At Quitman they had destroyed "two flour mills, a fine sawmill, railroad depot, and other storage buildings, with several thousand feet of lumber." Crocker's Fourth Division remained in Enterprise until the morning of the nineteenth, when it returned to Meridian. While Gresham's men recounted their experiences to fellow soldiers at Enterprise, Sherman, at Meridian, planned his continued destruction.[22]

Sherman issued orders to Hurlbut at Marion Station that morning, placing special emphasis on the destruction of the Mobile and Ohio Railroad north of Meridian and gathering intelligence information. A. J. Smith's Third Division continued to work on the Southern Railroad to Selma, east of Meridian, while James Veatch's Fourth Division destroyed the rails around Marion Station to the north. Sherman wanted Hurlbut to send Winslow's cavalry eastward to search for the Confederate army so that he would know its exact location. How far had they gone to the east, and were they planning to retake Meridian? The commanding general urged his subordinate to relay any information about the location of Sooy Smith's cavalry force, now long overdue. Sherman was growing anxious over the lack of information about Smith, as the Federal cavalryman had supposedly left Collierville, Tennessee, on February 1 with orders to meet with Sherman around the tenth. It was now the seventeenth, and Sherman had not heard any word. He told Hurlbut that the Union army would remain near Meridian "until Smith is definitely heard from."[23]

Hurlbut ordered A. J. Smith to move one of his infantry brigades from the railroad to Selma toward Veatch at Marion Station to open a line of communication between the two divisions. The Confederate army was somewhere east of Meridian, and the exact location of their cavalry was not known. Veatch's and Smith's divisions needed to be able to support one another in case of an enemy attack. Smith replied that he had less than two brigades with him. He had sent his First Brigade back to Meridian, after it had "completed their portion of [destruction on] the road," to finish work on the rails near town. Sherman ordered Smith to send Winslow far down the railroad toward Selma to destroy any large bridges the cavalry could find. With all large bridges gone, the Confederate army would have difficulty launching a rapid attack on A. J. Smith's weakened division. With the extra time, Smith's division could fall back to Meridian safely. Sherman rode out the following day to survey Smith's progress on the Southern Railroad.[24]

A cool wind blew all afternoon that February 17, and the sun shone brightly. The beautiful weather made working conditions bearable for the Federal soldiers who labored beside immense fires of burning timber along the Mississippi roads. Several wagons of foraging parties rambled down the paths and country roads, searching for smoked hams and local jams. Sherman's congratulatory order had reached the Union army's ranks. "It seemed to say that the object of the expedition was accomplished," a Union soldier commented, "so we will be very likely to return to some point on the Mississippi River."[25]

That afternoon, Veatch moved part of his command northward toward Lauderdale Springs, northeast of Marion Station. Manning Force's brigade from McPherson's Seventeenth Corps moved north from Meridian and camped near Marion Station. As they neared Hurlbut's headquarters, the marchers could see a large cloud of smoke pouring from the town. Reaching the settlement, Force's troopers found two locomotive engines and several railroad cars, together with the depot and some storehouses, burning. The newly arrived Union marchers searched through the smoldering buildings and discovered three barrels of peanuts that their comrades had somehow overlooked. The fires had roasted them. Delighted with their find, the hungry troopers gobbled down the goober peas. "Nearly all the male citizens of this place are held as prisoners," one Federal soldier said. "They evidently did not expect that the town would soon fall into our hands." Although the records do not indicate who these the prisoners were, they were most likely old men and teenage boys, the rest of the combat-age men having already left for the service or vacated the town at the Federals' approach. It was a common precautionary practice during Sherman's march to arrest any person deemed capable of joining a guerrilla organization or the Confederate army.[26]

The destruction continued at Meridian. Among the burned structures were the Ragsdale Hotel, Ball's Store, Terrill's Inn, and the Burton House. Twelve government warehouses and the soldiers' home for invalids all burned. The Federal soldiers located two large gristmills, and after grinding twenty thousand bushels of corn the troopers torched them. John Ball, owner of Ball's Store, had begun construction on two frame houses in earlier months, and the buildings were nearing completion. The exposed pine made excellent kindling, and each house went up in flames. Because of Leggett's protection, however, the Ball family's main residence did not burn. The Meridian House, where some of the citizens had taken refuge, also was spared the torch. Federal soldiers similarly did not destroy Dr. Johnson's or Richard McLemore's house. The Greer plantation home was spared and, much to his surprise, so was the shingle factory.[27]

Starke's Confederate cavalry had remained between Marion Station and Lauderdale Springs for the last three days, searching for an opportunity to hit any vulnerable openings in Hurlbut's column. On the afternoon of the seventeenth, with Hurlbut's infantry advancing on their position, Starke's and Ross's cavalry commands moved north of Lauderdale Springs. Ferguson and Adams followed the next day.[28]

Lee telegraphed Polk that he would "leave one regiment to cover Demopolis" but that he would take the rest of the cavalry with him and, as Polk had ordered, join Forrest to defeat Sooy Smith. While Sherman's army focused its attention on the destruction of Meridian and surrounding areas, rumors began to circulate that the Federals would soon return to Vicksburg. The Confederate army had almost reached Demopolis, and there was little need for Lee to continue screening its movement. Polk thought the key to keeping Sherman from marching on Mobile was stopping Sooy Smith's cavalry from joining the Union army at Meridian. "To crush that force is important," he said adamantly.[29]

From February 13 to 17 the telegraph wires between Dalton, Richmond, and Alabama hummed with flurried excitement over how to stop the advance of Sherman's army. In an effort to elicit reinforcements, on the thirteenth Polk telegraphed Joseph Johnston at Dalton and Jefferson Davis in Richmond, providing them with a report on his situation. Johnston responded later in the day: "Sherman's army must have a long wagon train. Cannot General Lee strike it? It seems to me that he can destroy it long before it reaches Mobile." Johnston clearly did not understand what Sherman was doing.[30]

Because of military precautions, communications to and from Polk had to travel through Montgomery, causing delay in their arrival. Davis's and Polk's communications crossed on February 13. Davis inquired as to Polk's situation. The president had "received nothing from you [Polk] since dispatch of 9th," and he was worried about the reports of Sherman's army moving east. Davis insisted that Polk stop the invading army before it reached the Gulf and "established a base to which supplies and reinforcements may be sent by sea." The Confederate high command still believed that Sherman was moving to attack Mobile. Davis also sent a message to Johnston, asking if he could assist Polk: "What can you do [to] strik[e] him [Sherman] while [he is] in motion and before he establishes a new base?" Davis supposed that the Federal command in the Western theater did not have sufficient men to field two large armies simultaneously in different locations. Therefore, he believed Johnston could send reinforcements to Polk because Dalton could not be seriously threatened when a large Union army was marching across Mississippi.[31]

The following day, Polk informed Davis that Sherman had turned toward Meridian. The Mississippi commander still erroneously assumed that the Union army's objective was Mobile and that Sherman was at Meridian to rendezvous with a cavalry force coming down from Collierville. Davis replied that the Union army's advance on Meridian might be a feint and that "his real purpose [might] be to move eastward for reasons you will readily anticipate." Perhaps the governor of Alabama could send a few militia troops, Davis added.[32]

After receiving no response from Johnston concerning possible support of

Polk, Davis sent another message to Dalton the morning of February 15. "You are probably informed of the condition of General Polk's command," he wrote, "and I have only to request that you will communicate with him freely." Davis asked Johnston to send any assistance to Mississippi that he could. Reminding his subordinate of the importance of Alabama to the Confederacy, the commander in chief concluded: "The interior of Alabama and the Tombigby [*sic*] valley are our reliance for supplies in the coming campaign." He sent the same message to Alabama governor Thomas H. Watts.[33]

Later that day, Davis received a reply that Johnston dated February 13. Scouts had reported enemy movement in his front, Johnston argued, and therefore he could not send Polk reinforcements. Davis responded that if the enemy army reached the interior of Alabama, "the most serious consequences must ensue." The scouting reports were wrong, Davis rebutted. There could not be a substantial enemy presence in the front of Dalton. Unless the Union army "immediately" threatened him, Davis commanded, Johnston should send enough infantry that, when combined with Polk's, it would defeat Sherman's invading army.[34]

Johnston responded to Davis's order the following day. He contended that he could not weaken his force at Dalton to provide Polk reinforcements and still protect the Atlanta front effectively. The Mississippi commander needed so many soldiers to bolster his beleaguered force that it would require two-thirds of Johnston's army to meet the requirement. Johnston insisted that it would take him at least a month to obtain transportation, supplies, and equipment for the massive force, and then he would still have to move it to Demopolis. "The enemy could therefore seize Atlanta before our return," he concluded. Johnston insisted again that a Federal force was in his front: "The enemy is so near to us here that we cannot hope for other warnings of his advance than the sight of his marching columns." He suggested that Davis allow him to send only a "spare" force to Polk.[35]

Polk's problem in Mississippi then became the topic of several discussions between Davis and Secretary of War James A. Seddon in Richmond. Davis argued that the loss of Mobile would prove devastating to the Confederacy. A Federal army sat perched near the Mississippi-Alabama border prepared for a march on Mobile, or so thought the Confederate high command. Sherman did have his army in Meridian, but he had no intentions of either moving on Mobile or moving deeply into the interior of Alabama. Either objective, Davis thought, would be damaging.

On February 17, Seddon promised Polk: "You will be reinforced." The war secretary told Polk to "make all necessary arrangements for immediate and active operations against the enemy." Seddon suggested that Polk add Forrest's cavalry command to Lee's and that the combined force continue to harass and delay Sherman's infantry while Davis arranged reinforcements. Polk responded that he had already concentrated his cavalry, not for an attack on the army at Meridian, but to "intercept a column of cavalry coming down . . . from West Tennessee."[36]

The same day, Davis ordered Johnston to send Patrick Cleburne's and Benjamin F. Cheatham's divisions from William J. Hardee's infantry corps to aid Polk. He was tired of his subordinate's excuses. The president said that he "expected" to return those troops to Dalton before the Federals would "seriously endanger" Johnston's position. Johnston sent a message to Hardee encouraging the general to travel to Demopolis quickly: "It is all important to crush the enemy in Mississippi with the least delay." Finally, it seemed, Polk would have a large enough force to throw back the Union army when it advanced into Alabama.[37]

The Union column from Chattanooga, which was supposed to move in concert with Sherman's advance, had not marched on Dalton as ordered. Ulysses S. Grant had told George H. Thomas on February 12 to attack Johnston's army at Dalton, but Grant discovered on February 17 that Thomas had still not moved. He sent another message explaining how important Thomas was to Sherman's success. Pressure on Dalton, Grant argued, would prevent the sending of any reinforcements to Mississippi. Thomas delayed for another five days, and as a result the Confederate reinforcements were able to leave Dalton, bound for Alabama, on February 19.[38]

While the Confederate government sent reinforcements to Polk, Sherman continued to worry about his cavalry force, sending messages to McPherson and Hurlbut on February 18 expressing his concern. Sherman knew that he could not remain in one place too long while waiting for Sooy Smith to arrive. His army was like a swarm of locusts, consuming huge quantities of supplies daily. The Union army would soon deplete Meridian and the surrounding areas of foodstuffs. Sherman's army had not established a supply or communication line, so it could move quickly across the state.[39]

As a result, Sherman's idea of destructive war continued to mature on his march to Meridian. Food, whether publicly or privately owned, was now militarily important. Federal soldiers, therefore, could take these products from Mississippi civilians, entering private dwellings to gather provisions. Taking food served a number of purposes in Sherman's strategy. He could feed his army without a supply line or large numbers of supply wagons. Whatever the hungry troopers did not consume, they destroyed, removing the foodstuffs from possible Confederate army use. When it confiscated or destroyed Southern provisions, Sherman's army often placed Southern civilians in a difficult position. They had to choose between continuing their support for the Confederate government or providing for their own families. After the Union army had passed through, they simply did not possess enough provisions to do both. More often than not, people chose to take care of their families, abandoning their material support for the Confederacy.

Sherman also counted on the psychological effect of this type of warfare. When the Union army came into Southerners' homes, took all their goods, killed or carried off the livestock, confiscated or destroyed their grain, and burned the barns and possibly the houses, these actions exerted an overwhelming emotional impact on these people. The Union army made it clear to Southern civilians that continued support of the Confederacy and the pursuit of an independent nationhood meant their possessions were subject to unrelenting destruction and confiscation. Many of them therefore decided to choose their own interests over those of the South.[40]

Sherman decided on the 18th that he could wait only one more day for Sooy Smith's cavalry. An officer reported that Sherman was "much disconcerted" about not hearing from the cavalry column, which, after all, he had made especially strong to cope successfully with any Confederate force it might encounter. Rumors circulated about a "forced retreat" by Sooy Smith, but these whisperings were unsupported. Sherman did receive news that Polk's army had crossed the Tombigbee River just west of Demopolis, reassuring the Federal commander that they were no longer a threat to his army at Meridian. Because Sherman had heard no reliable information about his cavalry commander, he decided to "change somewhat his former plans." He ordered McPherson to begin assembling his command "at or near Meridian . . . to prepare to march back to Vicksburg on the 20th." Hurlbut should send a portion of Hickenlooper's Pioneer Corps to repair the bridge across Okatibbee Creek, since the Union army would cross that structure on its return route. He should also prepare the rest of his corps for departure.[41]

Sherman then ordered Winslow to continue northward from Marion Station to Lauderdale Springs in an effort to contact Sooy Smith, a brigade of mounted infantry from Hurlbut's corps riding in support. When the Federal column reached Lauderdale Springs, they were to destroy the town. On the return march, the infantry should demolish as much of the "railroad, depot, bridges, [and] culverts" as possible. Sherman sent J. C. Audenreid, a member of his staff, to accompany Winslow. If the group found the missing cavalry commander, Winslow should relieve Sooy Smith and merge the two cavalry forces. Sooy Smith should then report "personally" to Sherman at Meridian. The combined Federal cavalry should then "move immediately upon Demopolis and destroy all property there that could be used in war, including the steamboats in the river and the railroads." If he did not discover any information before nightfall, however, Winslow should return to Marion Station. Sherman, as always, planned carefully.[42]

Snow began to fall heavily, and the wind blew cold, chilling the working soldiers. Throughout the day on February 18, the destruction of the railroads and bridges continued while Federal soldiers scraped together supplies for the return march to Vicksburg. "We run a mill and get 20 bushels of meal for the reg[iment]," an Illinoisan said. The mills in and around Meridian ran all day and all night, preparing food to fill the troopers' haversacks for the long trip back to the Mississippi River.[43]

Hurlbut's two divisions were working together near Marion Station. A. J. Smith's Third Division had finished its work on the railroad east of town and had moved northwestward to an area nearer Veatch. Since Smith's division had remained in the field away from any settlements along the railway to Selma, they had exhausted most of their supplies. Smith had to send "large foraging parties from each regiment in all directions." Because they now had shifted their positions further north, they reached an area where no Federal troops had previously visited and found several head of cattle and other foodstuffs. Few untouched areas remained in close proximity to Meridian, however.[44]

Sherman's army had spent a week thoroughly demolishing the railroads around Meridian and the surrounding towns while waiting for Sooy Smith. Since the Federal cavalry column had not arrived, Sherman was forced to alter his plans. His army was running out of food, and he could wait no longer. He had wanted to travel into the interior of Alabama and destroy railroads at Demopolis or Selma, but because of the lack of a large cavalry force he decided to return to Vicksburg. He would continue to search for Sooy Smith as the Union army marched westward.

That evening, Sherman issued Special Order 20, which explained his decision to return to Vicksburg: "Having fulfilled completely and well all the objects of the Expedition, the troops will return to the Mississippi River to embark on an equally important movement." He referred to Nathaniel Banks's proposed attack up the Red River. Hurlbut's infantry and Winslow's cavalry, which Sherman would accompany, would move from Marion Station through Union to Hillsboro. Simultaneously, McPherson's corps would travel from Meridian via Decatur to Hillsborough. Each corps would reach its destination in about four days, he estimated. Sherman would not retrace his line of advance along the Southern Railroad to Vicksburg. Instead, the army's path would be north of the Southern Railroad through areas where he could find substantial quantities of supplies for his army. At Hillsborough the commanding general would issue more orders concerning the army's next movement. The immense concentration of supply wagons, still camped between the Chunky River and Tallahatta Creek, would break up, each wagon returning to its appropriate command. Because of the fear that lurking Confederate cavalry might capture Federal stragglers or strike at exposed supply wagons, Sherman reminded his officers not to travel too quickly. Fifteen miles per day would be enough to keep the army from stringing out too far. The Federal troops cheered at the prospect of returning to Vicksburg. When they reached the Mississippi River, many of them could take their veteran furloughs and visit their families.[45]

Taking the new route back to Vicksburg served two purposes. First, the Union army was running short of provisions, and this rich farmland would serve to refill the supply wagons with much-needed rations. Sherman's soldiers had remained at Meridian for five days wrecking the railroads, but they had also taken all the food from the area. By February 20 many of the Union troopers had run low on or were out of victuals. One fellow reported that he had "done without Rations for three days." To remain potent, the army needed food and needed it soon. Second, Sherman chose to travel north of the Southern Railroad in order to search for Sooy Smith's missing cavalry.

While the Union army readied to march back to Vicksburg, Lee's Confederate cavalry rode northward to find Forrest.[46]

Lee moved his four brigades of cavalry toward Starkville and Forrest, leaving one regiment to observe the Federals at Meridian. The Confederate horsemen, worn and battered from their three-week skirmish with Sherman's army, took two days to reach their destination. The gray-clad horsemen were not the only Confederate soldiers who were weary that day.[47] The falling snow had melted quickly but added water to the slushy roads. The cold wind chilled Polk's retreating Confederate infantry. Mules and horses strained against the mud. Some marchers hacked and coughed, slipping and falling as they trudged forward. The march soon ended, however. The Confederates neared their destination of Demopolis, fifty-five miles northeast of Meridian.[48]

Winslow's cavalry reached Lauderdale Springs that morning and discovered news of Sooy Smith from local citizens, who informed the Union officers that the Confederate cavalry had left Old Marion to join with Forrest near Macon to meet the Federal cavalry. Before the war, Lauderdale Springs was known as a popular health resort because of its mineral springs. The town had nearly 175 homes, a depot, several warehouses, two doctor's offices, and two hotels. Winslow's cavalry burned the "station house, commissary, and other buildings at Lauderdale" and returned to Marion Station.[49]

While Winslow made his sweep on Lauderdale Springs, the only new development on the Confederate side came from Mobile. Dabney Maury reported that Federal gunboats had fired on Grant's Pass, a few miles south of the town. By the nineteenth, however, the weather had become so inclement that the Union gunboats had halted their attack and sat idly in the sound near Grant's Pass. No infantry had landed. Maury promised to keep Polk apprised of the situation if conditions changed. Polk remained stubbornly convinced that Sherman's ultimate objective was Mobile and that the Federal fleet was part of that operation. Stopping the Federal cavalry from joining the operation, therefore, became even more important.[50]

Polk, at Demopolis, scurried to collect enough troops to meet Sherman if he turned back to the east, his immediate hopes resting on the shoulders of Lee and Forrest. After a great deal of arguing, Johnston sent reinforcements to Polk. He was reluctant to send the troops, fearing the Federals would crush his weakened army at Dalton. In his opinion, Lee's cavalry alone could end Sherman's raid. By the time the reinforcements reached Montgomery, however, Sherman had already decided to go back to the Mississippi River. Meanwhile, Lee's cavalry moved north to reinforce Forrest in an effort to halt the Federal cavalry's advance and, Polk thought, thereby defeat Sherman.

The Confederates knew where Sooy Smith was. Recent reports to Lee placed the Federal column near Aberdeen. Lee's cavalry continued to ride to join Forrest, now reported north of Columbus near West Point. Polk ordered Lee to "urge all the people of the country through which you pass to mount and take the field against that column. Let them form companies or join those already with you. It is of the highest importance that the [Federal cavalry] command should be crushed." Polk's total attention now focused on Sooy Smith. Meanwhile, Sherman's main force began moving, unopposed, back to the Mississippi. Sherman had successfully marched across Mississippi and was now withdrawing virtually unmolested.[51]

7 / An Opportunity Lost

As February 19 came to a close, Sherman gazed into the distance and searched for dust rising on the horizon. He was looking for one of his couriers with news of Sooy Smith's arrival. He saw nothing. Sherman, thinking of Sooy Smith, now nine days late, may have remembered the words he had written to Grant in December: "I deem General Sooy Smith too mistrustful of himself for a leader against Forrest." His assessment, it seemed, had come true. The opportunity to continue into the heart of Alabama slipped away as the hours passed. Smith never arrived.[1]

The overall plan, in the beginning, had seemed well designed. Grant had written Halleck in December that he intended "to start a heavy cavalry force to move against Forrest [while he was] in West Tennessee." This cavalry command would cooperate with Stephen A. Hurlbut, whose forces garrisoned Memphis. General Benjamin H. Grierson, who commanded the combined cavalry force, however, proved unable to destroy Nathan Bedford Forrest's cavalry or even become fully engaged with the wily cavalryman. Grierson did, however, drive Forrest out of western Tennessee and into northern Mississippi in late December.

Another chance at hitting Forrest came when Sherman approached Grant about returning to Mississippi. It was then that he proposed using a cavalry force from Memphis to join him at Meridian. The Union column, moving through Forrest's vicinity, could meet the enemy, destroy him, and link with the main army. Forrest's "irregular force of cavalry was constantly threatening Memphis and the river above, as well as our routes of supply in Middle Tennessee," Sherman argued. Grant thought he knew the best man to lead such an expedition, thirty-three-year-old Brigadier General William Sooy Smith, a fine infantry commander and former civilian engineer. In November 1863, after recovering temporarily from a severe case of arthritis, Smith had become the chief of cavalry for the Military Division of the Mississippi. Grant had ordered Smith to move near Memphis on February 1 with twenty-five hundred cavalry from middle Tennessee to add to part of Hurlbut's cavalry of roughly seventy-five hundred men. The combined forces, with the best brigades chosen to ride with Smith, were to be a strong force of about seven thousand horsemen. Smith organized three brigades under the command of Colonel George E. Waring Jr., Lieutenant Colonel William P. Hepburn, and Colonel La Fayette McCrillis.[2]

Smith, an Ohioan, had graduated from West Point in 1856. He was assigned to an artillery post, but soon he resigned to work in the railroad industry as a civil engineer. When the war started he returned to service as an infantry colonel with the Thirteenth Ohio, Army of the Ohio. After fighting primarily in western Virginia, Smith commanded one of Don Carlos Buell's brigades at Shiloh, and later he participated in the Vicksburg campaign as a division commander in the Army of the Tennessee. After the fall of the river city, Smith became Grant's cavalry chief.[3]

Some of Smith's horsemen were no strangers to battle either, while some were untested. The veterans had fought in battles at Forts Henry and Donelson, Shiloh, Corinth, Vicksburg, Chickamauga, and Chattanooga. Although Hepburn's Second Brigade and McCrillis's Third Brigade contained many veterans, Waring's First Brigade was made up of regiments that had only recently formed. The Second New Jersey had organized in August 1863, the Seventh Indiana and Nineteenth Pennsylvania in October 1863. These men had seen little action, and their inexperience in combat would prove troublesome for Smith when he met Forrest's Confederate horsemen.[4]

As commander of Union cavalry in western Tennessee, Grierson expected to lead the cavalry expedition. He had caught Sherman's attention when he led an effective diversionary raid through Mississippi during the Vicksburg campaign. Sherman believed Grierson was the best man for this new command, but Grant thought otherwise. Sherman, not wanting to differ with his friend, placed all the Army of the Tennessee's cavalry under Smith's command. Understanding Grierson's disappointment, Sherman promised him that if he went along as second in command to Smith, who was unfamiliar with the territory, "after the cavalry reached him [Sherman] at Meridian he would relieve General Smith and send him back to [Nashville], giving [Grierson his] own independent command again." Grierson agreed but continued to harbor ill will toward Smith. Sherman, thus, had placed his cavalry force in the command of someone who had a very different relationship with his officers than Sherman did. Sherman's men looked up to him, while Smith's did not.[5]

Smith reached Memphis in the second week of January and set about preparing for the expedition, collecting horses and equipment from across western Tennessee and Missouri. He wrote to the Cavalry Bureau offices in St. Louis, stating that animals and supplies had to come as rapidly as possible and asking that the bureau "give this department preference for the present." The last line ironically read: "Time is everything." Smith found Grierson's command "even worse off than the cavalry of Middle Tennessee." In letters to Grant and General J. P. Hatch, Smith reported that many of the horses were shoeless and in need of forage and that the cavalry regiments were scattered. The bright side for Smith came when horses from St. Louis arrived in better condition than any he had gathered before. The number of serviceable horses continued to fall short, however, as new recruits arrived continuously, each needing a mount.[6]

Sherman met with Smith on several occasions and instructed him to leave Collierville on February 1, allowing ten days to travel the 250 miles, for arrival in Meridian on February 10. Sherman assured Smith that he commanded the best cavalry in the land, "better than the combined cavalry which the enemy [had] in all the State of Mississippi." He stressed to the cavalry commander that he should not allow the enemy to draw him into any "minor affairs" that would delay him from the rendezvous. "Disable the [Mobile and Ohio] as much as possible, consume or destroy the resources of the enemy along that road, [and] break up the connection with Columbus, Miss.," ordered Sherman. He also told Smith to sustain his force through "liberal" foraging of hay and standing corn. Mounts and pack mules could be obtained from the countryside, along with any cattle that might prove useful to the soldiers' diet. Sherman warned Smith to respect any inhabited homes and their families, as was the common policy. The "mills, barns, sheds, stables and such things" were "to be used for the benefit and convenience" of the cavalry. Although Smith had not been Sherman's first choice for the expedition, the commanding general felt confident that, since Grierson would go along, Smith would complete his assigned tasks. After the two forces united at or near Meridian, they would attack and defeat Polk's army stationed there.[7]

Two days before the command left Collierville, Smith issued Special Field Order 2. Among other things, this order included Smith's philosophy for success: "The strength of the cavalry consisting to a great extent in its momentum, the attack must be made en masse," and the column "must meet charge with charge." The former engineer, it seemed, thought he had calculated a formula for victory. In the beginning, too, Smith looked forward to finding Forrest. He wrote Grant: "I have been anxious to attack him at once, but General Sherman thinks that I had better await his movement, and in the meantime collect, organize, and supply my command."[8]

Smith had most of the column ready by the appointed time, the men and animals in fine shape. An observer commented: "The finest cavalry force which had operated in this department was now massed" and ready to move. Word then came from Union City, Tennessee, that Waring's First Brigade had encountered washed-out bridges and flooded plains. Smith decided to wait for the First Brigade, making the crucial mistake of the expedition. Waring had left Union City on January 22, but he did not reach Collierville until February 8. Finding the First Brigade's horses exhausted from battling the icy river, muddy roads, and inundated steams, Smith ordered Waring's men to rest while mule skinners arranged the pack train. The column, therefore, did not leave for Meridian until February 11, a full ten days after Sherman had instructed them to march.[9]

Many questions surround Smith's decision to wait for Waring's brigade. In his later report to Grant, Sherman chastised Smith for not moving sooner. To that, Smith later wrote to Sherman: "I asked you if I should wait its arrival, and you answered, 'Certainly, if you go without it, you will be too weak, and I want you strong enough to go where you please.'" Sherman always denied saying that Smith should wait, and Smith argued ceaselessly that he had. Nevertheless, the command left much too late to assist Sherman effectively. It did, however, draw Forrest away from Sherman's main infantry advance from Vicksburg to Meridian.[10]

In December, Forrest had made a recruiting pass through western and middle Tennessee. He had gathered more than three thousand men, and he would have gathered more had Grierson not gone after him. He spent most of January 1864 organizing the men and making them fit for service. Forrest created four brigades and placed them under Colonel James Richardson, Colonel Robert McCulloch, Colonel Tyree H. Bell, and his brother Colonel Jeffrey Forrest. He placed McCulloch's and Forrest's brigades into a division under the command of Brigadier General James R. Chalmers.[11]

Forrest had developed quite an enviable reputation as a hard-fighting common man, especially around his homeland of northern Mississippi and western Tennessee. Many Mississippi secessionists looked to him for protection, and wherever he traveled, people flocked to see him. In their opinion, he had become their "guardian angel," protecting them from the "evils" of the Union army. His band of cavalry, from the end of 1863 to March 1864, stood as the only sizable Confederate force in northern Mississippi. In early February, when he pardoned a group of deserters at the last minute, saving them from a firing squad, members of his command vowed never to desert again. Townsfolk rejoiced over Forrest's compassion. Forrest stood as a heroic symbol to the people of Mississippi.[12]

Soon after Polk had taken command of Confederate forces in Mississippi, Forrest received command of cavalry in northern Mississippi and western Tennessee, creating "Forrest's Cavalry Department." He made Oxford his headquarters from which he continually raided Union-held southern towns such as Corinth and supply depots like Grand Junction.[13]

Around the seventh of February, Polk wrote Forrest that a Federal army had left Vicksburg heading toward Jackson and that another had come up the Yazoo River. Spies and scouts also informed Forrest of a substantial cavalry unit equipping in the Memphis area. Forrest immediately dispatched several scouts to discover these units' plans.[14]

Smith decided that in order to mask his main movement toward New Albany, he would feint with Colonel McMillen's infantry brigade and a small number of cavalry to the south toward Panola, Wyatt, and Abbeville. He hoped to draw the Confederate cavalry's attention away from his main line of march and keep Forrest guessing about the Federal objective. Forrest, however, was not fooled. He wrote to Polk that he was sure that "this is only a feint" and that the Federals intended to attack the Mobile and Ohio Railroad from across the prairies near Okolona and continue down the railroad to join Sherman's army. Forrest insisted that Polk allow him to concentrate his forces "against Smith and whip him, after which attention could be given to Sherman." Polk agreed and added that he would send Forrest all the troops he could spare. As a safeguard, Forrest had sent portions of Chalmers's division down to guard crossings of the Tallahatchie River between Panola and Abbeville and to provide a report as to the Federal purpose. He also sent Bell's brigade to Grenada and Jeffrey Forrest's men to West Point to watch for any movement from the south.[15]

Smith's main force left Collierville around 2 P.M. on February 11, marching on the Moscow road toward the southeast to cross the Tallahatchie River. The men were in high spirits. One soldier commented on the rumor that they might catch Forrest on their way: "There lay before us a fair opportunity for dispersing the most successful body of cavalry in the Rebel service." Besides any danger that Forrest or the Mississippi state forces might pose, the Federal cavalry had constantly to guard against bushwhackers. A short time into the march, Smith confronted guerrilla troops who were using the swamps and wooded areas for cover. The nature of the land allowed for ease of concealment and a quick retreat for the native troops, and it also provided difficulties for the bluecoats in their detection and pursuit of the menacing lot. A sergeant wrote in frustration that "the first notice the advanced guard had [of] their [bushwhackers'] whereabouts was a volley." Confrontations with guerrillas, nonetheless, slowed the Federals very little, and they made a relatively swift movement across the highlands.[16]

Smith's trek across northern Mississippi passed through heavy timber and swampy lowlands containing few plantations. At this time of the year, these swamps were impassable except in areas where the only avenues across the murky water came from poorly constructed corduroyed roads and bridges. This factor, of course, limited the number of places where the Federal troops could move. Knowing the probable route of the enemy, Forrest would later use his acquaintance with the land to lay a trap for Smith's grand cavalry.

On February 13, the lead elements of the Federal horsemen had difficulty crossing the Tippah Creek on a bridge made from fence rails, but they traversed the Tallahatchie at New Albany "without firing a shot." As far as Smith was concerned, the feint toward Wyatt had worked; the Confederates had guessed wrong, and he was making excellent progress toward his objective. Moving southward to avoid impassable swamps, the Union cavalry passed through Pontotoc, caught its inhabitants unaware, and seized valuable provisions. At a swamp crossing near Houlka, a Mississippi state brigade under General Samuel J. Gholson met and clashed with the Federal cavalry. The "rabble of State forces" proved no match for Smith's men, and the inferior force of six hundred men "stampeded and drove pell-mell across the swamp." That night, guerrillas tried again to inflict casualties on the Union ranks. They dressed in women's clothing and attempted to take a sentry post under the cover of darkness. When one of them spoke, however, the alert pickets discovered the ruse and fired into the charlatans, wounding one of them. One Indiana volunteer remarked that the shots had "settled the question of sex beyond a doubt." Whether lit for the sake of retribution or from other motives, fires flamed in the buildings of New Albany.[17]

Forrest still clung to the idea that Smith intended to move south to join Sherman at Meridian. He was not sure, however, if Smith would move west via Houston or Okolona. By February 14, Forrest's brother had reached West Point to establish a communication line with Chalmers at Houston. Forrest himself ordered the balance of his forces to begin concentrating at West Point. Estimating his opposition at ten to twelve thousand cavalrymen, he wrote to Polk: "In the event that the enemy proves too strong for me I shall fall back in the enemy's front toward Meridian." Stephen D. Lee, commander of Confederate Cavalry Corps in Mississippi, had informed Forrest that if he needed it, Lee could send support north to Forrest's location. Forrest sent word to Chalmers that if he encountered the enemy he was not to bring about a general engagement. He was to delay the enemy as long as possible and fall back slowly toward West Point.[18]

Smith's swift movements had caused the Confederates confusion in the first days of the expedition, but now, at New Albany, the Federals had slowed down. Heavy rains the following day prevented Smith from challenging the swollen creeks and swamps; the command stayed in camp or foraged from the countryside. Smith's arthritis had flared again (possibly because of the persistent rains), and he was much fatigued. He also thought about Sherman's warning about Forrest. A commander always had to keep on his guard in areas where Forrest operated. If he came into contact with Forrest, Sherman cautioned, Smith must assume the role of aggressor and not allow Forrest to gain the upper hand. Smith became more cautious, and the rain-soaked roads added to his concern. He penned an order to Grierson not to "move more than ten miles in advance" until supported. Although he had no word of substantial Confederate forces in the immediate vicinity, he still issued a cautious order. In addition, Smith continued to exaggerate the number of Confederate forces to his front, the result of inaccurate reports. However, he always believed the higher numbers rather than the lower ones.

Meanwhile, many Union soldiers worried that this sluggish pace might allow the Confederate forces to concentrate and move into a blocking position.[19]

Forrest scrambled to do just that. He sent his troops to a site near Starkville, his new headquarters, just twenty-five miles west of Columbus, and sent his brother straight to Aberdeen, a settlement roughly thirty-five miles northeast of West Point. Forrest ordered his brother to harass and delay any Federal advance and to communicate with Chalmers at Tampico. Again, the instructions were not to instigate a general engagement but to fall back slowly to the south toward West Point.[20]

Forrest had begun to concentrate the main body of his troops near West Point, and he prepared to check Smith's advance to determine his enemy's strengths and weaknesses. Word reached Forrest that Polk had ordered Lee to send a force to assist in halting the invaders. Polk had come to believe that stopping the Federal cavalry was paramount to stopping Sherman's army.[21]

As the temperature dropped, the rains turned to snow, and the freezing affected both man and beast. The Federals slogged and sloshed their way toward Okolona, passing the small town of Redland on their way, burning it to the ground along with its cotton gins, corncribs, presses, fence posts, and gristmills. Many of Smith's soldiers had interpreted their foraging orders broadly and had torched some of the private buildings as they burned the public property. As an observer later noted in his memoir, "In every direction, except the immediate front, as far as the eye could see smoke and flames shot up." The destruction continued as the Union forces reached Okolona on February 18.[22]

Waring later wrote that for two days after reaching Okolona, "the sky was red with the flames of burning corn and cotton." Smith ordered Waring to take his brigade on the road toward Egypt Station (near Aberdeen) to camp and to send out parties to destroy the railroad and any Confederate supplies that farmers had placed along its edges. Hearing that a Union brigade might make an attack on their nearby town, Columbus citizens decided to evacuate. A member of the Sixteenth Mississippi described what occurred there in a letter to his wife: "There was a great fluttering among the telegraphic wires over which orders came leaping with lighting speed startling the quiet and honest citizens of the loyal city of Columbus into a fearful panic—first—all the commissary and quartermaster stores were ordered to be carried across the river—secondly every wagon was ordered to be impressed to carry the stores to Demopolis (Ala.) with dispatch—thirdly the 'Bloody 43rd' just as it was ready to take the cars were ordered to remain at Columbus and to be mounted as rapidly as possible as the enemy were approaching the place and so we are still here." The Mississippi soldier wrote that he had never seen "so causeless, so senseless, so shameful a panic" in his life. The people of Columbus feared the worst, but fortunately for them, the Federal cavalrymen never reached their town.[23]

Around and near Okolona, the Federal troops noted how the landscape had changed. North of Okolona, the countryside was hillier. South of Okolona begins the rich, black soil that stretches across Alabama into Georgia, a prairie that grew bountiful corn crops and hefty hogs. One Iowan remarked, "We were now in one of the most beautiful prairies in the United States [with] millions of bushels of corn, thousands of bales of cotton, and well filled smoke houses on every plantation." The Union troops took advantage of this concentration of goods and efficiently destroyed all they did not use. One Tennessee rider under Forrest noted in his memoir the destruction's effect. "Up to that date, nothing like this had been seen in our part of the country," he wrote, and "our soldiers were aroused by the reports brought in [of the large-scale destruction]." Confederate soldiers angrily vowed that they would avenge the suffering of their people.[24]

The bluecoats were not the only ones dispensing fire and devastation on the Southern populace, however. Great numbers of fugitive slaves had begun to flock to the Federal troops, seeking freedom and safety. As they left their plantations, they often left destruction behind. Waring reported that the former slaves were "driven wild [and] set the torch to mansion houses, stables, cotton gins, and quarters." Smith could do relatively little about the slaves' actions, but he did issue instructions to his soldiers not to participate in widespread and wanton destruction of private property. Many of them did not obey.[25]

Sergeant James Larson of the Fourth United States Cavalry remarked that "the behavior of some of the troops was rather disgraceful and not as we had been in the habit of seeing cavalry act." Sherman had instructed Smith to destroy Confederate supplies, railroads, and machinery, but that did not include thievery or demolition of private property. Smith, disturbed at some troopers' disobedience, ordered "the first man caught in the act" of such damage "to be shot" and offered a reward of five hundred dollars for any culprit's detection.[26]

Later, as Smith moved from Okolona to West Point along the Mobile and

Ohio Railroad, his cavalry continued the devastation. Smith's men burned so sizable a quantity of corn that "there was a line of fire leading from place to place." Smith estimated that the blazes consumed one to two million bushels of corn and two thousand bales of cotton. Runaway slaves by the hundreds, riding on stolen horses and mules, came into the lines for sanctuary, lengthening the growing column. Sergeant Larson questioned the amount of time spent on foraging and burning. The expedition seemingly had "turned into a raid with no other object than to destroy Confederate property," he wrote, and "there appeared to be no haste to join Sherman." Smith used valuable time destroying supplies—time he could have used moving to Meridian.[27]

The night of February 17, Smith called all of his officers together for a council. Scouts continued to report a large concentration of Confederate forces at West Point, and this news deeply concerned Smith. He questioned the prudence of continuing the expedition. Seven days past the date he was to join Sherman, the Union general wavered. His officers pleaded with him to continue. Grierson asked for and received permission to take the Second Brigade and make a run for Meridian through a river crossing at Aberdeen, but before he could carry out the movement Smith withdrew his consent. The officers did, nonetheless, convince Smith that night that the expedition could and should proceed. It was, however, a reluctant commander leading the Union cavalry through Mississippi.[28]

On February 19, elements of Waring's and Colonel Forrest's brigades skirmished briefly between Aberdeen and Egypt Station. Colonel Forrest, following his brother's orders, commenced a slow, methodical movement back toward West Point. He sent Colonel Barteau, commanding Bell's brigade, to watch the Federals in case they tried to move to the east side of the Tombigbee River and make a dash for Columbus. Barteau arrived near Columbus in the late afternoon and crossed the river to the east. General Forrest, meanwhile, placed his remaining troops into position to meet the enemy at the edge of West Point. He decided to use the rivers, creeks, and swamps to his advantage.[29]

To the east of Forrest's position near West Point lay the Tombigbee, a formidable river, and about ten to twelve miles to the west flowed Sakatonchee Creek, which ran for many miles parallel to the Tombigbee until it joined the latter near Columbus. The recent heavy rains had swollen each of the streams to overflowing. These waterways formed a perfect blind alley into which Forrest intended to draw the Federal forces in order to detain them long enough for Lee to arrive. He had positioned himself so Smith would have to turn and move west instead of continuing south. If Smith continued on his southerly march, Forrest could get at his rear. The next morning, Forrest received a dispatch informing him that General Lee would arrive in two days.[30]

Smith continued southward and skirmished again with Colonel Forrest. General Forrest left Starkville in the early morning hours, taking portions of Chalmers's and Richardson's brigades and some artillery with him. He joined his brother three miles from West Point, ordering the entire group to an area southwest of Sakatonchee Creek. The graycoats camped near Ellis' Bridge, the closest crossing to Forrest's "trap," and across the river near Siloam. Located about four miles west of West Point, the thirty-yard-long bridge could only be approached by a corduroyed road located between two steep, rain-filled creek banks. Forces traversing either way had to travel with great caution and could not move in great force through the dangerous causeway. Forrest ordered the nearest bridge, eight miles upriver from Ellis' Bridge, destroyed after he discovered that a number of Federals had crossed and burned the local mill there. Nightfall found nearly all of Forrest's forces camped behind the Sakatonchee awaiting the Federal advance. Barteau's brigade, earlier sent to Columbus, had crossed the Tombigbee and ridden hard to reach this location. As they neared Waverly plantation, twelve miles from West Point, a member of Barteau's brigade wrote in his diary that "the whole country northward was illuminated by burning" and that this scene inspired the Confederates to try to "punish such an unmanly, heathenish method of warfare."[31]

Smith arrived at West Point around three o'clock in the afternoon. The Northern troops, greatly pleased with the abundance of forage and supplies collected for their camp messes and stew pots, looked forward to meeting the enemy on an open field. Scouts and patrols reported back to Smith that four enemy brigades, between six and seven thousand men, held the waterways to the south and west. Information of Lee's possible reinforcement had also reached the Union commander, and prisoners and deserters from the day's skirmish had confirmed its validity. Smith, feeling ill from both stress and arthritis and believing that Forrest had set a trap for him, called for another officers' council around midnight.[32]

When Grierson reported, he observed that his superior was "absolutely sick and unable to command in such an emergency." Smith informed the group that he believed that Sherman, having taken Meridian by now, was returning to Vicksburg and that Forrest and Lee would destroy Smith's entire command if he did not turn back. He had no direct knowledge of Sherman's whereabouts, of course, because the two had not communicated since shortly after Sherman's departure for Meridian. Smith later wrote that he had only one trustworthy brigade, the other two having displayed a lack of discipline in the previous days, leaving "the most serious apprehensions as to what would be their conduct in action." His column had added three thousand contrabands with all types of baggage, horses, and mules. Maneuvering, therefore, would be difficult. All of the cavalry officers opposed a return to Memphis, so, in desperation, the general declared himself too sick to lead and turned the command over to Grierson. When he inquired as to what Grierson intended to do with the men, Grierson declared that he intended to continue toward Meridian. Smith quickly responded: "No! That will never do. General Stephen D. Lee is in front of us with his whole force, including infantry and artillery." In Smith's opinion, continuing the march, Sherman or not, would result in the menacing Confederate force crushing his army. He retook command and ordered a countermarch to Memphis.[33]

In the early hours of February 21, Smith's raiders turned back toward Memphis. Smith decided to conduct a strong rearguard action to allow his bulky main force to get under way undisturbed. Reports traveled up and down the Federal line that they had accomplished the object of their mission: they had created an effective diversion for Sherman's army. Some of the men were confused. After venturing deep into enemy territory, they had heard no word about why they were returning to Memphis, and they did not understand why the officers had issued instructions to move in the opposite direction when they had met only slight resistance. One brigade commander commented: "We might have . . . given him [Forrest] successful battle, but, at every suggestion of this, we received from our general . . . the order to push forward," back to Memphis.[34]

Early that morning, General Forrest sent Colonel Forrest to the west side of Ellis' Bridge across the Sakatonchee River and placed McCulloch's brigade in support. Around 8 A.M., gunfire from the Second Iowa and the Sixth Illinois drove the Confederate pickets in, and they reported that the enemy was advancing in great force. General Forrest sent Chalmers forward to support the two engaged brigades. Colonel Forrest had thrown up a breastworks

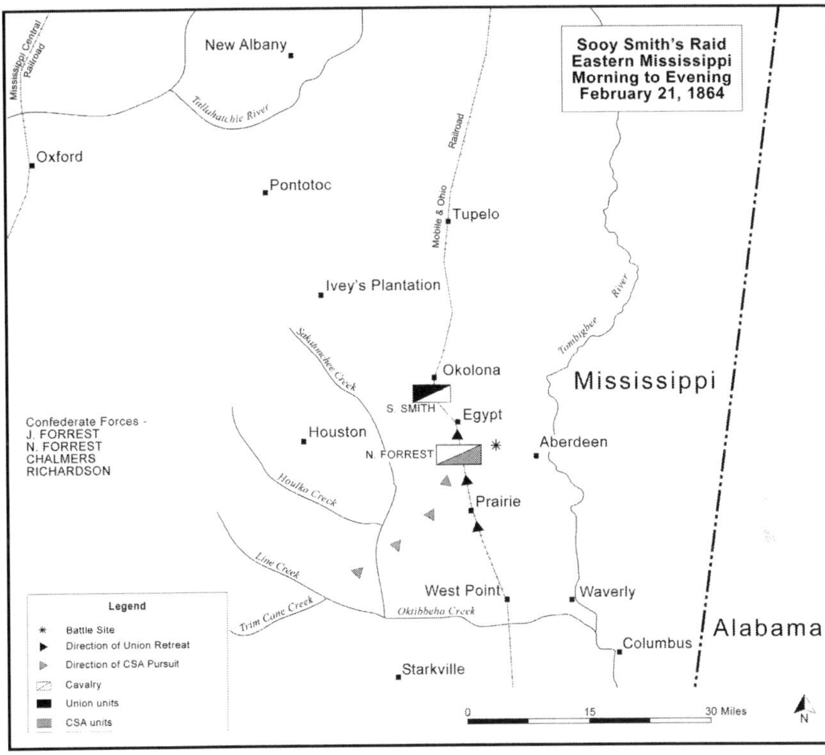

of logs and fence rails, which provided excellent protection. The Confederates repulsed several attempts to dislodge them. After two hours of fighting, the Federal attackers started to withdraw.[35]

Chalmers, the Mississippi lawyer turned cavalryman, was sitting on his horse at the rear of the action when he observed General Forrest riding hastily toward him with a portion of Faulkner's Kentuckians and some artillery. The excited general reined in his horse in front of his subordinate. "What are the conditions of affairs in the front?" he snapped. Chalmers replied that he had heard nothing from Colonel Forrest except that there was "some skirmishing." The general, unimpressed with the answer, shot back, "Is that all you know?" Before Chalmers could answer, the general spat out, "Then I'll go there and find out myself." With that statement, he spurred his horse in the direction of the gunfire. Chalmers followed on his heels.[36]

When Forrest reached the front, he realized that the Federals were heading back toward Memphis. He sent Chalmers to the rear with orders to regroup the remaining men, to hold the bridge, to send a patrol to watch the river crossing to the north for a flanking movement, and to send reinforcements, including artillery, to his location. Forrest commanded Jeffrey Forrest's and McCulloch's brigades to advance. The general led the group, with the Kentuckians and his escorts riding hard alongside him. They charged headlong into the rear guard, while McCulloch struck on their flank. Finding the pressure too hot, the Union cavalrymen fell back. Throughout the rest of the afternoon and evening the Federal rear guard attempted to make stands along the way, and each time Forrest, with McCulloch and Colonel Forrest in support, dislodged them, inflicting thirty-six casualties over the day's action. Bell's brigade had moved in a northwesterly direction to watch for Federal flanking movements, paralleling the Mobile and Ohio and Smith's path as they went. The running fight lasted until the battlers came near Okolona. By the time night fell, the pursuit became hazardous.[37]

Forrest and his escorts, riding through a series of deep ditches to cut off the retreating Federals, appeared on the road ahead of a group of Confederates. In the darkness, the two forces fired into one another. One ball passed through General Forrest's clothing, killing a man to his rear. Under these treacherous conditions, Forrest decided to end the attack and ordered his command to camp. Finding a generous portion of forage and supplies that the retreating rear guard had left behind on their old campground, the weary Confederates, content with their bounty, settled in for a night's rest.[38]

Confusion was not limited to the Confederate camp. Throughout the day's action, both Smith and Grierson gave orders without consulting one another. What followed was a series of conflicting movements that exhausted the Union cavalrymen both mentally and physically. Upon reaching camp late in the night at Okolona, for example, having received five conflicting orders throughout the day, the Seventy-second Indiana (mounted) Infantry became so confused that the men did not know whether they were to leave their horses saddled or to unsaddle them. The situation for the Federal soldiers in this column was quite different from that of those in Sherman's main column. Sherman and his officers commanded their men with proficiency, keeping communication open and clear between the officers, continuing down the ranks.[39]

Before dawn on February 22, the Confederates moved toward Okolona. Forrest learned that the enemy's rear guard had formed a line of battle near

Egypt Station, positioning themselves between his forces and Okolona. He sent Colonel Forrest to hit the right flank and McCulloch to hit the left. Forrest took his escort and attacked from the front. The combined activity drove the Federals back into Okolona, where they re-formed.[40]

Bell's brigade, which had camped nearer to Okolona and left earlier than Forrest that morning, had awaited his attack on the rear guard. They had halted one and a half miles west of town and had thrown out mounted skirmishers, who had soon clashed with Federal pickets. The sound of musket and cannon fire boomed in the distance. Forrest had attacked the rear guard, driving it toward town. A messenger soon arrived ordering Barteau to continue the flanking maneuver on the far right. Just outside Okolona, Bell's brigade realized that they were paralleling a Federal regiment (Fourth United States Regulars), the contending units about half a mile apart. Both forces eyed one another warily and continued on their path until the head of each force reached a few hundred yards north of town. Then they turned and faced one another, the Federals lined up along the southwest side of town and the Confederates along the northeast with the railroad between them.[41]

The Fourth United States Regulars had waited until their supply train had passed before they formed to repulse the Confederate attack. As the main column had passed near Okolona earlier, Waring had ordered the Seventh Indiana to fall out and support the Regulars. The Third Brigade, under Colonel McCrillis, brought up the rear of the main column, which moved northwest along the Pontotoc road. When word reached the main column that the rear guard might need further support, Smith ordered McCrillis to send a portion of the Third Brigade there.[42]

Forrest and his escorts continued moving northward until they discovered the Federals' strong line on a slight rise west of town. The general then noticed Bell's brigade in an opposing line. Realizing that he had outrun both Jeffrey Forrest's and McCulloch's brigades, and without adequate men to attack such a substantial Union force, the general left his escorts and rode around the edge of town to Bell's men. The men cheered the sight of their general, and as he quickly galloped toward the commanding colonel he called out to the soldiers, "Mount your horses."[43]

"Where is the enemy's whole position?" Forrest asked Barteau. "You see it, General, and they are preparing to charge," came the reply. Looking over to the Federal line, Forrest remarked, "Then we will charge them." And with

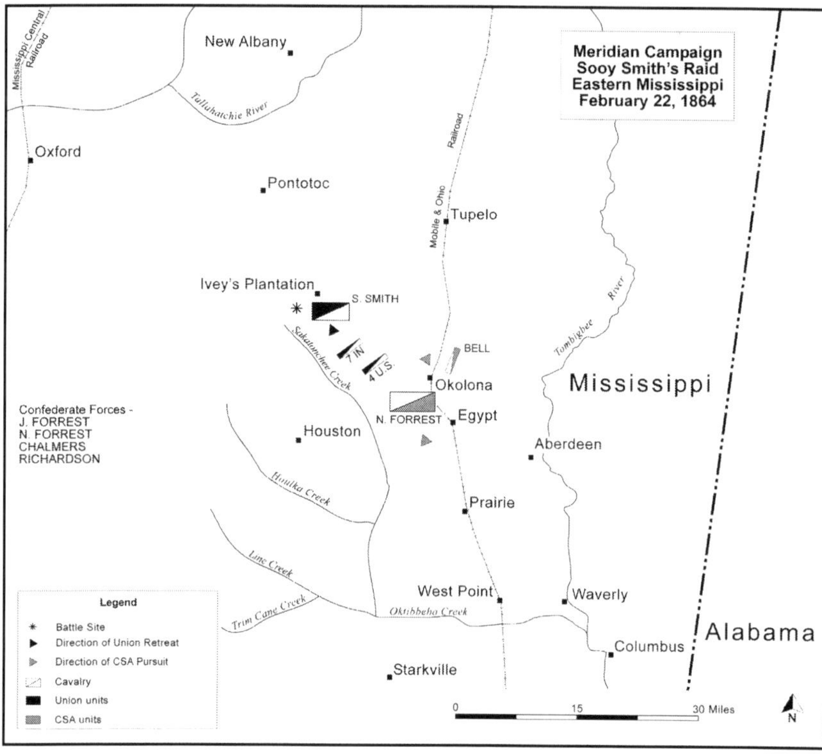

that he rushed down across the railroad track north of town with part of the brigade in tow and the other portion headed directly into Okolona.[44]

Many of the citizens of Okolona watched curiously from their second-story windows. The women leaned out and waved small Confederate flags, telling their cavalrymen to give the "'Yanks' Hail Columbia." Old men and children whooped and screeched.[45]

The Seventh Indiana, one of the regiments of newly recruited troopers, broke in frenzied confusion under the fierce Confederate fire and rushed headlong into elements of the Third Brigade, which had still not reached the town. Some of the stampeding soldiers screamed out, "Go ahead, or we will be killed." This caused a chain reaction, and before long the entire group was scurrying down the Pontotoc road in complete disorder. Many of the frightened men had lost their hats and thrown away guns and supplies, anything that might encumber their swift retreat. The mob, in its wild confusion, drove a six-gun battery off the road and into a field, where it became stuck, causing its gunners to spike five of the guns and destroy the carriages and ammunition. The rush continued into the main column, through the contraband slaves and animals, causing even greater pandemonium. An Iowan described the scene: "To the train of contrabands, 1,500 strong, was added double that number of demoralized soldiers . . . these, with 3,000 lead horses and mules . . . all mingled in one stampeded mass. At one time, this mob, which was over one fourth of a mile wide and miles in length, was moving off without advance or flank guard, or commander." The Fourth United States Regulars, now greatly outnumbered, angrily withdrew from the town. Waring recalled the growing despair of the Union troops: "When we left Okolona we left hope behind, for our road struck at once into a wooded, hilly country, full of by-ways and cross-roads known to the enemy and unknown to us." The chase continued.[46]

The Union horses, mules, and men moved over a relatively narrow piece of ground and cut deep into the rain-soaked ground, slowing the retreat but also making the pursuit difficult for the Confederates. Forrest and his men caught the rear of the column nonetheless and continued the assault. Over the next five miles, the swiftest Confederate horsemen battled the rear elements of Smith's line. Forrest realized that many of his men had become scattered, so he halted the line to regroup around five o'clock that afternoon.[47]

The temporary reprieve gave the Union officers time to react. Realizing that a firm stand was in order, Smith noticed an open ridgetop, thickly covered with underbrush and small oak trees, with high rail fences and log houses. There, at Ivey's Plantation, he decided to make a stand. The sides of the ridge, sloping steeply into the deep valleys on either side, protected his flanks from a rapid Confederate assault. A battery stationed along the edge of the road provided excellent cover for the men whom Smith dismounted and rallied into line.[48]

As the Confederates climbed the end of the ridge, they found the Federals well positioned and awaiting their arrival. Just as Colonel Forrest's and McCulloch's brigades came into full view of the defensive line, the men of the Fourth Missouri opened up with their mountain howitzers, blasting the Confederates with showers of hot metal and ball. Colonel Forrest moved to the right, McCulloch to the left; they rushed forward to carry the enemy's advance position. Fire poured from the Federal carbines at a terrific pace and staggered the gray line. Jeffrey Forrest, at the head of his men, fell mortally wounded in the neck. There was a lull in the action.[49]

After a few minutes, word reached his older brother, who rode quickly to his dying sibling's side. When he arrived, Forrest realized that Jeffrey had not yet perished. He knelt down, taking his brother's crumpled body into his hands, and raised him up into a seated position. Quiet words passed between the two, and then silence. The general leaned down, kissed his brother's brow, and placed him back on the battlefield with his hat across his face. Forrest remounted, took out his handkerchief, and tied it around his head, covering his face. The somber mood of the moment broke when Forrest shouted to his bugler, "Gaus, sound the charge!"[50]

Inspired, the men charged ahead and struck the Federals just as they had started to remount to continue the retreat. A fierce skirmish ensued, the Federals massing behind a makeshift breastwork of logs and rails in a new defensive position a few miles to the rear. Forrest repeated, "Charge them! Charge them!" as he continued forward. The Union line held the charge as long as possible and poured heavy fire into the attackers. Moving to the top of a rise, Lieutenant Colonel James A. Barksdale of the Fifth Mississippi, near the head of the line, reeled as a ball passed through his chest. As he fell mortally wounded, he continued to shout, "Charge!"[51]

The terrible hiss of passing musket balls continued, while cannon fire screamed over the embattled troops. Riding hard toward the enemy, Forrest felt his horse crumble underneath him and was thrown to the ground by the violent lurch. He gathered himself and continued his attack on foot until a trooper offered his horse, a gesture that Forrest quickly accepted. He had scarcely ridden a hundred yards when Federal fire claimed that horse's life too. Men fell wounded and were dying all around the general, including Colonel McCulloch, who, though wounded severely in the hand, refused to retire from the field. The Union soldiers could not halt the rush, however, and withdrew once again.[52]

His furious pace caused Forrest to outrun the bulk of his force once again. As a small number of Confederates continued the assault they came upon the enemy in four long lines of two thousand men, a few hundred yards apart on a small, open ridge known as Prairie Mound. Forrest could see that the Federals intended to smash his three-hundred-man force, and he quickly ordered it to take cover in a ditch that crossed the field, allowing time for the rest of his column to advance.[53]

The first, second, and third lines of Federals moved down toward the gully with determination, meeting deadly musket fire from Forrest's position. The attacking lines stumbled under the vicious defense, but remnants soon reached the gully. The small Confederate force, with most of its ammunition exhausted, used revolvers and bayonets to try to repulse the attack. Just as the Federals were about to overrun the enemy position, McCulloch's brigade arrived, with Bell's brigade in support. McCulloch flew into the fight and turned the portion of the enemy that had broken through, killing and wounding many Federals.[54]

Waring, believing that the Union force had an opportunity to end Forrest's pursuit, asked Smith to allow a saber charge against the enemy. He believed the Confederates were off balance and that a fierce strike could force the enemy to retreat. Smith uncharacteristically agreed, and the Fourth United States, Seventh Indiana, and Third Tennessee mounted their horses, ready to charge the enemy's position. Captain Charles S. Bowman, commander of the Fourth United States cavalry, rode forward as he shouted to his men, "Draw saber!" A loud "shrick" sounded across the battlefield as the men drew their swords. He called out "Charge!" and the men spurred their horses forward.[55]

Forrest, who preferred to be the attacker, rallied his men and proceeded to meet the "grandest cavalry charge ever witnessed" with a head-on charge of his own. The two forces clashed with a tremendous force as metal flashed, horses screamed, and pistols popped. The Federals, showing the greatest determination of the entire expedition, threw back the enemy's lead elements.[56] The main body of Confederates, however, remained well concealed behind a high rail fence and forced the attacking cavalry to sheathe their sabers and rely on their pistols. The Federals, unable to get at the entrenched enemy through or around the fence and under "heavy fire at close range," broke in confusion, losing another piece of artillery.[57]

The Confederates, critically low on ammunition and totally exhausted from clambering over the hills and fighting for the past two days, realized that they were too worn out to continue. The Federals had mounted a stiff resistance in their latest encounter, and the Confederates had had enough. Therefore, Forrest decided to end the pursuit. He slowly withdrew his troops to the rear and bivouacked for the night.

Lee had reached the Sakatonchee River. He learned of Forrest's pursuit of the retreating Federal cavalry. Satisfied that all was well, he fell back to Forrest's headquarters at Starkville and awaited word.[58]

The Federals continued their retreat. Smith, at the head of the line, had halted to stop some of the stampeding regiments. With the assistance of the Fourth United States cavalry, the general managed to collect most of the Seventh Indiana. He scathingly accused both officers and men of cowardice. He said that he had sent them to assist the Fourth United States at Okolona equipped with Spencer repeating rifles and that all that they had done with them had been to "render no assistance to the regiment then hard pressed by the advancing enemy." They had "stampeded in plain view of the enemy, and went to the rear in a complete panic that caused the loss of one battery." He ordered the officers of the regiment to turn over their Spencers to the Fourth United States. The officers complained that this order would have ill effects on the men in the future, so once again Smith proved his indecisiveness and withdrew the order. The hour being late, the general returned to his sickbed when his main column came to rest near Pontotoc. A soldier from the Second Brigade explained that Grierson, "rather by common consent, as well as the necessity of things, assumed the direction of affairs as soon as darkness put an end to the battles . . . and [to] him we owe our salvation."[59]

Late into the night, Gholson arrived with some eight hundred to a thousand relatively fresh state guardsmen. Forrest ordered him to continue the pursuit the following morning, which he did, harassing the long, demoralized Federal line. A Tennessean described the feeling of the downtrodden Union force: "There was little organization left in this command, which, scarcely a fortnight before, had left West Tennessee seven thousand strong, and as splendidly equipped a corps of cavalry as ever took the field." Waring further commented: "The retreat to Memphis was a weary, disheartening, and almost panic-stricken flight, in the greatest disorder and confusion." Although the Confederate main column had ended the chase, the Federals did not have an easy path to travel. Guerrilla troops and Gholson hung on their heels like bulldogs, sniping at them at every turn. In addition, they had moved back into a fire-scorched area, and forage became scarce. Men and animals went hungry.[60]

The long mass of fugitive slaves and animals continued to encumber the steady movement of the cavalry column. At one point the contrabands balked and blocked the way at a fork in the road, unclear on where to go.

Officers and enlisted men alike shouted and threatened the confused crowd, but to no avail. Smith, disturbed at the news, rode to the location, stood at the front of the line, and shouted: "Follow me, I'll show you where to go!" While the frustrated general led the freedom seekers forward, snickering flankers "shooed" the mass from the rear. They laughed that their general was at the head of an army of "darkies." He could not lead the cavalry. Now, he might be able to lead the contrabands. Only after great effort did the column move. As he rounded a bend in the road, Smith bluntly called out, "Now there's the road I want you to travel; don't you let me catch one of you out of it."[61]

Meanwhile, Forrest detailed burying parties to tend to the dead, both Confederate and Federal, and then returned to his headquarters near Starkville. He had lost twenty-seven men in his pursuit of Smith, with another ninety-seven wounded. The Federals had lost one hundred during the day's fight from West Point to Ivey's Plantation. The number of total Confederate casualties came to 144 when an additional twenty missing men were added to the final tally. Forrest had lost only half as many men as Smith. The majority of his men reached Starkville on February 24, with the rest (parts of two brigades) returning over the next two days. Forrest had once again frustrated the Federal efforts, and with the action he raised his status even higher among the common folk in Mississippi. He later wrote of the operation: "Considering the disparity in numbers and equipment, I regard the defeat of this force, consisting as it did of the best cavalry in the Union army, as a victory of which all engaged may feel justly proud." He believed that "peace and security" had returned to the land and that his men had been "inspired . . . with courage and given . . . confidence in themselves and their commanders."[62]

While a weary Forrest penned his preliminary report to Polk, the Federals stumbled into camp at Germantown and Camp Grierson near Memphis. The cold northern winds swept down across Tennessee for the following two days. By February 28, as if it were nature's last insult, it began to snow and did not stop for two days. The exhausted men and horses felt the brunt of the cold. The animals, having had little to eat since Okolona and worn from the long march, grew weaker from the icy blast, effectively removing them from action in the coming spring campaigns. General Hurlbut, examining the command a month later, remarked: "The cavalry of Grierson, now at Memphis, is of little value. Horses are run down, what there are of them."

Smith reported total casualties for the expedition at 319, with 47 killed, 152 wounded, and 120 missing, a relatively small loss considering the amount of skirmishing.[63]

Few Union citizens had known about Smith's predicament until the main force returned to Memphis. On February 29 the *New York Tribune* printed a dispatch from that city reporting that some Union cavalry coming into Memphis had stated that forces of "Rebel Gens. Forrest, Adams, Lee and Roddy [had] concentrated their forces against those of Gen. Smith" and that Smith "is slowly falling back toward Memphis." The last line of the print read, "but the report is not generally believed, as little credit can be placed in the statements of stragglers." Perhaps Waring was not wrong in his interpretation as to why the young recruits broke on the field near Okolona. These "stragglers" believed they had met a combined superior force; even more significantly, Smith had thought so too.[64]

Smith, however, had many other excuses for failing to meet Sherman in Meridian, let alone for being out-generaled by Forrest. The alleged combination of Forrest's forces with Lee's proved false, so Smith listed other reasons for his premature return. In his official report, the general complained that the "clumsiness of so large a command, encumbered as it was with pack trains and captured stock," made his movement extremely slow, opening it to enemy attacks. He protested that the "peculiar formation of the country," well known to the enemy but unfamiliar to the Federals, made finding and defending against or attacking the Confederates difficult. He argued that the march "was ten days behind time; could get no communication to you [Sherman]," and that as far as he knew, his superior had captured Meridian and had returned back to Vicksburg. The tardy arrival of Waring's brigade caused the delay in leaving for Meridian, he contended, blaming Sherman for verbally ordering him to wait until it arrived before leaving the post, thus throwing the entire movement behind time. Lastly, the enemy, armed with rifled muskets as opposed to the Union carbines, could fight much better dismounted than his men could in the terrain of northern Mississippi. The only positive section in Smith's report was his list of supplies destroyed and stock captured. Those actions, nonetheless, constituted only part of Sherman's plan for him. He was supposed to have gone to Meridian too.[65]

After the war, Smith argued that subsequent information substantiated the reasons for his withdrawal at West Point and that Sherman had, in fact, begun his return to Vicksburg. Lee had made a movement to reinforce Forrest and had come within a day's hard ride of doing so. Smith did, however, misstate that "Forrest's force is ascertained to have been rather above than below my estimate." Forrest had only thirty-five hundred men, and Smith's estimates ran from five thousand to twelve thousand men.[66] Much of Smith's report defended his reasoning for ordering a retreat and highlighted the property confiscated and destroyed. A marked exception was a special comment in his report concerning the conduct of General Grierson. Smith, realizing that the young general had played a significant role in the defense of his command, acknowledged that Grierson had "behaved nobly, and is a man of more capacity than either you or I have credited him with."[67]

Grierson did not feel the same about Smith. He regained command of his cavalry for the second time in five days, and this time it was more permanent. The grand force that had left Memphis so few days before had returned to camp as worn and tired as an old, weathered boot. Earlier convinced that Sherman wanted him to lead the column, he now cheered at the prospect that Sherman's attitude toward Smith might prevent the unsuccessful general from commanding a cavalry detachment again. Grierson wrote to his wife on February 28: "The command were very much dissatisfied with his mode of procedure," and "all wished to go on when he decided to turn back." Grierson remained convinced that he could have joined Sherman at Meridian had Smith not stopped the action the night of February 20. He later wrote in his memoirs that if he had seen the contents of Sherman's orders to Smith about reaching Meridian "at all hazards," he would have taken the Second Brigade on to Meridian alone. Although Grierson was furious at Smith, he did not publicly chastise the general until after the war.[68]

Waring also harbored a strong dislike for Smith's actions. After the war, he wrote: "All of us who were in a position to know the spirit with which we were commanded were conscious of a gradual oozing out at the finger-ends of the determination to make a successful fight." Realizing the extent of damage that the expedition had caused to morale, Waring concluded that the action had "filled every man connected with it with burning shame."[69]

Grant and Sherman saw the "Sooy Smith Raid" for what it meant to their overall plans. Sherman blasted Smith for not starting his movement at the agreed-upon time (on or before February 1). He insisted that although the orders he gave Smith called for the destruction of "railroads, bridges, and corn," the "sole purpose" of Smith's expedition was to link with him at Meridian on February 10. The cavalry had remained in Memphis till February

11, a delay that Sherman considered "unpardonable." He had ordered Smith not to allow minor obstacles to impede him, but Smith had ignored these directions. In Sherman's view, Smith's failure to link with him at Meridian forced the end to his Meridian expedition. Had a substantial force of cavalry been combined with his imposing army, he could have gone much further, at least to Demopolis. Sherman had also intended to strike at Polk's army, if the bishop would give him a fight. Sherman, who had always held grave doubts about the effectiveness of cavalry, now had Smith's disappointing performance to fortify his position.[70]

Grant agreed that Smith, with "nearly double [the men] of Forrest," should have acquitted himself better. He added, however, that the two forces were "not equal man to man," because Forrest's men had more battlefield experience. Grant either did not know or had forgotten that Forrest, just prior to meeting Smith, had come from a recruiting run through western Tennessee. He had gathered over three thousand men to his lines, and although many of these recruits had served in other companies, many were new enlistees. Therefore, both forces had new recruits within their ranks.[71]

Smith's conduct and personality certainly had a negative impact on Sherman's Meridian expedition. Smith had been slow in getting away from Memphis and had balked in the face of a smaller enemy force. Indecisiveness plagued him the entire time and cost him a partial success when he ordered Grierson away from a dash to Meridian. Unlike Sherman's men, Smith's did not respect him or think him a capable leader. Smith had allowed his men to spend too much time destroying property instead of traveling toward Meridian. Ironically, destruction was Sherman's main success on the expedition, while it was one of the factors that caused Smith to fail.

Although contemporary military strategists considered Sherman's new type of warfare unconventional, it relied upon a conventional factor: cavalry support. When Smith did not arrive, Sherman could not continue his expedition because he did not believe he had enough men to enter Alabama. He was racing against time. The Union army had to enter Alabama, complete its mission, and return to the Mississippi River before the Confederates could reinforce Polk. In the future, Sherman would make a point to have a leader he could trust supporting such an operation.

From the beginning, Smith's movement had suffered from a lack of celerity. Had the column started on time, a chance existed that Sherman, while near or at Meridian, could have sent reinforcements to him from the south. The two Federal forces might have caught Forrest off balance, causing him to fight vastly superior numbers on two fronts. Sherman's main column was successful because of good planning and rapidity of movement. Smith failed because he did not follow Sherman's plan, leaving Memphis ten days late and then wasting too much time destroying Mississippi provisions. The question arises of just how realistic Sherman and Smith had been in January about the ability of the cavalry to reach Meridian in ten days. Knowing the deplorable winter conditions of Mississippi's rivers, swamps, and roads and considering the copious amounts of time that Smith would have to spend breaking up railroads and destroying supplies, did Sherman's original plan allow Smith enough time? The Union army had also already experienced multitudes of fugitive slaves hampering their movements as they passed through the South. Sherman was aware of these factors, yet he expected Smith to travel an average of twenty-five miles a day across guerrilla-infested swamplands, meet and defeat a sizable cavalry force, and rendezvous with him 250 miles away. Undeterred cavalrymen could move across good ground at the rate of forty to fifty miles a day, but the road from Memphis to Meridian contained too many hindering factors for quick travel. Sherman may have realized his miscalculation when he waited at Meridian until February 20, thus providing Smith with another nine days to reach him there. With this extra time, Smith should have reached Meridian with an average daily ride of twelve miles, but his continued indecisiveness and failure to move quickly caused the mission to fail.

Even that extra time made no difference, however, because by the time Smith neared West Point, Sherman had already begun his march homeward, and the unfettered Lee had the chance to support Forrest. Smith's expedition, instead of disabling Forrest and linking with Sherman to defeat Polk's army, rendered a Federal cavalry force useless for a time, demoralized it, heightened northern Mississippi Confederate spirits, gave Forrest another victory, cemented Sherman's dislike for the cavalry, and caused the main Federal column to return to Vicksburg.

8 / "Meridian . . . No Longer Exists"

When William T. Sherman's army left Meridian, the town and the surrounding region lay devastated. The commanding general later noted in his report: "For five days 10,000 men worked hard and with a will in that work of destruction, with axes, crowbars, sledges, clawbars, and with fire, and I have no hesitation in pronouncing the work well done. Meridian, with its depots, storehouses, arsenal, hospitals, offices, hotels, and cantonments no longer exists." Sherman's main objective was to demolish the railroad into and out of Meridian so the Confederacy could not use the road to transfer men and supplies into Mississippi. He indeed tore up the rails in many directions from Meridian, but it remained to be seen if that was enough to halt any serious Confederate threat to the Mississippi River.[1]

Sherman had not destroyed indiscriminately on the march, however. Each burned corncrib, rail tie, and building fit into his plan and served to accomplish his overall purpose of injuring Confederate resources in Mississippi and convincing civilians to end their support of the Southern cause. Sherman believed that destruction of less militarily significant towns was not needed to accomplish his plan, and he attempted to stop pillaging and plundering in these locations, hoping to keep damage to a minimum. A careful examination of his actions at these locations along the march provides a good insight into his belief that it was more necessary to destroy and damage some Mississippi towns than others. More often than not, he looked the other way when his men stole and pillaged in the places he believed most important to the Confederate government. Yet, he and his officers issued orders prior to leaving Meridian, reminding their men that they should not destroy any buildings without express instructions from an officer. Before the Union army reached Vicksburg on its return march, Sherman even acted against his soldiers to protect Mississippi towns that he deemed unimportant to the Confederacy's war effort.

On the return march, Sherman's army witnessed examples of Mississippi citizens' favorable attitudes toward the Union. On more than one occasion, the populace openly embraced a return to the United States. Conversations and actions from several Mississippians illustrated their support of the Federal government. But at the moment, Mississippians in Meridian were witnessing the final Federal destruction as the army pulled out of town.

February 20 was a cold day, and it started with several large fires throughout the railroad town. Andrew Hickenlooper and his Pioneer Corps torched "all that remained of the town, including the Ragsdale House, the Arsenal containing about 1000 stands of old muskets, depots, warehouses, etc. at 6:30 A.M."[2]

James B. McPherson's Seventeenth Corps marched lively out of town westward toward the Okatibbee bridge headed to Decatur. Their course took them parallel to Stephen A. Hurlbut's Sixteenth Corps, which was further to the north, moving toward Union, a small community of less than a hundred souls. Some of the Federal soldiers, happy to get under way, sang as they walked. Many soldiers' haversacks, however, carried very little food. In the last two days, foraging parties had begun returning with very few goods, if any, so many of the soldiers had been living on parched corn. Their best hope for provisions was moving through an area that they had not earlier traversed. The first day's march, unfortunately, passed through some newly plowed farmlands, which contained few provisions. Little food remained from the earlier harvests, and the new plants had not produced.[3]

A long line of black and white unionist refugees trailed behind the Federal columns in "all manner of vehicles, drawn by horses, mules and oxen" as well as on foot. The worn and gaunt animals could hardly bear their burdens. A witness described what he saw:

> From four to seven thousand slaves accompanied the return of the expedition. I defy any human being to look on the scene unmoved. Old men with frosts of seventy years upon their heads; men in the prime

> of manhood; youths, and children that could barely run; women with their babes at their breasts. They came, some of them, it is true, with shouts and careless laughter, but silent tears coursed down many a cheek—tears of thankfulness for their great deliverance. There were faces in that crowd which shone with a joy almost inspired. Smile who will, but the story of the coming of the children of Israel out of the land of Egypt can never recall to my mind a more profound emotion than the remembrance of that scene.

Some of the slaves had been marching with Sherman's troops since they had departed from Vicksburg. They were now returning the 150 miles to the Mississippi River. The walking was hard, but the goal of freedom made it worthwhile.[4]

Although the wind blew cold and it had snowed the last two days, the peach and plum trees had blossoms on them. The snow had ended, and it was a bit warmer than it had been the last few days. The weather was still cold but cloudless. Hickenlooper remained behind at the Okatibbee bridge with a few cavalrymen, watching as all the infantry passed, and torched the bridge after all the marchers had crossed. McPherson's Seventeenth Corps camped near Tallahatta Creek with the wagon trains. Hurlbut's Sixteenth Corps moved out of Marion toward Union at daylight. They made fine progress throughout the day, crossing Chickasawhay Creek near dark and camping.[5]

Sherman sent Edward Winslow with three regiments of cavalry toward Philadelphia and Louisville, fifty miles north of Union, in search of William Sooy Smith. If Winslow could not locate Smith immediately, Sherman wanted him to send scouts into northern Mississippi to locate the missing Federal cavalry column. When the scouts found Smith, they were to instruct him to meet Sherman at Canton, twenty-five miles north of Jackson. After Winslow had sent the scouts, he should move via Kosciusko, further to the west, to meet with the Union army at Canton as well. Sherman wanted Smith found.[6]

While Sherman searched for Smith, Leonidas Polk waited for William J. Hardee's men from Dalton. The Confederate infantry would "take the offensive" as soon as they arrived, he wrote Stephen D. Lee. The vanguard of Hardee's corps from Dalton had reached Montgomery. Polk wired Hardee to proceed with haste to Demopolis. The Mississippi commander needed the reinforcements as soon as possible.[7]

R. O. Perrin, commander of the remaining Confederate cavalry regiment near Meridian, reported to Polk that the Union army was moving out of the town westward. A prisoner had informed the cavalryman that Sherman intended to move eastward into Alabama as soon as he found Smith's column. If the Union army did advance eastward, Polk thought, he now would have enough soldiers to meet and defeat Sherman in the field.[8]

McPherson's corps continued on the road to Decatur throughout February 21, reaching the town just before sundown and camping east of the "ruins" of the burned community. Along the route the Federal soldiers had marched through a Choctaw Indian settlement not far from Tallahatta Creek. The men had marveled at the Native Americans, and despite their marching orders the Union soldiers had taken time to meet some of the people in the village.[9]

Hurlbut's Sixteenth Corps left the banks of Okatibbee Creek and marched westward toward Union, twenty-one miles distant. A soldier summed up the size of the settlement in one sentence: "Reached the town of Union, consisting of one house." The continual marching and working had taken its toll on the Federals' appearance. "O! Heavens what a dirty lot," one soldier remarked, assessing the condition of his fellows. The men's clothes and shoes had become ragged. Without needles and thread, the soldiers could not mend their tattered clothes, and they had another hundred miles still to go. The weary and famished infantry waited anxiously for the arrival of their wagon train.[10]

A Confederate cavalry force of about a hundred riders attacked the Sixteenth Corps' wagon train just outside Decatur as it prepared to move toward Union to link up with the main column. The train guards formed into a line of battle, ready to repulse a larger attack that never came. While the command was motionless, some of the blue-clad soldiers "amused themselves by setting fire to the few remaining houses of the town." A search for the culprits ensued, but no soldiers were arrested. After waiting an hour without any further sign of Confederates, the wagon train continued its path along the swampy roads to Union.[11]

When the wagon train reached the Sixteenth Corps' camp around 2 A.M., the bivouacked soldiers were as happy to see the supply trains as the teamsters were to see the infantry. The foot soldiers rushed to greet their comrades, cheering and hollering. Some soldiers leaped into the wagons and tossed rations into the ranks. The food "set us all right again," one hungry Indianan said. "We have hardtack, coffee, and sugar," an Illinoisan commented, provisions that many of the men had not tasted for some time.[12]

While the Federal infantry marched along westward, Winslow's cavalry rode toward Louisville for the next two days, sending scouts in all directions to search for any news of Smith. Upon reaching the crossroads between Louisville and Kosciusko, Winslow halted his men to await the arrival of his scouts. The Federal riders returned from the countryside, reporting that they had heard no information about Smith but that there was a large body of Confederate cavalry near Starkville, about thirty miles to the northwest. West Point, the location where Forrest had met and fought with Smith three days earlier, was only fifty miles northwest, but oddly, the Union cavalry never did discover any sign of the lost Union cavalry commander.[13]

Winslow knew that if he continued north the Confederate cavalry might cut his horsemen off from Sherman's infantry. Since he had heard no information about Smith, he decided that he should continue westward and not travel any farther north. Winslow believed that Lee's and Forrest's cavalry had joined somewhere near Starkville and that the larger combined force could rout his four regiments of cavalry. He did not want to take the risk without a good chance of finding and joining with Smith. Sherman had ordered him to find Smith and not to bring about "a general engagement unless compelled." Sherman had also ordered Winslow to send scouts further northward, if the command could not continue for any reason. After a call for volunteers, the main cavalry command headed down the road to Kosciusko, while a few Union scouts rode north alone in a hazardous search for Smith. By February 25 they reached Canton and waited there for the infantry to arrive.[14]

Polk telegraphed Richmond and informed President Davis that he expected all of Hardee's corps to reach Demopolis in the next day or two. In anticipation of their arrival, Polk moved his army back across the Tombigbee River to the west. He planned to "push the whole force forward . . . and move upon the enemy" when Hardee arrived. Unless Sherman delayed his march back to Vicksburg, however, the Confederate army would never catch the Federals before they reached the Mississippi River. If Joseph Johnston had released Hardee's troops when Polk had first requested reinforcements, they would have arrived in Alabama while Sherman's army still occupied Meridian.[15]

If the nearly twenty thousand Confederate troops had attacked the twenty-five-thousand-man Union army at Meridian, Johnston's meeting with Sherman's army at Dalton the following spring might have had a different outcome. The action might have delayed the Atlanta campaign, if not thwarted it. At the very least, a battle in Mississippi, no matter the victor, would have cost Sherman men, reducing the number he could field against Johnston during the spring conflict.[16]

On Washington's birthday, February 22, 1864, McPherson's Seventeenth Corps left their camps near Decatur, finding pleasant weather and decent roads until they struck the Tuscalemeta Swamp around midmorning. Hickenlooper's Pioneer Corps worked quickly to repair and corduroy the sunken swamp thoroughfare. Covering seventeen miles during the day, McPherson's marchers camped near Untuckaloo Creek, seven miles east of Hillsboro.[17]

Some of McPherson's troops believed that the army should "have a National Salute to Washington Birthday," but it did not occur. The date was significant to many Federal soldiers, and many of them noted the special time in their diaries. The Confederates were defeated at Vicksburg and Gettysburg the previous Fourth of July, which some believed as a sign from God that the Federals would win the war. Henceforth, dates acquainted with the foundation of the United States became even more important to battling Union soldiers in the field. One marcher penciled in his diary before he bedded down: "I will not soon forget this birthday of Washington." His division had marched through fifteen miles of swamp in seven hours. Maybe God was on their side after all.[18]

Sherman, who continued to travel with Hurlbut's Sixteenth Corps, told A. J. Smith to keep his Third Division from foraging. Since the army had made contact with their supply trains, there was no longer a need to search for food. There were enough victuals to last until they reached Canton, a region that the Federals had not marched through before. The Confederates were still capturing foraging parties, and there was no need to take further risks obtaining more provisions. Stragglers were still a concern, and Sherman ordered Smith to arrest and punish any men who fell behind. There was little reason to have Union soldiers captured on the return trip just because they would not keep up with their commands. In addition, stragglers were those most responsible for unwarranted damage to nonmilitary supplies. Sherman wanted these men where their officers could keep an eye on them.[19]

Lee, after learning that Forrest had Sooy Smith's cavalry on the run, sent his own horsemen to continue the harassment of Sherman's infantry column. The Confederates rode hard from Starkville toward the southwest to intercept the marching Federals.[20]

On February 22, General George H. Thomas finally headed to Dalton from Ringgold Gap with four divisions of the Army of the Cumberland, and scouts noted them and reported to Johnston. He placed his troops near Tunnel Hill, north of the city, and prepared to repel the advance. Because President Davis had ordered Hardee's corps to Alabama, Johnston had only half of his infantry force. Johnston had been right, he thought; the Federals did have enough soldiers to attack two areas simultaneously. If he lost now, it would not be his fault; it would be Davis's.[21]

The next morning, while the Federals met the Army of Tennessee between Ringgold Gap and Tunnel Hill, Johnston wrote Davis in Richmond and James Longstreet in eastern Tennessee to beg for more soldiers. He ordered Hardee to return quickly from Alabama: "The enemy is advancing; is now in force at Tunnel Hill. Lose no time." Polk had informed Davis that Hardee's corps had come too late to assist him because Sherman was already marching back to Vicksburg. Therefore, Davis sent word to Hardee to return to Dalton.[22]

Johnston fell back to a stronger defensible position near Dalton while he continued to search for reinforcements. Thomas, meanwhile, wrote Grant that, because of starving horses and lack of supplies, he could not remain at Tunnel Hill. Therefore, Thomas ordered the Union army to fall back into Tennessee because of the food shortages and his belief that Johnston's army "largely outnumbered" his four divisions. Grant noted disgustedly in his memoirs: "[John] Schofield also had to return [from Rome] for the same reason." Although Thomas reported later that operations at Dalton had been "a complete success, inasmuch as it caused the recalling of the reinforcements sent to oppose General Sherman's expedition against Meridian," it mattered little. By the time Thomas and Schofield made their attacks, Sherman was already on his way back to Vicksburg, and Johnston had sent reinforcements to Alabama. Johnston's delay, not Thomas's actions at Dalton, caused Hardee's delay in supporting Polk. The only success that Thomas had at Dalton was obtaining information about the Confederate position at Buzzard's Roost, knowledge that the Union army would use in the coming spring campaigns. Johnston similarly considered his army's actions at Dalton a success. It had thrown back the Federal onslaught and saved Georgia, he believed.[23]

On February 22, Polk reported to Davis that his defense of Mississippi was a success. Lee's cavalry "kept him [Sherman] so closed up that he could not spread out and forage," saving vast amounts of public and private property. The bishop insisted that his quick action had saved most of Mississippi's military supplies. "I have already taken measures to have all the roads broken up by [the Union army] rebuilt," he said. Polk believed that restoring the rail link to Meridian would prove to be "of the highest importance" and that Davis should place any materials needed for its repairs at his disposal. While crews worked on the fifty miles of destroyed rail around Meridian, he said, the Army of Mississippi would pursue Sherman's army until it vacated the field.[24]

McPherson's Seventeenth Corps and Hurlbut's Sixteenth Corps continued their march westward, meeting little resistance except from an occasional Confederate cavalry dash at the trains or the capture of a few foragers. During the march, the 117th Illinois infantry passed "a comfortable looking farm house" with some ladies sitting on the porch. One of the women called out to the men: "Will you unfurl the flag so we can see it?" The color-bearer untied the string, unbinding the flag, and a slight breeze caught its folds, opening it as if on cue. An Illinoisan commented about the ladies' reactions: "They seemed to[o] glad to look once more on the 'old flag' which they had very likely loved so well in days gone by. They watched us as far as they could see us." "I have no doubt but what down deep in the secret heart of a majority of the southern people there still exists a love for our National Banner," he pondered, "remember[ing] the privileges they enjoyed under its protection." The private remarked about how during the march to Meridian, "citizens frequently compare[d] the present condition of things to what they were before the war and add[ed] with a sigh 'Well I hope this trouble will be ended some way before long.'"[25]

Before the fall of Vicksburg in July 1863, northernmost and southernmost Mississippi had experienced Federal occupation, compelling many citizens there to sign an oath claiming they had always been loyal to the Union. Whether to secure protection for their property, to trade with Union-controlled New Orleans and Memphis, to avoid Confederate conscription, or because they were unionist or tired of the war, Mississippians had visited Federal provost marshals to sign the oath. When Sherman had marched to Jackson in late July 1863, prominent citizens like William Sharkey, J. O. Poindexter, and William Yerger had pledged to create a new state government there. Sherman encouraged the move, arguing that "if the prominent men in Mississippi admit the fact of being subdued, it will have a powerful effect all over the South." When the Union army marched from Vicksburg to Meridian, nearly three hundred white citizens joined the column for many of the same reasons that their fellow citizens had in 1862 and 1863.[26]

Any family that had its own transportation could travel along with Sherman's supply wagons. The Union army provided empty wagons for those citizens who did not have a means of conveyance but were deemed "worthy" of assistance. Only personal baggage would be allowed in the empty wagons, not cotton.[27]

Sherman theorized that the South's ability to continue to wage war depended upon the willingness of Southern civilians to support the Confederate government. He had campaigned in Mississippi to break Southern unity by taking or destroying railroads and provisions and pressuring the citizens to make a choice—protect their private interests or continue to support the Confederacy. As the ladies on that porch near Hillsboro exemplified, many Southerners had realized that after years of struggle, chances for Southern independence had already slipped away. They decided to end their support of the Confederacy and return to the Union. Sherman's theory of destructive war seemed to be working.

Within two weeks of Sherman's departure from Meridian, the Confederate government asked Lieutenant A. H. Polk (no relation to Leonidas Polk) to travel to the area to ascertain the extent of Federal damage around the town. He reported that W. W. Hall, a former member of the Mississippi legislature, had provided information concerning the formation of a company of men from western Lauderdale County who were going to join the Union army. Lieutenant Polk compared these citizens to those "tories and deserters in Jones County." "They are becoming troublesome, as well as dangerous, to the country around," he said. If the men in western Lauderdale County to whom he referred were not unionist prior to the Union army's visit, or even if they were lukewarm in their feelings, then their actions exceeded Sherman's expectations in Mississippi. These men now not only ceased supporting the Confederacy, as Sherman had hoped, but they were now also planning to join the fight to end the war with a Union victory.[28]

By February 23, Leonidas Polk had learned of Sooy Smith's retreat. He wired Davis that his cavalry was pursuing Sherman's main column and that he would have his infantry move westward as soon as possible to reestablish his former position in Mississippi. He was arranging for transportation of Hardee's troops back to Dalton as soon as they came in. Polk asked Davis just how far he should move westward after the Union army; he was unsure, and the president knew the country. "I think [it is] now certain that the campaign of the enemy is broken up," the bishop said contentedly. As far as he was concerned, Sherman had not accomplished one thing on his expedition that the Confederates could not quickly overcome.[29]

Richmond believed that as well. J. B. Jones, a Confederate government clerk, described in his diary the feeling around the capital about Sherman's campaign: "The column of Federal cavalry from Memphis, destined to co-operate with Gen. Sherman, has been intercepted and a junction prevented. And both Sherman and the cavalry are now in full retreat—running out of the country faster than they advanced into it. The desert they made as they traversed the interior of Mississippi they have now to repass, if they can, in the weary retreat, with no supplies but those brought with them. Many will never get back."[30]

In reality, Sherman's men were not having a difficult time finding provisions along the return track. Reaching areas that had not been searched earlier, Federal quartermasters and contrabands found the smokehouses and corncribs filled with supplies. Private Charles H. Snedeker of the 124th Illinois, Seventeenth Corps, remarked at the army's success in locating victuals: "Made a big haul of Meat, Poultry, Meal, Flour & c. Our Regt. got a wagon load of forage and a wagon and Ox team to bring it to camp." Henry Fike of the 117th Illinois "captured ten head of mules and horses" the next day. Sherman's plan to resupply his army had worked.[31]

By February 26 the Federal infantry had recrossed the Pearl River into Canton, the seat of Madison County, "a beautiful town on the Great Northern RR" of about twenty-five hundred citizens. "It had the appearance of comfort and thrift. Several very nice dwellings and beautiful yards were on the street along which we passed," remarked one Illinoisan. Other marchers commented about how wealthy the town looked with several fine, large houses. Trees and shrubs lining the streets and filling the front yards were neatly trimmed. It seemed as if Canton was not suffering as much as other towns in Mississippi. Madison County had good soil, making farming the major occupation, and the cotton trade had brought wealth to the town. As A. J. Smith's division marched by a "neat little residence," a young woman stepped forward as the colors passed. "O double-quick a little won't you? I want to see how you look," she said. She giggled as the color-bearer threw out his chest and picked up his pace. Federal officers estimated that there were about "400 ladies here [at Canton], refugees from Memphis and other places." They had tried to flee the Union army to a location they deemed safe from invasion. Some of the women now realized that there was no place in the Confederacy that the Union army could not reach. Sherman hoped that all Southerners would get that message.[32]

Sherman decided that he needed to hasten his return to Vicksburg to prepare for his joint operation with Nathaniel Banks on the Red River. Banks hoped to take Shreveport and clear the Mississippi Valley of significant Confederate forces. Sherman ordered the railroads destroyed within a five-mile radius of Canton. He instructed Hurlbut and McPherson to send all the soldiers due veteran furloughs to Vicksburg as soon as practicable so they could begin their homeward journeys. He ordered the remainder of the army to camp at Canton until the destruction of the railroad and Confederate property was complete. Sherman also hoped that Sooy Smith's cavalry might link up with the infantry there. He would give the horsemen a few additional days to turn up. Then, all of the command would return to Vicksburg around March 3 (unless they heard from Smith sooner) to prepare themselves for departure to Louisiana. Before Sherman left, however, he reminded his officers about keeping nonmilitary damage in Canton to a minimum.[33]

The taking of nonmilitary possessions during the march to Meridian had served a military purpose: to strike terror into Mississippi civilians while simultaneously removing supplies. Allowing some stealing served to terrorize Southern civilians, perhaps enough to cause them to stop supporting the Confederacy. When Sherman believed that excessive pillaging was not essential to his plan, however, he and his officers issued orders against it. The general never publicly condoned the pillaging of Southern homes, but he did allow it on those occasions when it coincided with his other destructive war operations, especially railroad demolition. Throughout the campaign, the destruction of railroads remained his most important action, and the Mississippians living along the rails experienced the most damage from the Union army.

For example, Decatur, unlike Lake Station or Meridian, was not militarily significant to the Confederacy. It was not on any railroad, nor did it contain large amounts of supplies. It was merely a sleepy farming community. Although the Federal soldiers did not understand the distinction between one Mississippi town and another, Sherman and many of his officers did. The Union soldiers had burned and pillaged since leaving Vicksburg, marching along the rails eastward. These actions had conditioned them to continue their destruction without thinking about its significance. Since Decatur was not of great military importance, however, Federal officers attempted to push their command quickly through town, placing guards on the town's buildings in an attempt to prevent any further destruction of private residences or property. Unfortunately for Decatur's citizens, events occurred that brought Federal vengeance on the town, and it burned anyway.

Sherman's attempts to limit the damage in Decatur failed because of the Confederate attack on the Union wagon train. Since a member of the town had taken part in the attack, officers were hard pressed to prevent their men from burning most of the town in retaliation. Instead, his officers cautioned their men to keep such burning and plundering to a minimum.

Some of the Federal soldiers continued to dislike the harsh treatment their army was inflicting on Southern civilians. A Wisconsin soldier penned his thoughts about what the Union army was doing in Mississippi: "Sherman is taking everything—horses, mules, wagons. He leaves nothing but women, children and old men with enough to feed them. All men capable of bearing arms are arrested, and held as prisoners." Another soldier commented on the destruction: "Nearly every building in Meridian was destroyed, save those which were occupied, and the smoking ruins, with their blackened walls and chimneys standing as giant sentinels over the sorrowful scene, sent a thrill of pity to the hearts of those whom stern war and military necessity compelled to apply the torch."[34]

Some Union soldiers, however, relished the destruction. An Iowan in Hurlbut's corps wrote after the war: "Those people were responsible for the condition, and it was their fortune to take the consequences." The South had started the war, and now they had to pay the price, many Union soldiers believed. If Southerners had to pay a high enough price, they would stop supporting the Confederacy and the war would end. The Meridian populace felt especially the hard hand of war because they lived in and around a militarily significant location, one that both Sherman and his men believed needed to be destroyed.[35]

After the fall of Vicksburg, Sherman considered Meridian the most important military target in Mississippi. Here he unleashed his army to do its most extensive destruction during the campaign to both public and private property. Sherman had reached his objective, however, and his return march was different. Then he issued orders to cease the unauthorized burning of any building, no matter what the nature of its use.

Before leaving Meridian, Sherman had added a provision to his Special Order 20, which explained the post-Meridian objective to his army: "Buildings must not be burned on the return march save by order of the Comdg General of a Corps or Division," he said. In a situation where the enemy might use structures as cover to snipe at the Federal soldiers, "then any commissioned officer may cause them to be destroyed and report the fact to his Division commander." Before the army's departure from Vicksburg, Sherman had not issued any orders dealing with pillaging or looting. His soldiers marched along the railroad for most of the way to Meridian. These were the areas where Sherman wanted to cause the most damage, both physically and psychologically. Therefore, although not issuing orders that supported taking of nonmilitary goods, he did not prevent it in the Mississippi towns that the Union army marched through, the exception being Decatur because of its nonmilitary nature.[36]

The return march took Sherman's army, not along the railroad as they had come, but through a less militarily significant region—farmlands with little industry. In Sherman's opinion, there was no need to bolster the terrorization of the Mississippi farmers with anything more than his presence and the destruction of Confederate property. Therefore, there was no need for his soldiers to take anything from the people other than food or items of military value. Pillaging and plundering would not serve further to stop these people from supporting the Richmond government, and therefore Sherman issued orders against burning buildings, or even entering a house, without permission from a commanding officer. If the commanding general "deemed it necessary," he could issue orders for further destruction, but it was his decision, not his soldiers'. Corn and foodstuffs were the primary products that people not living along the railroads could offer to the Confederacy. If the Union army consumed or destroyed that, then there was little left with which these inhabitants could support the Southern cause.

McPherson added a strong interpretation to Sherman's order for the destruction of occupied dwellings: "The commanding general trusts that no pillaging, burning, or wanton destruction of private property will mark our course, but that our march will be orderly and systematic, creditable to you as soldiers, and worthy [of] the cause for which we are fighting. Should it be deemed necessary to destroy any buildings, mills, or tanneries on the line of march, orders will be given and the proper details made to do the work."[37]

Other Federal officers also issued orders to halt pillaging of nonmilitary items during the return march. William T. Shaw, commander of the Third Brigade in Hurlbut's Third Division, penned an order to his brigade: "It is hereby ordered that hereafter during the march no soldier shall enter a house occupied by a family unless under direction of a commissioned officer." Furthermore, the soldiers should not take anything from Southern civilians "except provisions and such articles as are necessary for the subsistence of the army." The looting of valuable articles such as silverware, cash, and clothing was to cease.[38]

Canton, although located on a railroad, was not as militarily significant as other towns Sherman had burned. In addition, he had already achieved his objective at Meridian and thought that his army's actions there were enough to remove Mississippi from the war. He could spare the nonmilitary possessions of Canton's citizens without sacrificing his objective. Furthermore, if the private buildings and property of Canton were spared, the benefits of nonresistance would be demonstrated to the rest of the state and the South. Those who were anti-Federal had already left Canton before the Union army's arrival, so Sherman emphasized that his men should not steal or destroy nonmilitary items and property. To illustrate his severe attitude toward such actions, Sherman severely punished a lieutenant from the Tenth Missouri after he was caught burning a slave cabin near Canton without permission.[39]

On February 27, Sherman left Canton and returned to Vicksburg, leaving the army under the command of Hurlbut, the senior major general. When he reached Vicksburg, Sherman found a letter from Banks saying that he would be ready for the Red River expedition by March 5. Sherman decided that he would travel to New Orleans to meet Banks the following day. A letter from Grant ordered Sherman's army to cooperate with Banks for a limited time, but Grant wanted Sherman himself to return to Huntsville, Alabama, and prepare for the coming spring campaigns. Grant did not want his favorite general down in Louisiana while preparations were being made for more significant plans to move into the interior of the Confederacy.[40]

For the next three days, the Union army at Canton destroyed the rails in all directions. In addition, twenty-four locomotives were destroyed, along with cars and Confederate workshops and warehouses. Foraging parties went out and brought back mules, horses, cattle, and food. Rain and snow fell for three straight days and the temperature dropped, making work uncomfortable for the weary soldiers. Throughout the week, supply wagons from Vicksburg arrived with provisions for the men. While the healthy soldiers worked, sick and wounded soldiers, along with the contrabands, left town sporadically in the empty supply wagons headed to Vicksburg.[41]

Wagon trains and foragers continued to be easy targets for Confederate cavalry, which had now caught up with the Federal column and continued to harass its movements and railroad work. Peter Starke, Wirt Adams, and William H. Jackson hovered all around the Federal position, taking prisoners and skirmishing with the Federals on a daily basis. The Confederate horsemen remained a small but constant threat to the Union soldiers in and around Canton.[42]

For example, one of Winslow's Union scouts, Charles G. Loesch from the Tenth Missouri, had ridden only a few miles from his column when Confederate horsemen captured him. After Sherman's army departed, he was thrown together with twenty-seven other Federal prisoners and held at Canton for a month, awaiting exchange. Because Sherman left for the Atlanta campaign, however, there were no exchanges. After the Confederates moved him from one town to another for a month, Loesch reached Andersonville Prison in Georgia, where he remained until the end of the war. Most of the Federal prisoners taken in the Meridian expedition ended up at Andersonville Prison, one of the most notoriously harsh military prisons in the war.[43]

When word reached Hurlbut and McPherson on February 29 that Sooy Smith had already arrived back at Memphis, they prepared the command to leave Canton and return to the Mississippi River. On March 1 the lead elements of the army reached Livingston, camping for the night before the final march into camp along the Big Black River near Vicksburg. The final few days of the expedition proved to be the worst. The Federal column endured muddy roads, tattered clothes, sore and aching muscles and feet, and wet and freezing conditions. Mule teams stalled, soft mud froze to the soldiers' feet, and marching became difficult. Division commander James Veatch noted in his report, "Weather freezing. Troops suffering." These factors, however, did little to dampen Union spirits. They were too close to Vicksburg and the end of the long expedition.[44]

By March 3, lead elements of Sherman's army began reaching their old camps along the Big Black River near Vicksburg. The soldiers had not faced large numbers of the enemy, but they were tired and worn, having endured two weeks of marching through hostile territory, suffered from want of provisions, and tramped more than a hundred miles back to their base. The men were overjoyed to see their old campgrounds. One observer commented on the men's spirits as they reached the Mississippi River: "Twenty thousand bronzed warriors, carrying hats and caps aloft on the muzzle of their guns, were lustily singing, 'John Brown's body lies a moldering in the ground,' while thousands of 'contrabands,' following the marching column[s], now getting their first taste of freedom, joined heartily in the chorus." The marchers were a scruffy and dirty-looking lot when they tramped into town and camp. "At least one man in every five or six came back barefooted," a member of the Twelfth Wisconsin remembered. Some soldiers had torn their pants so terribly that they hung secured only at the waist. One fellow took his knife and cut his pants legs, which were in fairly good condition, into long strips, poking fun at the motley condition of his fellow soldiers. "He went in on the home stretch with the ribbons floating gaily about him in the breeze."[45]

While the Federal soldiers marched into their old campgrounds along the Big Black River, heads held high in triumph, Bishop Polk, still in Alabama, issued his own congratulatory order to his men: "The lieutenant-general commanding takes pleasure in congratulating the officers and men of the commands of Major-General Lee and Major-General Forrest upon the brilliant and successful campaign just closed. Their [the Federals'] proclaimed and boasted object was to overrun and desolate our country, if not strike a death-blow to our cause. They have been forced to return, beaten and distracted and pursued by our cavalry. Their retreating column may be tracked by their dead and their lost arms and equipments." Polk sent similar words of contentment to Richmond, saying that by preventing Sooy Smith's cavalry from linking with the Federal infantry at Meridian, he had "destroyed his [Sherman's] campaign." Lee's cavalry was now chasing "a very exhausted" Federal infantry, "cutting up his rear." Polk forgot that his men were as tired as Sherman's, that the Confederate cavalry had been useless against the large Federal infantry force, and that now that the Union marchers were close to their base at Vicksburg, Lee's cavalry would accomplish even less. Nevertheless, Polk was confident that he had thwarted Sherman's plan and that he and his skillful cavalrymen were the victors of the campaign. This belief laid the groundwork for much disagreement after the war about who had actually triumphed during the Meridian expedition.[46]

Once the Union army reached Vicksburg, the Confederate cavalry fell back into the interior of Mississippi, scattering across the state. There, most of them remained until the spring, recuperating from their skirmishes with the Union army. The infantry remained for the most part in Alabama. They too were recuperating, not from battle, but from marching and working to save goods from Sherman's army. Spring would bring them another chance to meet the Federals in the field. Many of them hoped that next time they might have a commander who would fight instead of retreat. To them, the expedition had indeed been a failure. Many Mississippians had been forced to abandon their native state. For many this was too much to bear, and they deserted, returning to their homes and families. Upon returning, many found that Sherman, although passing near their homes, had not burned the place to the ground. Those from the Meridian area, however, did find their property burned or confiscated.

During the entire march, Sherman had exhibited a different attitude toward various Mississippi towns his army had passed through. At those he considered more militarily significant, he allowed pillaging and plundering as well as the burning of some private homes. He believed it was more important that these people end their support for the Confederacy than it was for those living in areas that were less militarily significant. In areas such as Decatur, where railroads did not pass, and Canton, where manufacturing centers did not exist, he took measures to prevent the taking of nonmilitary items and protected private property and buildings. In some cases, extenuating circumstances had thwarted his attempts to protect a town, such as the raid on the wagon trains at Decatur. In any case, he was not the brutal barbarian of Lost Cause mythology. He had not destroyed indiscriminately on the march, and the majority of buildings burned and articles taken served to accomplish his overall purpose of injuring the Confederate resources in

Mississippi and urging civilians to end their support of the Southern cause. Just as Sherman planned his actions on the battlefield, so too did he plan the destruction his army wrought on this march.

Sherman learned that some Southerners were indeed ready to end the war. White families joined his column and returned to Vicksburg. On more than one occasion, white Mississippians openly supported the Union cause. In Lauderdale County, the scene of Sherman's most significant devastation, a company of Mississippi men formed together to join the Union army after it had wrought destruction on the location. These factors, coupled with his other experiences on the Meridian expedition, laid the groundwork for future operations and assisted in the creation of Sherman's unique style of war.

Conclusion

The significance of William T. Sherman's Meridian campaign can be assessed on several levels: its immediate impact on the war and its participants, on Mississippi's inhabitants, and on Sherman in his first major attempt at hard war. The short-term consequences of the expedition proved far less important than the campaign's role in the shaping of Sherman's distinctive type of warfare. The new combination of tactics that the Union general used for the first time in Mississippi led the way to their application on a wider scale later, when they played a key role in ending the war. This combination became what scholars refer to as Sherman's style of warfare. By taking or destroying supplies from Southern citizens, Sherman tried to prevent the Confederates from sustaining the fight while simultaneously punishing Southerners for supporting the Confederacy. On a grander scale, he sought to strike at all Southern military resources and infrastructure, hoping thereby to destroy the Confederacy's ability and will to keep fighting. It is because Sherman finally found the correct combination for success in Mississippi that the Meridian expedition is so important to the study of the American Civil War and military history.

The total loss in men on both sides in the campaign is difficult to determine because of the duration and extent of the operation. Sherman's report listed Stephen Hurlbut's corps as having 52 killed, wounded, and missing and James B. McPherson's having 74. Edward Winslow's cavalry division, acting as an independent unit, lost 44 troopers, bringing the grand total of

Union losses to 170. William Sooy Smith lost around 150 horsemen on his ride.[1]

The Confederate losses are more uncertain because of conflicting reports. William H. Jackson, commander of the Confederate cavalry division containing Wirt Adams's, Lawrence Sullivan Ross's, and Peter Starke's brigades, reported his total loss at 225 killed, wounded, and missing. Stephen D. Lee, overall commander of Confederate cavalry forces in Mississippi, although writing his report two weeks after Jackson, listed the division's loss at only 104. Total losses for the Confederates, according to Lee, were 279. Nathan Bedford Forrest's losses from West Point to Ivey's Hill numbered around 80. Considering the length of the expedition and the number of troops involved (40,000), it is remarkable that fewer than 750 men were lost on both sides during the entire campaign.[2]

The campaign was designed to destroy as many Confederate resources as possible, with particular emphasis on the Mississippi railroad lines and depots. According to Sherman's chief engineer, Andrew Hickenlooper, the Union army destroyed "59 miles of railroad, 3 miles of trestle, 6 bridges, 21 locomotives, 45 cars, 10 depots, 6 warehouses, 5 mills, and over 1000 small arms." Besides damaging property, the Union army captured 3,000 mules, horses, and oxen—so many animals, in fact, that the departmental quartermaster "replenished the teams he had with him [on the march and] those he left in camp." Although no exact numbers were kept on the bushels of corn, pieces of meat, or portions of other foodstuffs that the Federals confiscated or burned, the amount must have been staggering. For example, Sooy Smith, after his comparatively brief operation, reported that he had destroyed three million bushels of corn. The main Federal column must have taken or destroyed three to five times that amount. Sherman insisted that his army was in better shape materially after the expedition than it was before it made the march.[3]

The Confederates insisted that the Federals had directed their destructive energies mainly at private property. Stephen D. Lee later wrote several articles about his experiences during the Meridian expedition, castigating Sherman and his actions: "There never was an army in a civilized country that laid waste and destroyed public and private property as did Sherman's army." Lee estimated the damage at more than fifty million dollars, three-fourths of this being private property. The Confederate cavalryman insisted that history would condemn Sherman and the Meridian campaign. The destruction of private property, however, was the much lesser portion of the total destruction than Lee argued.[4]

Memphis and Charleston Railroad president Samuel Tate, the individual in charge of Confederate repair work in Mississippi, said that the Federals damaged only about thirty miles of track and that the railroad could quickly be repaired. The most extensive damage was done to the tracks between Marion Station and Enterprise. Tate insisted, on March 8, 1864, that he needed "5,000 crossties, 300 bars of iron, and 500,000 feet of bridge timbers to complete the work." He could repair the entire line in less than forty days if he had this material. Besides the railroad destruction, Leonidas Polk reported that sixty miles of telegraph wires and poles had been destroyed. The Confederates could repair these as they laid new track.[5]

Tate and his subordinates, under Confederate authority, impressed slaves from the countryside to work on the railroads. In a short time, large gangs of slaves were laboring up and down the Mobile and Ohio and Southern railroads. With the needed supplies procured from the Railroad Bureau, the work went quickly. By April 1, within twenty-five days of beginning the repair, Tate had most of the roads back in order.[6]

In a multivolume study published not long after the war, Columbia University historian John W. Draper argued that the breaking of railroads in Mississippi had a great impact on other 1864 operations. He contended that the campaign "greatly aided [George H.] Thomas in obtaining his victory at Nashville" because the destruction of the railroad "compelled [John Bell] Hood to linger long at Florence, waiting to obtain supplies for his men." Hence Thomas had the time to prepare his army at Nashville for Hood's advance. This could not be the case, however, because the battle for Nashville occurred in December, a full eight months after the Meridian expedition. By that time the railroads, although not in perfect shape, were repaired to about the same condition they had been prior to the Meridian campaign. The rolling stock, of course, could not be replenished. Still, the results of Sherman's march had little impact on Thomas's victory at Nashville.[7]

Sherman's campaign had perhaps its greatest impact on Alabama and Georgia in the summer of 1864. Ties, spikes, and timber needed for repairing and maintaining railroads in those states were unavailable because they were being used to mend Mississippi's roads. Confederate efforts to shore up their faltering supply and troop transportation system were thereby thwarted, making it difficult for them to rebound from Sherman's attack on the railroads there during his march to Atlanta.[8]

Additionally, although the Confederates had performed a remarkable feat with their quick repair work in Mississippi, Sherman had disrupted Southern shipping in the West for more than a month with his destruction of significant sections of the Magnolia State's railroads. Reports indicate that the supply routine for the region continued to be intermittent at best, even after the railroads were repaired. The chief commissary of subsistence, W. H. Dameron, could not procure enough wagons to compensate for the disruption in rail service. The Confederacy continued to have difficulty drawing supplies from the region. Food continued to spoil at depots in north-central and southwestern Mississippi while awaiting transport. Sherman's march also stopped a major Confederate offensive against the Mississippi River during that winter and spring. Joseph Johnston had ordered Polk to retake lost ground in Mississippi just before he left the Army of Mississippi in late 1863. Polk remained on the defensive because Sherman took the offensive first. This stopped the Confederate attempt to reclaim Southern territory before it even began. Instead of gaining ground, Polk retreated and Sherman advanced as far as he wished in Mississippi.[9]

Sherman had also intended to remove Mississippi from the war and make the region unusable for any sizable enemy force as a base of operations against the Mississippi River. He wanted to free the men garrisoning the river for use during offensive campaigns deeper into the Confederacy. In these plans he both failed and succeeded. After the Meridian campaign, Mississippi did not support a sizable Confederate force capable of retaking the Mississippi River or a major city along its banks. Mississippi did, however, continue to harbor Confederate cavalry, which used the state as a base to strike at Union supply lines in Tennessee, northern Mississippi, Alabama, and Georgia. These Confederate horsemen prevented the release of Union troops garrisoning the Mississippi for campaigns deeper into the Confederacy. Instead, they had to take garrisoning positions along Union-held railroads. For example, instead of marching with Sherman to Atlanta, thousands of soldiers had to remain behind to protect railroads from Confederate cavalry raids.[10]

The Meridian campaign not only damaged Mississippi's infrastructure and removed large amounts of supplies and equipment from the state, but it also removed slave labor that both planters and the Confederacy needed to continue the war. By the time Sherman reached Vicksburg, between five and seven thousand slaves had attached themselves to his column. Because the Federal government was still unprepared to supply and care for large numbers of contrabands, many of the blacks who made it to Vicksburg continued to suffer from want of food and clothing. Settling into makeshift camps around Vicksburg, they passed the time, wondering about their future. After the war, a Wisconsin trooper wrote about the fate of some of the black men who had followed him across Mississippi: "Large numbers enlisted in colored regiments then forming, and aided our army materially in fighting for the old flag." He guessed that some were killed during the massacre at Fort Pillow later that year. Thus, Sherman's march helped provide black volunteers for the Union army.[11]

Planters who lived in Sherman's path found it difficult to plant in the spring of 1864. Disrupted in their daily duties because of the Federal march, farmers were barely able to plant enough food for themselves, let alone the Confederacy. In the spring of 1864, visitors who passed through the region between Jackson and Meridian found few crops in the ground and discovered many unplowed fields.[12]

Some white Mississippians even took the opportunity to leave the Confederacy. Along with the thousands of blacks marching to Vicksburg came a thousand white refugees. Whether they were tired of the war or were unionists, wagonloads of white Mississippians flocked to Sherman's lines as he passed through the state. By the end of March 1864, unionism had spread across the state. Reports passed through Richmond about significant unionist activity in Jones, Lauderdale, Lowndes, and Hinds counties.[13]

These civilians were not the only Mississippians tired of the war, however. When Polk's army "abandoned" the state to Sherman's army, many Mississippi soldiers deserted the Confederacy and went home. One Confederate trooper described his feelings that winter:

> Those who are here [Mobile] are dispirited, and can not fight, they, as well as those who left us, would have made a splendid fight in Mississippi, but since the whole State was given up without striking a single blow, the men have lost confidence in the Government, and especially in its representatives [officers]. Most of those who have left us, have left the service for good, so far as the regular army is concerned. It is a

> shame!—a stigma on the fair fame of the Confederacy that thirty-five thousand hostile men should march entirely through Miss[issippi] and Ala[bama] and no obstacle be placed in the way to impeded [*sic*] their progress![14]

Some Confederates went even further than deserting the Confederacy. An Illinoisan writing to his brother after the march remarked, "A few rebels has [*sic*] enlisted in our Army." The Federals captured approximately four hundred prisoners on the march, some of whom decided that they wanted "a Change."[15]

Union soldiers had little time to contemplate their month-long march because they were off to Tennessee and to Louisiana within a few days of returning and refitting at Vicksburg. Most blue-clad soldiers, however, considered the march a success. "You may ask what we accomplished," one marcher said. "That I cannot answer satisfactorily to myself but I do know we have accomplished one of the hardest marches that has been made in this war." Indeed, a 350-mile round trip in thirty days was a significant achievement. Sherman wrote in his report about the march's impact on his men: "The great result attained is the hardihood and confidence imparted to the command, which is now better fitted for war."[16]

But did the Meridian campaign have a victor? Polk argued that with Forrest's defeat of Sooy Smith's cavalry, Sherman could not continue on to his main objective, Mobile. Stephen D. Lee echoed Polk, saying that his cavalry had kept Sherman's troops closed up and did not allow them to impose irreparable damage on Mississippi. He pointed out that the Confederates repaired the railroads within twenty-five days of Sherman's departure.

There is, however, a problem with these contentions. Sherman never intended to march on Mobile. His main objective was to destroy the railroads around Meridian with only the possibility of continuing on into Alabama—and not to Mobile, but to Demopolis or Selma. One kernel of truth in Polk's argument is that the defeat of Sooy Smith did hurt Sherman's campaign. Without his main cavalry force, Sherman decided to return to Vicksburg and not continue into Alabama. In this the Confederates were successful.

The Meridian campaign, for Sherman, was the final step in his transition to a hard war mind-set. His attitudes had been changing throughout the first three years of the war as he developed and experimented constantly with different tactics to deal with guerrillas and secessionist civilians. His experience with partisan activity along the banks of the Mississippi in 1862 and 1863 pushed him to become harsher on the local populations who served as a support base for the bushwhackers. Punishing the populace for supporting the Confederates worked hand in hand with his philosophy of removing the resources from his enemy's use. He could perform both activities simultaneously in an effort to force the South to end the war, making them suffer from the lack of supplies and military goods.

Sherman knew that his venture into Mississippi was a risk. He would travel 150 miles through hostile country without reinforcements. The application of several different tactics allowed him to ensure that a larger enemy force did not catch his army in the open, far from safety. One of the first measures he decided upon was the cutting of his supply and communication lines, a tactic he had watched Grant use in 1863. By establishing no such lines, he made his column invulnerable to attack on the rear, always an army's weakest part. Sherman believed his army could live off the countryside and on the supplies they carried along. This was not a new concept, but it served to achieve three goals in Mississippi. First, Sherman could feed his army while simultaneously removing food from Confederate use. Second, the confiscation and destruction of foodstuffs served to punish Mississippians for supporting the Confederacy. And third, secessionists would be encouraged to choose their own needs over Richmond's and give up their support of the Southern cause.

Sherman also knew that deception was essential to his campaign's success. Feints, although used commonly in the war, proved invaluable in his march across Mississippi. They kept the Confederate authorities guessing about Sherman's true objective until it was too late to prevent his attack on Meridian. Feints up the Yazoo River and at Mobile, Dalton, and Rome convinced Polk, Johnston, and Jefferson Davis that Sherman was headed to Mobile. By the time they realized he was marching to Meridian, Confederate reinforcements could not arrive in time to prevent the destruction of the town and railroads. Additionally, Sherman pressed his army forward at a furious pace, knowing that celerity of movement was crucial. If the feints did not work, he needed to reach Meridian as soon as possible before the Confederates could combine into a force large enough to meet and rout his army. The Federals' quick movement kept the Confederates off balance throughout the entire campaign.

For his army to move quickly across the swampy lowlands of Mississippi,

Sherman relied heavily upon his Pioneer Corps. Hickenlooper's troops performed admirably throughout the march, repairing roads and bridges and building pathways across the swamps. Because of their knowledge of construction, the Pioneer Corps also played a large part in the destruction of railroads and bridges. In the Meridian campaign, Sherman developed an efficiency at destroying the Confederate infrastructure that he would use for the remainder of the war. The Federal soldiers burned the ties and bent the iron rails, rendering them unusable. Sherman, after learning that the railroads around Meridian were repaired within twenty-five days, made sure that future railroad destruction centered on the rendering the iron rails absolutely irreparable. He made sure that, at all times, his men made the extra effort to bend the rails so Confederate workers could not run them through a straightening machine, quickly making them usable again.

The Meridian campaign also illustrates Sherman's sense of which targets were significant military resources and which were inappropriate for demolition. On his march across Mississippi, Sherman distinguished between targets that were militarily significant and those that were not. He made a distinction between those towns most important to the Confederate war effort and those that were not. In those locations he deemed most important, Sherman allowed his men a wide range of latitude in their destructive activity. When he deemed the locations less important militarily to the South, he made efforts to prevent needless destruction and to focus attention only on public property.

Sherman's men, too, developed their own sense of hard war as they marched the roads in Mississippi. Whether for better or worse, Union soldiers' attitudes toward civilians varied from hatred and vengeance to condolence and sympathy. Whether or not Federal soldiers approved of the destructiveness of Sherman's style of war may be beside the point; the Meridian campaign unquestionably made them efficient in its practice.

Sherman took what he learned in the Meridian expedition and used that knowledge for the rest of the war. He became famous for his style of hard war, and many historians and military strategists argue that it significantly shortened the duration of the conflict. Few, however, appreciate the fact that he placed the final touches on his new style of warfare along the roads of Mississippi in February and March 1864.

Notes

Abbreviations

CHS	Cincinnati Historical Society, Cincinnati, Ohio
DUL	Duke University Library, Durham, North Carolina
IHS	Indiana Historical Society, William H. Smith Library, Indianapolis
ISHL	Illinois State Historical Library, Springfield
ISL	Indiana State Library, Indianapolis
LC	Library of Congress, Washington, D.C.
OR	*The War of the Rebellion: A Compilation of the Official Records of the Union and Confederate Armies.* 128 vols. Washington, D.C.: Government Printing Office, 1880–1901.
USMHI	United States Army Military History Institute, Carlisle Barracks, Pennsylvania
WHMC	Western Historical Manuscript Collection, Columbia, Missouri

Preface

1. Victor, *History of the Southern Rebellion,* 4:351.

Chapter 1

1. During operations in western Tennessee and northern Mississippi in July 1862, Sherman sent out a patrol to shoot on sight any soldiers engaged in robbery or pillaging. If any perpetrators were captured, they received bread and water until Sherman decided to end the punishment. General Order 49, July 7, 1862, *OR,* ser. 1, 17, pt. 2:81.

2. Mary Chestnut calls Sherman a "nightmare, ghoul, [and] hyena," in Woodward, *Mary*

Chestnut's Civil War, 740. For studies arguing Sherman was the inventor of "hard war," see Walters, *Merchant of Terror* and "General Sherman and Total War"; and Brinsfield, "Military Ethics of William T. Sherman." For studies arguing that someone other than Sherman invented hard war, see Sutherland, "Lincoln, Pope, and the Origins of Total War"; and Janda, "Shutting the Gates of Mercy."

3. Jomini, *The Art of War,* 212. For examples of contemporary works influenced by Jomini see Halleck, *International Law;* and Mahan, *Naval Strategy.*

4. William T. Sherman to Ellen Sherman, July 28, 1861, in Simpson and Berlin, *Sherman's Civil War,* 125; *Cincinnati Commercial,* October 17, 1861.

5. Sherman to Henry W. Halleck, July 14, 1862, *OR,* ser. 1, 17, pt. 1:23.

6. Halleck to Ulysses S. Grant, August 2, 1862, *OR,* ser. 1, 17, pt. 2:150; General Order 107, August 15, 1862, and General Order 109, August 16, 1862, *OR,* ser. 3, 2:388, 397.

7. Grimsley, *Hard Hand of War,* 100; General Order 49, July 7, 1862, and General Order 45, June 21, 1862, *OR,* ser. 1, 17, pt. 2:81, 23.

8. Sherman to Grant, August 17, 1862, *OR,* ser. 1, 17, pt. 2:178.

9. Grant quoted in *Memphis Bulletin and Appeal,* August 20, 1862; for more on the move away from the conciliatory stance in Missouri, Kentucky, Tennessee, and western Virginia, see Grimsley, *Hard Hand of War.*

10. Sherman to John Sherman, September 22, 1862, in Simpson and Berlin, *Sherman's Civil War,* 301–2.

11. Sherman to Charles C. Walcutt, September 24, 1862, *OR,* ser. 1, 17, pt. 2:235.

12. Sherman to Grant, October 4, 1862, and Special Order no. 254, September 27, 1862, ibid., 235, 240.

13. Special Order no. 283, October 18, 1862, ibid., 281; Grimsley, *Hard Hand of War,* 117.

14. General Order no. 7, December 18, 1862, *OR,* ser. 1, 17, pt. 1:618–19; Sherman to James Guthrie, August 14, 1864, in Lewis, *Fighting Prophet,* 398.

15. Sherman to James Guthrie, August 14, 1864, in Lewis, *Fighting Prophet,* 398.

16. Grimsley, *Hard Hand of War,* 101; Grant to J. C. Kelton, December 25, 1862, *OR,* ser. 1, 17, pt. 1:477–78; Grant, *Memoirs,* 1:435.

17. Grant, *Memoirs,* 1:368–69.

18. *OR,* ser. 3, 124, pt. 3:149–51.

19. Sherman to Frederick Steele, March 31, 1863, *OR,* ser. 1, 24, pt. 3:158; Report of Frederick Steele, April 10, 1863, *OR,* ser. 1, 24, pt. 1:501–2.

20. Sherman to Steele, April 19, 1863, *OR,* ser. 1, 24, pt. 3:209.

21. Grant to Sherman, May 14, 1863, ibid., 312.

22. Special Order no. 105, May 14, 1863, Sherman to Mower, May 15, 1863, Grant to Peter J. Osterhaus, May 26, 1863, ibid., 315, 351; Grimsley, *Hard Hand of War,* 158–59; Grant to Sherman, July 18, 1863, *OR,* ser. 1, 24, pt. 3:528; Sherman to Grant, July 14, 1863, *OR,* ser. 1, 24, pt. 3:525–27; Sherman to David D. Porter, July 19, 1863, *OR,* ser. 1, 24, pt. 3:531.

23. Sherman to Halleck, September 17, 1863, in Sherman, *Memoirs,* 335–42; Sherman to John Sherman, December 29, 1863, in Simpson and Berlin, *Sherman's Civil War,* 576–78.

24. Quoted in Kennett, *Sherman,* 235; Merrill, *Sherman,* 239–40; Marszalek, *Sherman,* 249; Sherman to A. J. Smith, January 6, 1864, *OR,* ser. 1, 32, pt. 2:36.

25. Sherman to John A. Logan, December 21, 1864, *OR,* ser. 1, 32, pt. 3:459–60.

26. Quoted in Kennett, *Sherman,* 232.

27. Marszalek, *Sherman,* 249–50.

28. Sherman to R. M. Sawyer, January 31, 1864, William T. Sherman Papers, LC.

Chapter 2

1. Shank, "Meridian" (*Journal of Mississippi History*), 275.

2. Sherman, *Memoirs,* 388; William T. Sherman Report, March 7, 1864, *OR,* ser. 1, 32, pt. 1:173–75.

3. Westwood, "After Vicksburg," 169; Grant to Halleck, July 18, July 24, 1863, *OR,* ser. 1, 24, pt. 3:529–30, 546–47.

4. Halleck to Nathaniel Banks, July 24, 1863, *OR,* ser. 1, 26, pt. 1:652–53; Lincoln to Grant, August 9, 1863, *OR,* ser. 1, 24, pt. 3:584. See also Halleck to Grant, January 8, 1864, *OR,* ser. 1, 32, pt. 2:40–42.

5. Sherman to Elias F. Dennis, August 28, 1863, and Sherman to L. Rawlins, September 12, 1863, *OR,* ser. 1, 30, pt. 3:198, 557.

6. Sherman to John Rawlins, September 22, 1863, and Sherman to S. A. Hurlbut, September 25, 1863, ibid., 773, 844–45.

7. Sherman to Rawlins, October 14, 1863, *OR,* ser. 1, 30, pt. 4:355–56; Hurlbut to Halleck, October 12, 1863, *OR,* ser. 1, 30, pt. 2:734.

8. Sherman to McPherson, October 24, 1863, *OR,* ser. 1, 32, pt. 1:720–21.

9. Sherman to Halleck, November 18, 1863, *OR,* ser. 1, 32, pt. 3:185.

10. For the best sources on Chattanooga see McDonough, *Chattanooga;* and Peter Cozzens, *Shipwreck of Their Hopes.*

11. Sherman, *Memoirs,* 387.

12. Ibid.

13. Castel, *Decision in the West,* 18; Dodge, *Personal Recollections,* 142–43; George H. Thomas report, March 10, 1864, *OR,* ser. 1, 32, pt. 1:8–9. Also see Grant to Halleck, December 7, 1863, *OR,* ser. 1, 31, pt. 3:349–50.

14. Marszalek, *Sherman,* 247; Dodge, *Personal Recollections,* 140–42.

15. W. Sherman to John Sherman, December 1863, in Thorndike, *Sherman Letters,* 220. For Sherman's battle with the press see Marszalek, *Sherman's Other War.*

16. Keim, *Sherman: A Memorial,* 244.

17. Hurlbut to Smith, and Hurlbut to Sherman, January 2, 1864, *OR,* ser. 1, 32, pt. 2:13, 14.

18. Sherman, *Memoirs,* 388; Sherman to Ellen Sherman, January 11, 1864, Sherman Family Papers, University of Notre Dame.

19. Castel, *Decision in the West,* 81; for a study of Hurlbut see Lash, *A Politician Turned General.*

20. Sherman to Hurlbut, January 11, 1864, *OR,* ser. 1, 32, pt. 1:179–80; Sherman to McPherson, January 10, 1864, Sherman Papers, LC. Sherman ordered Paducah and Columbus, Kentucky, and Cairo, Illinois, reduced.

21. Sifakis, *Who Was Who,* 600.

22. Hurlbut to A. J. Smith, January 11, 1864, *OR,* ser. 1, 32, pt. 2:67.

23. Ibid.; Sherman to Halleck, January 12, 1864, ibid., 75; Grant to Halleck, and Grant to Sherman, January 15, 1864, in Simon, *Grant Papers,* 10:15, 19.

24. Grant to Halleck, January 15, 1864, in Simon, *Grant Papers,* 10:15.

25. Sherman to Ellen Sherman, January 28, 1864, in Simpson and Berlin, *Sherman's Civil War,* 592–94.

26. Sherman to Nathaniel P. Banks, January 16, 1864, Sherman Papers, LC; Sherman to Frederick Steele, January 23, 1864, *OR,* ser. 1, 32, pt. 2:189–90.

27. Sherman to James B. McPherson, January 17, 1864, Sherman Papers, LC; W. F. Scott, *Story of a Cavalry Regiment,* 186.

28. Sherman to Ellen Sherman, January 11, 1864, in Simpson and Berlin, *Sherman's Civil War,* 584–85.

29. "Edward Francis Winslow," in Sifakis, *Who Was Who,* 724.

30. Andrew Hickenlooper Report, March 25, 1864, *OR,* ser. 1, 32, pt. 1:214; "Andrew Hickenlooper," in Sifakis, *Who Was Who,* 306–7.

31. Sherman to Ellen Sherman, January 19, 1864, Sherman Family Papers, University of Notre Dame.

32. Sherman to John Sherman, January 20, 1864, Sherman Papers, LC.

33. Banks believed that a Federal raid up the Red River would open the door for the Union into Texas. Lincoln thought after the French invasion of Mexico in 1863 that the United States should show a presence in Texas. The expedition was to cross the interior of Louisiana from southeast to northwest near Shreveport. For more on the Red River campaign see Joiner, *One Damn Blunder;* and Halleck to Grant, January 17, 1864, *OR,* ser. 1, 32, pt. 2:122–23.

34. Sherman to Grant, January 24, 1864, *OR,* ser. 1, 32, pt. 2:201–2; D. D. Porter to E. K. Owen, January 24, 1864, Sherman Papers, LC.

35. Waring, "Sooy Smith Expedition," 417–18; Sherman to Smith, January 27, 1864, *OR,* ser. 1, 32, pt. 1:181–82.

36. Sherman to Ralph P. Buckland, January 27, 1864, Ralph P. Buckland Papers, Rutherford B. Hayes Presidential Library, Fremont, Ohio; Sherman, *Memoirs,* 389.

37. Field Order no. 11, *OR,* ser. 1, 32, pt. 1:182.

38. William B. Westervelt diary, January 28, 1864, William B. Westervelt Papers, Civil War Miscellaneous Collection, USMHI; Luther Frost to Parents, January 31, 1864, in Frost, *Letters,* 18–22.

39. Sherman to John Sherman, January 28, 1864, in Thorndike, *Sherman Letters,* 221; Sherman to Ellen Sherman, January 28, 1864, in Simpson and Berlin, *Sherman's Civil War,* 592–94. Spring campaigns consisted of Sherman's invasion deep into the interior of the Confederacy. Sherman would make his march through Georgia in the spring of 1864.

40. Grant to Sherman, January 15, 1864, in Simon, *Grant Papers,* 10:19; Grant to Thomas, January 15, 1864, *OR,* ser. 1, 32, pt. 2:142–43. At the time Sherman left Vicksburg toward Meridian in February, Memphis had only five regiments of infantry, fourteen hundred artillerymen, and two regiments of cavalry to garrison the town; Hurlbut to F. Steele, January 15, 1864, ibid., 106–7.

41. Thomas, *General George H. Thomas,* 453; Grant, *Memoirs,* 1:112–13.

42. Grant to George H. Thomas, January 19, 1864, in Simon, *Grant Papers,* 10:45–46; Grant to John A. Logan, January 24, 1864, *OR,* ser. 1, 32, pt. 2:198–99.

43. Sherman to Halleck, January 29, 1864, *OR,* ser. 1, 32, pt. 2:259–61; Sherman to McPherson, January 30, 1864, *OR,* ser. 1, 32, pt. 1:183.

44. Sherman to Owen, and Sherman to Porter, January 30, 1864, *OR,* ser. 1, 32, pt. 1:183, 184–85.

45. Grimsley, *Hard Hand of War,* 1–6.

46. Ibid., 7–17.

47. Ibid., 48, 85–87, 130–38.

48. Hattaway and Jones, *How the North Won,* 492.

49. Grimsley, *Hard Hand of War,* 151–52.

50. Hattaway and Jones, *How the North Won,* 489–93; Grant to Halleck, January 15, 1864, in Simon, *Grant Papers,* 10:15.

51. Hattaway and Jones, *How the North Won,* 492.

52. Ibid.

53. Sherman to John A. Rawlins, August 4, 1863, *OR,* ser. 1, 24, pt. 3:574–75.

54. James B. McPherson report, March 16, 1864, and Order of March, *OR,* ser. 1, 32, pt. 1:209, 168–72.

55. Bettersworth, *Confederate Mississippi,* 150–51.

Chapter 3

1. Sword, *Southern Invincibility,* 229.

2. Vandiver, "Joseph Eggleston Johnston," 217–18.

3. Heidler and Heidler, *Encyclopedia of the American Civil War,* 4:1537–38.

4. Raab, *W. W. Loring,* 133; Lee, "The War in Mississippi," 47.

5. Haas, *Mountain of Fire,* 110; French, *Two Wars,* 185.

6. French, *Two Wars,* 188.

7. Leonidas Polk to Jefferson Davis, January 14, 1864, Dabney H. Maury to Polk, January 15, 1864, Polk to Maury, January 22, 1864, and Polk to Cooper, January 26, 1864, *OR,* ser. 1, 32, pt. 2:553, 564, 601, 616–17. See also Davis to Johnston, Cooper to Johnston, and Polk to Johnston, January 14, 1864, ibid., 554, 555.

8. Joseph Johnston to Davis, January 2, 1864, ibid., 510–11; see also Johnston to Polk, January 23, 1864, ibid., 603–4.

9. Command Circular, January 23, 1864, ibid., 608; Raab, *W. W. Loring,* 133; W. D. Gale to French, January 22, 1864, *OR,* ser. 1, 32, pt. 2:602.

10. Heidler and Heidler, *Encyclopedia of the American Civil War,* 4:1220.

11. Ibid., 788–89.

12. E. C. Bearss, *The Siege of Jackson,* 124–26; Order of March, February 20, 1864, *OR,* ser. 1, 32, pt. 2:332–34.

13. Polk to Cooper, January 26, 1864, *OR,* ser. 1, 32, pt. 2:616–17.

14. Stephen D. Lee report, April 18, 1864, *OR,* ser. 1, 32, pt. 1:365; William A. Montgomery memoir, William A. Montgomery Papers, Mississippi Department of Archives and History, Jackson.

15. Loring to Stephen D. Lee, January 31, 1864, *OR,* ser. 1, 32, pt. 2:637; "Another Account," February 29, 1864, in Moore, *Rebellion Record,* 8:479.

16. Loring to Stephen D. Lee, January 31, 1864, *OR,* ser. 1, 32, 2:637.

17. Polk to Johnston and Polk to Davis, January 31, 1864, and Johnston to Polk, January 30, 1864, ibid., 636, 637, 638.

18. Polk to Lee, February 1, 1864, and Polk to Maury, February 2, 1864, ibid., 648, 655; Harris Reynolds Daniels diary, February 1, 1864, Harris Reynolds Daniels Papers, Mullins Library, University of Arkansas; Albert O. Allen to Jap Pinnell, December 3, 1864, Robert L. LaValle Letters, Loesch Collection, WHMC.

19. Charles Snedeker diary, January 3, 1864, Charles Henry Snedeker Papers, Civil War Miscellaneous Collection, USMHI.

20. McPherson, *For Cause and Comrades,* 158, 160, 180; Glatthaar, *March to the Sea and Beyond,* 17–18.

21. Glatthaar, *March to the Sea and Beyond,* 32.

22. Ibid., 21; Howe, *Home Letters of William T. Sherman,* 339.

23. Burke Wylie to mother, April 2, 1865, quoted in Glatthaar, *March to the Sea and Beyond,* 26.

24. Bishop, *The Story of a Regiment,* 154.

25. W. F. Scott, *Story of a Cavalry Regiment,* 56; Westervelt diary, January 23, 1864, Westervelt Papers, USMHI.

26. William Stubbs Elliot diary, January 30, 1864, William S. Elliot Collection, IHS; Aldolphus P. Wolfe to Parents, February 2, 1864, Adolphus P. Wolfe Papers, Civil War Times Illustrated Collection, USMHI; Westervelt diary, January 29 and 30, 1864, Westervelt Papers, USMHI.

27. Henry Fike diary, January 31, 1864, Henry Fike Papers, WHMC; Westervelt diary, January 31, 1864, Westervelt Papers, USMHI.

28. J. Scott, *Story of the Thirty-second Iowa,* 121; John H. Pierce to Mother, February 2, 1864, Letters, John H. Pierce Papers, DUL; John B. Rice to Wife, February 2, 1864, John B. Rice Papers, Rutherford B. Hayes Presidential Library.

29. *Experiences in the War of the Great Rebellion,* 96; Elliot diary, January 31, 1864, Elliot Collection, IHS.

30. David W. Poak to Sister, February 1, 1864, Letters, David W. Poak Papers, ISHL; Benjamin Hieronymous diary, February 1, 1864, Benjamin Hieronymous Papers, ISHL; Henry Fike diary, February 1, 1864, Fike Papers, WHMC; Elliot diary, February 1, 1864, Elliot Collection, IHS.

31. Sherman, *Memoirs,* 389.

32. Grant to Sherman, February 1, 1864, *OR,* ser. 1, 32, pt. 2:310–11. Sherman later learned that Johnston had not sent a division of men to Polk, but only four brigades that Longstreet returned.

33. Ira Blanchard, "Recollections of Civil War Service with the 20th Illinois Infantry Company H," February 2, 1864, Ira Blanchard Papers, Champaign County Historical Archives, Urbana, Illinois; Sherman to Ellen Sherman, February 2, 1864, Sherman Family Papers, University of Notre Dame.

34. Sherman to J. M. Tuttle, February 2, 1864, *OR,* ser. 1, 32, pt. 2:316.

35. Lee report, April 18, 1864, *OR,* ser. 1, 32, pt. 1:365.

36. Elliot diary, February 3, 1864, Elliot Collection, IHS.

37. Kennedy, *Agriculture of the United States,* 84–87; Walker, *Statistics of Wealth and Industry,* 184–85.

38. Thaddeus Packard diary, February 3, 1864, Diary, Thaddeus Packard Papers, ISHL; W. F. Scott, *Story of a Cavalry Regiment,* 189; McPherson report, March 16, 1864, and Wirt Adams report, March 12, 1864, *OR,* ser. 1, 32, pt. 1:209, 372.

39. "Wirt Adams," in Warner, *Generals in Gray,* 35.

40. McPherson report, March 16, 1864, *OR,* ser. 1, 32, pt. 1:209; Hieronymous diary, February 3, 1864, Hieronymous Papers, ISHL; Fike diary, February 3, 1864, Fike Papers, WHMC; Snedeker diary, February 3, 1864, Snedeker Papers, USMHI.

41. Edward F. Winslow report, February 29, 1864, *OR,* ser. 1, 32, pt. 1:248–49; Packard diary, February 4, 1864, Packard Papers, ISHL; W. F. Scott, *Story of a Cavalry Regiment,* 190; Wirt Adams report, March 12, 1864, *OR,* ser. 1, 32, pt. 1:372–73.

42. McPherson report, March 16, 1864, Walter Q. Gresham report, March 5, 1864, Marcellus M. Crocker report, March 6, 1864, "Another Account," February 29, 1864, in

Moore, *Rebellion Record,* 8:477; Hickenlooper report, March 25, 1864, *OR,* ser. 1, 32, pt. 1:209, 215, 237–38, 247.

43. Castel, *Decision in the West,* 79–81.

44. Barber, *Army Memoirs,* 133–34; John Ritland diary, Meridian entry, http://www.ehistory.com/uscw/library/letters/ritland/02.cfm.

45. McPherson report, March 16, 1864, Walter Q. Gresham report, March 5, 1864, Marcellus M. Crocker report, March 6, 1864, and Hickenlooper report, March 25, 1864, *OR,* ser. 1, 32, pt. 1:209, 215, 237–38, 247; for more details of the skirmish see Simon Peter Duck diary, February 4, 1864, Simon Peter Duck Papers, Civil War Miscellaneous Collection, USMHI; Barber, *Army Memoirs,* 133–34; Cyrus Hall report, March 7, 1864, *OR,* ser. 1, 32, pt. 1:246; Luther Frost to Parents, February 6, 1864, Luther Frost Papers, ISHL.

46. Wirt Adams report, March 12, 1864, *OR,* ser. 1, 32, pt. 1:372–73.

47. Elliot diary, February 4, 1864, Elliot Collection, IHS; Starke report, March 13, 1864, *OR,* ser. 1, 32, pt. 1:375. Joseph Davis was Jefferson Davis's brother.

48. "Peter Burwell Starke," in Sifakis, *Who Was Who,* 617.

49. Deupree, "The Noxubee Squadron," 88–89; Montgomery, *Reminiscences,* 149–50.

50. Noah Gebbart diary, February 4, 1864, Noah Gebbart Papers, DUL; Barber, *Army Memoirs,* 133–34.

51. Massey, *Women in the Civil War,* 197–200; T. P. August to G. W. Lay, August 10, 1863, *OR,* ser. 4, 2:76–762. For works on women and the Civil War also see Clinton, *Tara Revisited;* Clinton and Silber, *Divided Houses;* Edwards, *Scarlett Doesn't Live Here Anymore;* Massey, *Refugee Life in the Confederacy;* and Simkins and Patton, *Women of the Confederacy.*

52. Fike diary, February 21, 1864, Fike Papers, WHMC.

53. Gebbart diary, February 14, 1864, Gebbart Papers, DUL.

54. Hieronymous diary, February 21, 1864, Hieronymous Papers, ISHL.

55. Ballard, "Yankees in the Yard," 9, 13; Faust, *Mothers of Invention,* 200. For more about soldier attitudes see Mitchell, *Civil War Soldiers.*

56. Haas, *Mountain of Fire,* 107; Rood, *Story of Company E,* 242–43.

57. Johnston to Polk, and Polk to Loring, February 4, 1864, *OR,* ser. 1, 32, pt. 2:670, 671.

58. McPherson report, March 16, 1864, *OR,* ser. 1, 32, pt. 1:209–10.

59. Wirt Adams report, March 12, 1864, and Lucius M. Rose report, March 8, 1864, ibid., 222, 373–74.

60. Wirt Adams report, March 12, 1864, and Lucius M. Rose report, March 8, 1864, ibid., 222, 373–74; Stevenson, *History of the Seventy-eighth,* 267–74.

61. Rood, *Story of Company E,* 244; "Another Account," February 29, 1864, in Moore, *Rebellion Record,* 8:477; Wirt Adams report, March 12, 1864, *OR,* ser. 1, 32, pt. 1:373–74.

62. Peter B. Starke report, March 13, 1864, *OR,* ser. 1, 32, pt. 1:375–76; Hieronymous diary, February 5, 1864, Hieronymous Papers, ISHL; Howard, *History of the 124th,* 184.

63. Starke report, March 13, 1864, *OR,* ser. 1, 32, pt. 1:375–76; Westervelt diary, February 6, 1864, Westervelt Papers, USMHI.

64. John A. Griffin journal, February 5, 1864, John A. Griffin Papers, ISHL; "Another Account," February 29, 1864, in Moore, *Rebellion Record,* 8:478.

65. W. F. Scott, *Story of a Cavalry Regiment,* 191.

66. Samuel French to William Loring, and Loring to French, February 5, 1864, *OR,* ser. 1, 32, pt. 2:674.

67. Lee to French, and French to Loring, February 5, 1864, ibid., 675–76.

68. Polk to Loring, and Loring to Polk, February 5, 1864, ibid., 676.

69. John H. Howe report, March 7, 1864, *OR,* ser. 1, 32, pt. 1:235; Duck diary, February 5, 1864, Duck Papers, USMHI; Letter to the editor, *Clinton Public and Central Transcript,* February 18, 1864.

70. Stevenson, *History of the Seventy-eighth,* 273–74; Andrew Hickenlooper, February 5, 1864, unpublished memoir, Andrew H. Hickenlooper Papers, CHS.

71. Snedeker diary, February 5, 1864, Snedeker Papers, USMHI.

72. W. F. Scott, *Story of a Cavalry Regiment,* 191.

73. Ibid.; Winslow report, February 29, 1864, *OR,* ser. 1, 32, pt. 1:249.

74. W. F. Scott, *Story of a Cavalry Regiment,* 191; Winslow report, February 29, 1864, *OR,* ser. 1, 32, pt. 1:249; Lee to Jackson, February 6, 1864, *OR,* ser. 1, 52, pt. 2:609.

75. W. F. Scott, *Story of a Cavalry Regiment,* 191; Winslow report, February 29, 1864, and McPherson report, March 16, 1864, *OR,* ser. 1, 32, pt. 1:209–10, 249.

76. French, *Two Wars,* 188.

77. W. F. Scott, *Story of a Cavalry Regiment,* 191; Winslow report, February 29, 1864, and McPherson report, March 16, 1864, *OR,* ser. 1, 32, pt. 1:209–10, 249.

78. McPherson report, March 16, 1864, *OR,* ser. 1, 32, pt. 1:209–10; Bundy G. Smith, February 5, 1864, unpublished memoir, Bundy G. Smith Papers, WHMC; Snedeker diary, February 5, 1864, Snedeker Papers, USMHI.

79. "Another Account," February 29, 1864, in Moore, *Rebellion Record,* 8:478; Rood, *Story of Company E,* 245. In 1860, Mississippi contained 436,631 slaves and 775 free blacks and "other." Economic Research Department Mississippi Power & Light Company, "Mississippi Statistical Summary of Population, 1800–1980" (February 1983), Mitchell Memorial Library, Special Collections, Mississippi State University.

80. Rood, *Story of Company E,* 245.

81. Marszalek, *Sherman,* 254–55; Sherman to John Sherman, September 3, 1864, Sherman Papers, LC.

82. Sherman report, March 7, 1864, *OR,* ser. 1, 32, pt. 1:175; Sherman to Buckland, James C. Veatch to William Heath, February 6, 1864, *OR,* ser. 1, 32, pt. 2:346, 343; W. F. Scott, *Story of a Cavalry Regiment,* 191.

83. McMurry, "Sherman's Meridian Campaign," 24–32.

Chapter 4

1. Sherman to Tuttle, February 6, 1864, Sherman Papers, LC.

2. Hickenlooper memoir, February 6, 1864, Hickenlooper Papers, CHS.

3. Elliot diary, February 6, 1864, Elliot Collection, IHS.

4. Wilfred B. McDonald, February 6, 1864, Journal, Wilfred B. McDonald Collection, ISL.

5. Kennedy, *Agriculture of the United States,* 84–87.

6. Haas, *Mountain of Fire,* 107; "Another Account," February 29, 1864, in Moore, *Rebellion Record,* 8:478; Snedeker diary, February 6, 1864, Snedeker Papers, USMHI; Howard, *History of the 124th,* 184.

7. Hieronymous diary, February 6, 1864, Hieronymous Papers, ISHL.

8. Sherman to Ellen Sherman, February 7, 1864, in Simpson and Berlin, *Sherman's Civil War,* 602; *New York Tribune,* February 25, 1864. Also see Griffin journal, February 6, 1864, Griffin Papers, ISHL. All of the Mississippi city population numbers come from one source—

Economic Research Development Mississippi Power and Light Company, "Mississippi Statistical Summary of Population, 1800–1980" (February 1983), Mitchell Memorial Library, Special Collections, Mississippi State University.

9. Hickenlooper report, March 25, 1864, *OR*, ser. 1, 32, pt. 2:215; Gebbart diary, February 6, 1864, Gebbart Papers, DUL.

10. Lee report, April 18, 1864, and Samuel Ferguson report, March 31, 1864, *OR*, ser. 1, 32, pt. 1:365–66, 379; Lee to Loring, February 6, 1864, *OR*, ser. 1, 32, pt. 2:683–84; Packard diary, February 7, 1864, Packard Papers, ISHL.

11. Loring to French, and Thomas Jack to French, February 6, 1864, *OR*, ser. 1, 32, pt. 2:684, 683; Daniels diary, February 6, 1864, Daniels Papers, University of Arkansas.

12. Polk to Davis, and Polk to Forrest, February 6, 1864, *OR*, ser. 1, 32, pt. 2:334–5, 684–85.

13. Snedeker diary, February 7, 1864, Snedeker Papers, USMHI.

14. James H. Howe report, *OR*, ser. 1, 32, pt. 1:207; Hieronymous diary, February 7, 1864, Hieronymous Papers, ISHL; Westervelt diary, February 7, 1864, Westervelt Papers, USMHI.

15. "A National Account," March 5, 1864, in Moore, *Rebellion Record*, 8:471; Kennedy, *Agriculture of the United States*, 206.

16. Lucius M. Rose report, March 8, 1864, *OR*, ser. 1, 32, pt. 1:222.

17. Gebbart diary, February 7 and 8, 1864, Gebbart Papers, DUL; McDonald journal, February 7, 1864, McDonald Collection, ISL; General Field Order no. 1, February 7, 1864, *OR*, ser. 1, 32, pt. 2:350; Snedeker diary, February 7, 1864, Snedeker Papers, USMHI.

18. Unknown Ohio Soldier Diary, February 7, 1864, Ohio Historical Society, Columbus; McPherson report, March 16, 1864, *OR*, ser. 1, 32, pt. 1:210; "Another Account," February 29, 1864, in Moore, *Rebellion Record*, 8:479.

19. *New York Tribune*, March 21, 1864; "Journal of the March," March 6, 1864, in Moore, *Rebellion Record*, 8:470.

20. "A National Account," March 5, 1864, in Moore, *Rebellion Record*, 8:472; soldier quoted in M. R. Bearss, *Sherman's Forgotten Campaign*, 89. "Jayhawked" refers to the bloody conflict between pro-slavery and anti-slavery settlers in Kansas during the 1850s. Each side resorted to violence and theft during numerous clashes. A "Jayhawk" was an anti-slavery advocate, and the word became synonymous with stealing and violence.

21. "Another Account," March 4, 1864, in Moore, *Rebellion Record*, 8:476.

22. Quoted in Parks, *General Leonidas Polk*, 359; "Another Account," February 29, 1864, in Moore, *Rebellion Record*, 8:480; French, *Two Wars*, 188.

23. A. J. Lawson to Polk, and Lee to Loring, February 7, 1864, *OR*, ser. 1, 32, pt. 2:688, 690; Polk to Beauregard, and Polk to Maury, February 7, 1864, ibid., 686, 688–89.

24. Polk to Beauregard, and Polk to Johnston, February 7, 1864, ibid., 686; Beauregard to Polk, February 9, 1864, ibid., 700.

25. William H. Jackson report, March 21, 1864, *OR*, ser. 1, 32, pt. 1:369.

26. Fike diary, February 8, 1864, Fike Papers, WHMC; Albert Underwood diary, February 8, 1864, Albert Underwood Collection, IHS; Stephen H. Smith diary, February 8, 1864, Stephen H. Smith Papers, Civil War Miscellaneous Collection, USMHI.

27. Philip Roesch memorandum, February 8, 1864, Roesch Papers, USMHI.

28. McPherson report, March 16, 1864, *OR*, ser. 1, 32, pt. 1:210–11; J. Scott, *Story of the Thirty-second Iowa*, 122.

29. Hickenlooper memoir, February 8, 1864, Hickenlooper Papers, CHS.

30. W. F. Scott, *Story of a Cavalry Regiment*, 200.

31. French, *Two Wars*, 188; Loring to Lee, February 8, 1864, *OR*, ser. 1, 32, pt. 2:694.

32. Polk to T. F. Sevier, February 8, 1864, *OR,* ser. 1, 32, pt. 2:695.

33. French, *Two Wars,* 188.

34. Loring to Polk, February 8, 1864, *OR,* ser. 1, 32, pt. 2:693. French mentions a council held that afternoon in Morton at which they decided to fall back to Newton; French, *Two Wars,* 188. Also see Loring to Thomas M. Jack, February 8, 1864, *OR,* ser. 1, 32, pt. 2:693, where he orders Jack to halt all reinforcements at Newton to concentrate with the retreating forces there. See also the comments of W. S. Featherston, commander of a Confederate brigade at Morton, as to when Polk actually arrive on the scene and took command. By the time he reached his army, it was already falling back toward Newton. This further supports the theory that he did not make the decision to abandon Morton; W. S. Featherston, unpublished memoir, 68, W. S. Featherston Papers, USMHI.

35. W. F. Scott, *Story of a Cavalry Regiment,* 202; Packard diary, February 9, 1864, Packard Papers, ISHL.

36. J. A. Cates to Wife, February 9, 1864, J. A. Cates Papers, Civil War Miscellaneous Collection, USMHI; Bevier, *History of the First and Second Missouri,* 229.

37. Griffin journal, February 9, 1864, Griffin Papers, ISHL; James S. Reeves to Thomas Stevenson, March 9, 1864, in Stevenson, *History of the Seventy-eighth,* 269.

38. Westervelt diary, February 9, 1864, Westervelt Papers, USMHI.

39. Gebbart diary, February 9, 1864, Gebbart Papers, DUL.

40. Griffin journal, February 9, 1864, Griffin Papers, ISHL; Unknown Ohio Soldier Diary, February 9, 1864, Ohio Historical Society; Hieronymous diary, February 9, 1864, Hieronymous Papers, ISHL. Also see J. Scott, *Story of the Thirty-second Iowa,* 124.

41. French, *Two Wars,* 188; Raab, *W. W. Loring,* 137; Polk to Lee, *OR,* ser. 1, 32, pt. 2:700; Ferguson report, March 31, 1864, *OR,* ser. 1, 32, pt. 1:379–80. Also see Special Order, February 9, 1864, *OR,* ser. 1, 32, pt. 2:702; Lee report, *OR,* ser. 1, 32, pt. 1:366.

42. Polk to Richmond, February 9, 1864, *OR,* ser. 1, 32, pt. 1:335; Polk to Maury, February 9, 1864, *OR,* ser. 1, 32, pt. 2:701; *Mobile Tribune,* February 10, 1864.

43. W. F. Scott, *Story of a Cavalry Regiment,* 202; Veatch report, *OR,* ser. 1, 32, pt. 1:201; Westervelt diary, February 10, 1864, Westervelt Papers, USMHI.

44. Fike diary, February 10, 1864, Fike Papers, WHMC; Underwood diary, February 10, 1864, Underwood Collection, IHS.

45. Unknown Ohio Soldier Diary, February 10, 1864, Ohio Historical Society; Haas, *Mountain of Fire,* 110; "Journal of the March," March 6, 1864, in Moore, *Rebellion Record,* 8:470; L. M. Dayton to Hurlbut, February 10, 1864, *OR,* ser. 1, 32, pt. 2:362.

46. French, *Two Wars,* 188; Special Order, February 9, 1864, *OR,* ser. 1, 32, pt. 2:702.

47. Lee to Polk, February 10, 1864, *OR,* ser. 1, 32, pt. 1:358.

48. Thomas M. Jack to B. G. Bidwell, February 10, 1864, *OR,* ser. 1, 32, pt. 2:705.

49. Lee to Adams, February 9, 1864, *OR,* ser. 1, 52:617–18.

50. General Order no. 19, February 10, 1864, *OR,* ser. 1, 32, pt. 2:711–13.

51. W. F. Scott, *Story of a Cavalry Regiment,* 202.

52. Hickenlooper report, March 25, 1864, *OR,* ser. 1, 32, pt. 1:216–17; McDonald journal, February 11, 1864, McDonald Collection, ISL.

53. Hieronymous diary, February 11, 1864, Hieronymous Papers, ISHL.

54. Howard, *History of the 124th,* 189.

55. Hickenlooper memoir, February 11, 1864, Hickenlooper Papers, CHS; Lucius M. Rose report, March 8, 1864, *OR,* ser. 1, 32, pt. 1:222; "Another Account," February 29, 1864, in Moore, *Rebellion Record,* 8:482.

56. Special Field Order no. 16, n.d., *OR,* ser. 1, 32, pt. 1:185–86.

57. Lee report, April 18, 1864, and Ferguson report, March 31, 1864, *OR,* ser. 1, 32, pt. 1:366, 380.

58. Polk to Loring, and Polk to Lee, February 11, 1864, *OR,* ser. 1, 32, pt. 2:717–18, 719.

59. Polk to Lee, February 11, 1864, ibid., 718–19; Lee to Polk, February 11, 1864, *OR,* ser. 1, 32, pt. 1:359, 359–60.

60. Sherman report, March 7, 1864, *OR,* ser. 1, 32, pt. 1:175.

61. Liddell Hart, *Sherman,* 225.

62. Polk to Sevier, February 11, 1864, *OR,* ser. 1, 32, pt. 2:721.

63. Polk to Lee, February 11, 1864, ibid., 720.

64. Polk to Loring, February 11, 1864, ibid., 720–21.

65. Davis to Johnston, Johnston to Davis, and Johnston to Polk, February 11, 1864, ibid., 716.

66. Grant, *Memoirs,* 2:113–14.

67. Ferguson to Loring, February 11, 1864, *OR,* ser. 1, 32, pt. 2:722, 723; "Journal of the March," March 6, 1864, in Moore, *Rebellion Record,* 8:470; Ferguson to Loring, February 11, 1864, *OR,* ser. 1, 32, pt. 1:378; Polk to Loring, February 12, 1864, *OR,* ser. 1, 32, pt. 2:725.

68. "Another Account," March 4, 1864, in Moore, *Rebellion Record,* 8:476; Veatch report, *OR,* ser. 1, 32, pt. 1:202; Westervelt diary, February 12, 1864, Westervelt Papers, USMHI; "Another Account," February 29, 1864, in Moore, *Rebellion Record,* 8:482.

69. Dayton to Hurlbut, and Sherman to Hurlbut, February 11, 1864, *OR,* ser. 1, 32, pt. 2:383.

70. Sherman, *Memoirs,* 391.

71. Montgomery memoir, February 12, 1864, Montgomery Papers, Mississippi Department of Archives and History; "Another Account," February 29, 1864, in Moore, *Rebellion Record,* 8:482.

72. Sherman, *Memoirs,* 391.

73. Barber, *Army Memoirs,* 135; Rood, *Story of Company E,* 246; Lee report, April 18, 1864, *OR,* ser. 1, 32, pt. 1:366. See also Force, *Great Commanders,* 184; Adams report, March 12, 1864, *OR,* ser. 1, 32, pt. 1:374.

74. Barber, *Army Memoirs,* 135; for other retaliation arguments see also McDonald journal, February 12, 1864, McDonald Collection, ISL; Howard, *History of the 124th,* 190; Hieronymous diary, February 12, 1864, Hieronymous Papers, ISHL.

75. Polk to Loring, February 12, 1864, *OR,* ser. 1, 32, pt. 2:723–24.

Chapter 5

1. "Mississippi Statistical Summary of Population," Lauderdale County, Mitchell Memorial Library, Special Collections, Mississippi State University.

2. Shank, "Meridian" (M.A. thesis), 29–30.

3. "Roster of the Meridian Invincibles," Meridian Public Library, Meridian, Mississippi.

4. Kennedy, *Agriculture of the United States,* 84–86.

5. Stover, *Railroads of the South,* 17; Desha, *Directory of Meridian,* 62.

6. William D. McCain to Henry S. Loeb, January 21, 1954, Vertical Subject File, Meridian Public Library; Shank, "Meridian" (M.A. thesis), 31; *Meridian Daily Mississippian,* August 29, 1863; Snedeker diary, February 16, 1864, Snedeker Papers, USMHI.

7. *Meridian Daily Mississippian,* August 29, 1863.

8. Fike diary, February 14, 1864, Fike Papers, WHMC; Elliot diary, February 13, 1864, Elliot Collection, IHS; Westervelt diary, February 13, 1864, Westervelt Papers, USMHI.

9. Hieronymous diary, February 13, 1864, Hieronymous Papers, ISHL; Underwood diary, February 13, 1864, Underwood Collection, IHS; Gebbart diary, February 13, 1864, Gebbart Papers, DUL.

10. "Another Account," March 4, 1864, in Moore, *Rebellion Record,* 8:476; Hieronymous diary, February 13, 1864, Hieronymous Papers, ISHL; John Ritland diary, February 13, 1864, in http://www.ehistory.com/uscw/library/letters/ritland/02.cfm.

11. Abram Fulkerson diary, February 13, 1864, Abram Fulkerson Papers, Civil War Miscellaneous Collection, USMHI.

12. Hurlbut to A. J. Smith, February 13, 1864, *OR,* ser. 1, 32, pt. 2:389.

13. W. F. Scott, *Story of a Cavalry Regiment,* 203.

14. Polk to Maury, February 13, 1864, *OR,* ser. 1, 32, pt. 2:733–34.

15. Lee report, April 18, 1864, *OR,* ser. 1, 32, pt. 1:366; Lee to Polk, February 13, 1864, ibid., 361, 362.

16. Polk to Lee, February 13, 1864, *OR,* ser. 1, 32, pt. 2:733.

17. Polk to Loring, February 13, 1864, ibid., 732.

18. Loring to Polk, and Polk to Loring, February 13, 1864, ibid., 732, 733.

19. Hieronymous diary, February 14, 1864, Hieronymous Papers, ISHL.

20. McPherson to Chamber, February 14, 1864, *OR,* ser. 1, 32, pt. 2:393.

21. McPherson to Mortimer Leggett, February 13, 1864, Manning Ferguson Force Papers, Suzzallo Library, University of Washington.

22. Snedeker diary, February 14, 1864, Snedeker Papers, USMHI.

23. Manning Force to J. C. Douglas, February 14, 1864, Force Papers, University of Washington; John O. Duer report, March 8, 1864, and John H. Howe report, March 7, 1864, *OR,* ser. 1, 32, pt. 1:233–34, 235–36; Job Yaggy diary, February 14, 1864, quoted in M. R. Bearss, *Sherman's Forgotten Campaign,* 154.

24. Hickenlooper report, March 25, 1864, *OR,* ser. 1, 32, pt. 1:217.

25. Packard diary, February 14, 1864, Packard Papers, ISHL.

26. W. F. Scott, *Story of a Cavalry Regiment,* 204.

27. Packard diary, February 14, 1864, Packard Papers, ISHL.

28. Starke report, March 13, 1864, *OR,* ser. 1, 32, pt. 1:376; W. F. Scott, *Story of a Cavalry Regiment,* 206.

29. Hieronymous diary, February 14, 1864, Hieronymous Papers, ISHL; Underwood diary, February 14, 1864, Underwood Collection, IHS; Smith diary, February 14, 1864, Smith Papers, USMHI.

30. Westervelt diary, February 14, 1864, Westervelt Papers, USMHI.

31. Dayton to McPherson, February 14, 1864, *OR,* ser. 1, 52, pt. 1:519.

32. McPherson to Chambers, and McPherson to Leggett, February 14, 1864, *OR,* ser. 1, 32, pt. 2:393. McPherson ordered Chambers to assist in protecting the wagon train prior to receiving news that the Confederates had attempted an attack.

33. W. B. Smith, *On Wheels and How I Came There,* 111–12.

34. Special Order no. 45, February 14, 1864, *OR,* ser. 1, 32, pt. 2:738; Lee, "The War in Mississippi," 54.

35. L. J. Fleming to Polk, February 14, 1864, *OR,* ser. 1, 32, pt. 2:768.

36. Special Order no. 17, February 14, 1864, *OR,* ser. 1, 32, pt. 1:186.

37. Special Field Order no. 18, February 15, 1864, ibid., 187.

38. Ira Blanchard, "Recollections of Civil War Service with the 20th Illinois Infantry, Company H," February 15, 1864, Blanchard Papers, Champaign County Historical Archives.

39. Howard, *History of the 124th,* 192; McDonald journal, February 15, 1964, McDonald Collection, IHS; "Journal of the March," March 6, 1864, in Moore, *Rebellion Record,* 8:470. On the return march, Federal soldiers found the graves of two soldiers of the Thirteenth Iowa near Hillsboro.

40. McPherson report, March 16, 1864, *OR,* ser. 1, 32, pt. 1:211; Underwood diary, February 16, 1864, Underwood Collection, IHS.

41. T. H. Harris to Smith, T. H. Harris to J. C. Veatch, T. H. Harris to Winslow, and Hurlbut to Smith, February 15, 1864, *OR,* ser. 1, 32, pt. 2:399.

42. Howe report, March 7, 1864, *OR,* ser. 1, 32, pt. 1:207; Packard diary, February 17, 1864, Packard Papers, ISHL; Clarke, *Thunder at Meridian,* 168.

43. Jim Dawson, "Paths to the Past: Board of Police, 1832–1870, Board of Supervisors, 1870–1992," Meridian Public Library, 26; *Eighth Census of the United States.*

44. Lee report, April 18, 1864, *OR,* ser. 1, 32, pt. 1:366–67.

45. McPherson to Leggett, February 15, 1864, *OR,* ser. 1, 32, pt. 2:399.

46. Special Field Order no. 19, February 15, 1864, *OR,* ser. 1, 32, pt. 1:187; McPherson to Crocker, February 15, 1864, *OR,* ser. 1, 32, pt. 2:400.

Chapter 6

1. Roesch memorandum, February 15, 1864, Roesch Papers, USMHI; "Campaigns of the 178th New York Volunteers," February 14, 1864, USMHI; Hickenlooper memoir, February 16, 1864, Hickenlooper Papers, CHS; Veatch to Harris, February 17, 1864, *OR,* ser. 1, 32, pt. 2:420.

2. Packard diary, February 16, 1864, Packard Papers, ISHL; Duck diary, February 16, 1864, Duck Papers, USMHI; A. J. Smith to Hurlbut, February 17, 1864, *OR,* ser. 1, 32, pt. 2:419–20.

3. Crocker to McPherson, February 16, 1864, *OR,* ser. 1, 52, pt. 2:520.

4. Walter Q. Gresham report, March 5, 1864, *OR,* ser. 1, 32, pt. 1:247.

5. Gault, *Roster,* February 16, 1864; McPherson report, March 16, 1864, *OR,* ser. 1, 32, pt. 1:211–12; Charles E. Smith diary, February 16, 1864, quoted in M. R. Bearss, *Sherman's Forgotten Campaign,* 171–72.

6. Charles E. Smith diary, February 16, 1864, quoted in M. R. Bearss, *Sherman's Forgotten Campaign,* 171–72.

7. French, *Two Wars,* 188; Circular, February 16, 1864, *OR,* ser. 1, 32, pt. 2:754.

8. Lee to Forrest, February 16, 1864, ibid., 753.

9. Fike diary, February 17, 1864, Fike Papers, WHMC; J. Scott, *Story of the Thirty-second Iowa,* 123.

10. Quoted in Howard, *History of the 124th,* 195–96; Business Directory of Meridian, Mississippi Department of Archives and History; O. G. Phillips letter, *New York Daily,* March 21, 1864.

11. *New York Times,* March 27, 1864.

12. Ibid.

13. McPherson, *For Cause and Comrades,* 148–55.

14. J. Scott, *Story of the Thirty-second Iowa,* 124–25.

15. James S. Reeves to Thomas Stevenson, March 9, 1864, in Stevenson, *History of the Seventy-eighth,* 267–74.

16. Mrs. Julie Greer Marechal interview, in Mrs. Henry Woods, "Growth and Development," Vertical Subject File, Meridian Public Library. For another description of Greer's actions to hide his goods see Nettie Henry interview in *Slave Narratives,* 61–67.

17. *New York Times,* March 27, 1864. For excellent sources on slave behavior and life see Blassingame, *The Slave Community;* Genovese, *Roll Jordan Roll;* Mohr, *On the Threshold of Freedom;* and Roark, *Masters without Slaves.*

18. "The Second Account," March 4, 1864, in Moore, *Rebellion Record,* 8:483.

19. "Another Account," February 29, 1864, in Moore, *Rebellion Record,* 8:482.

20. Crocker report, March 6, 1864, *OR,* ser. 1, 32, pt. 1:238; "The Second Account," March 4, 1864, in Moore, *Rebellion Record,* 8:484–85.

21. "The Second Account," March 4, 1864, in Moore, *Rebellion Record,* 8:484–85; *Mobile Daily Register,* February 27, 1864.

22. Cyrus Hall report, March 9, 1864, *OR,* ser. 1, 32, pt. 1:246; Crocker to McPherson, February 18, 1864, *OR,* ser. 1, 52, pt. 1:522; "Another Account," February 29, 1864, in Moore, *Rebellion Record,* 8:482.

23. Dayton to Hurlbut, February 17, 1864, *OR,* ser. 1, 32, pt. 2:418–19.

24. Harris to Smith, February 17, 1864, and Smith to Hurlbut, February 17, 1864, ibid., 419, 419–20.

25. Hieronymous diary, February 17, 1864, Hieronymous Papers, ISHL.

26. Snedeker diary, February 17, 1864, Snedeker Papers, USMHI; Underwood diary, February 17, 1864, Underwood Collection, IHS.

27. Clarke, *Thunder at Meridian,* 166–68; Business Directory of Meridian, 5; Mrs. Henry Woods, "Growth and Development," Vertical Subject File, Meridian Public Library.

28. Starke report, March 13, 1864, *OR,* ser. 1, 32, pt. 1:376–77.

29. Lee to Polk, February 17, 1864, ibid., 363; Daniel Ruggels to Polk, February 17, 1864, *OR,* ser. 1, 32, pt. 2:757–58; Polk to Seddon, February 18, 1864, *OR,* ser. 1, 32, pt. 1:336.

30. Polk to Johnston, and Johnston to Polk, February 13, 1864, *OR,* ser. 1, 32, pt. 2:729–30.

31. Davis to Polk, and Davis to Johnston, February 13, 1864, in Rowland, *Jefferson Davis,* 6:171, 172.

32. Davis to Polk, February 15, 1864, ibid., 175.

33. Davis to Johnston, February 15, 1864, ibid., 172; Davis to T. H. Watts, February 15, 1864, *OR,* ser. 1, 52, pt. 2:620.

34. Connelly, *Autumn of Glory,* 294–95. Johnston's telegraph has since disappeared, but Davis's responses provide clues as to what it contained; Davis to Johnston, February 15, 1864, in Crist and Williams, *Papers of Jefferson Davis,* 234–35.

35. Johnston to Davis, February 16, 1864, *OR,* ser. 1, 32, pt. 2:751–52.

36. J. A. Seddon to Polk, February 17, 1864, ibid., 755; Polk to Davis, February 17, 1864, *OR,* ser. 1, 32, pt. 1:336.

37. Davis to Johnston, February 17, 1864, and Davis to Hardee, February 21, 1864, in Rowland, *Jefferson Davis,* 6:177–78, 183.

38. Grant, *Memoirs,* 2:113–14.

39. Dayton to McPherson, and Dayton to Hurlbut, February 18, 1864, Sherman Papers, LC.

40. See also Ash, *When the Yankees Came.*

41. Hickenlooper memoir, February 16, 1864, Hickenlooper Papers, CHS; Sherman report, March 7, 1864, *OR,* ser. 1, 32, pt. 1:176.

42. W. F. Scott, *Story of a Cavalry Regiment,* 208; T. H. Harris to Veatch, and T. H. Harris to Winslow, February 18, 1864, *OR,* ser. 1, 32, pt. 2:426.

43. Snedeker diary, February 18, 1864, Snedeker Papers, USMHI; Griffin journal, February 18, 1864, Griffin Papers, ISHL; Frederick Pell journal, February 18, 1864, Frederick Pell Papers, Civil War Times Illustrated Collection, USMHI.

44. Smith to Hurlbut, February 18, 1864, *OR,* ser. 1, 32, pt. 2:424; see also Hieronymous diary, February 18, 1864, Hieronymous Papers, ISHL; Ezekial T. Willoughby diary, February 18, 1864, Ezekial Thomas Willoughby Papers, ISHL.

45. See sources cited in n. 44; also see Sherman report, March 7, 1864, *OR,* ser. 1, 32, pt. 1:176.

46. Packard diary, February 23, 1864, Packard Papers, ISHL.

47. Lee report, April 18, 1864, *OR,* ser. 1, 32, pt. 1:367.

48. French, *Two Wars,* 188.

49. W. F. Scott, *Story of a Cavalry Regiment,* 209; Winslow to Smith, February 19, 1864, *OR,* ser. 1, 32, pt. 2:430; Rowland, *Military History of Mississippi,* 57. Also see Packard diary, February 19, 1864, Packard Papers, ISHL.

50. Maury to Polk, February 19, 1864, *OR,* ser. 1, 32, pt. 2:769.

51. Lee to Polk, February 20, 1864, and Ferguson report, March 31, 1864, *OR,* ser. 1, 32, pt. 1:364, 380.

Chapter 7

1. Sherman to Grant, December 19, 1863, *OR,* ser. 1, 31, pt. 3:445.

2. Grant to Halleck, December 18, 23, 1863, ibid., 436, 473; General Order no. 5, November 11, 1863, ibid., 115; Heidler and Heidler, *Encyclopedia of the American Civil War,* 4:1822; Grant, *Memoirs,* 2:108; Sherman, *Memoirs,* 394; *OR,* ser. 1, 32, pt. 1:171–72.

3. Sifakis, *Who Was Who,* 609.

4. Glatthaar, *March to the Sea and Beyond,* 19; Dyer, *Compendium,* 111.

5. Benjamin H. Grierson manuscript, p. 299, Benjamin Grierson Papers, ISHL; Leckie and Leckie, *Unlikely Warriors,* 109; January 27, 1864, Sherman Papers, LC.

6. Smith to Hatch, January 14, 23, 27, 1864, *OR,* ser. 1, 32, pt. 2:97, 190, 241; Smith to Grant, January 17, 1864, ibid., 123.

7. Sherman to Smith, *OR,* ser. 1, 32, pt. 1:181–82.

8. Special Field Order no. 2, February 9, 1864, *OR,* ser. 1, 32, pt. 2:358; Smith to Grant, January 12, 1864, *OR,* ser. 1, 32, pt. 1:74–75.

9. Pierce, *History of the Second Iowa,* 56; Waring, "Sooy Smith Expedition," 417; Waring, *Whip and Spur,* 105–8.

10. Quoted in Waring, "Sooy Smith Expedition," 147.

11. N. B. Forrest to Jefferson Davis, February 5, 1864, *OR,* ser. 1, 32, pt. 1:346; Lytle, *Bedford Forrest,* 257; Hancock, *Hancock's Diary,* 308–9.

12. For a full description of the pardon and the action prior see Dinkins, *Personal Recollections,* 129–31.

13. Hurst, *Nathan Bedford Forrest,* 146; Hancock, *Hancock's Diary,* 303.

14. Jordan and Pryor, *Campaigns,* 385.

15. *OR,* ser. 1, 32, pt. 1:252; Lytle, *Bedford Forrest,* 260; *OR,* ser. 1, 32, pt. 1:347; Hancock, *Hancock's Diary,* 310–11; Quoted in Henry, *As They Saw Forrest,* 150; Jordan and Pryor, *Campaigns,* 386; Dinkins, *Personal Recollections,* 60; Young, *Seventh Tennessee Cavalry,* 75.

16. Waring, *Whip and Spur,* 116; Larson, *Sergeant Larson,* 217. For more instances of guerrilla attacks on Smith's expedition see Pierce, *History of the Second Iowa,* 84; William Records diary, February 11, 1864, William H. Records Papers, ISL; *OR,* ser. 1, 32, pt. 1:285; McGee, *History of the Seventy-second Indiana,* 267.

17. Quoted in Starr, *Union Cavalry,* 85–87; *OR,* ser. 1, 32, pt. 1:252; Cogley, *History of the Seventh Indiana,* 88; Records diary, February 13 and 14, 1864, Records Papers, ISL; McGee, *History of the Seventy-second Indiana,* 269.

18. *OR,* ser. 1, 32, pt. 1:348–49.

19. Smith to Benjamin Grierson, February 19, 1864, ibid., 317, 431; McGee, *History of the Seventy-second Indiana,* 269; Smith to Grierson, February 16, 1864, Grierson Papers, ISHL.

20. *OR,* ser. 1, 32, pt. 2:703, and ser. 1, 32, pt. 1:348; Young, *Seventh Tennessee Cavalry,* 75; Hancock, *Hancock's Diary,* 312.

21. Polk to Davis, February 17, 1864, *OR,* ser. 1, 32, pt. 1:336.

22. Records diary, February 18, 1864, Records Papers, ISL; McGee, *History of the Seventy-second Indiana,* 269; Cogley, *History of the Seventh Indiana,* 90.

23. Waring, *Whip and Spur,* 112–13; report of Colonel George E. Waring, *OR,* ser. 1, 32, pt. 1:267; Smith report, ibid., 252; Columbus Sykes to Wife, February 18, 1864, Columbus Sykes Papers, USMHI.

24. Pierce, *History of the Second Iowa,* 82; Hubbard, *Notes of a Private,* 55.

25. Waring report, *OR,* ser. 1, 32, pt. 1:267.

26. Larson, *Sergeant Larson,* 217; Smith to Grierson, *OR,* ser. 1, 32, pt. 1:431.

27. Smith report, *OR,* ser. 1, 32, pt. 1:252; Pierce, *History of the Second Iowa,* 85; Larson, *Sergeant Larson,* 221–22.

28. Grierson manuscript, p. 574, Grierson Papers, ISHL.

29. Young, *Seventh Tennessee Cavalry,* 76; Hancock, *Hancock's Diary,* 312–13. Tyree H. Bell was sick in Starkville and could not command.

30. Jordan and Pryor, *Campaigns,* 388; Starr, *Union Cavalry,* 382; Hancock, *Hancock's Diary,* 313–14; Lee, "Sherman's Meridian Expedition," 56.

31. Forrest report, *OR,* ser. 1, 32, pt. 1:352; Hancock, *Hancock's Diary,* 313–14.

32. Waring report, *OR,* ser. 1, 32, pt. 1:267; Smith report, ibid., 256–57, 352; Lee, "Sherman's Meridian Expedition," 56; Leckie and Leckie, *Unlikely Warriors,* 110.

33. Grierson manuscript, p. 579, Grierson Papers, ISHL; Smith report, *OR,* ser. 1, 32, pt. 1:252, 253, 257; Smith quoted in Lee, "Sherman's Meridian Expedition," 57.

34. McGee, *History of the Seventy-second Indiana,* 270; Waring, *Whip and Spur,* 117.

35. Forrest report, February 26, and March 8, 1864, *OR,* ser. 1, 32, pt. 1:349, 351, 352; Benjamin Grierson to Alice Grierson, February 27, 1864, Grierson Papers, ISHL.

36. Quoted in Hurst, *Nathan Bedford Forrest,* 149–50. While moving forward to the action, Forrest came upon a retreating Confederate cavalryman. Forrest caught him, slapped him around, and sent him back to the front.

37. Dinkins, *Personal Recollections,* 133–34; Forrest Report, *OR,* ser. 1, 32, pt. 1:352; Hancock, *Hancock's Diary,* 318–19.

38. Jordan and Pryor, *Campaigns,* 392; Forrest report, *OR,* ser. 1, 32, pt. 1:352; Dinkins, *Personal Recollections,* 133–34.

39. McGee, *History of the Seventy-second Indiana,* 271; Records diary, February 21, 1864, Records Papers, ISL.

40. Hancock, *Hancock's Diary,* 319; Dinkins, *Personal Recollections,* 134; Forrest report, March 8, 1864, *OR,* ser. 1, 32, pt. 1:353.

41. Hancock, *Hancock's Diary,* 320, 321.

42. Records diary, February 22, 1864, Records Papers, ISL; Waring, "Sooy Smith Expedition," 417; Smith report, March 4, 1864, *OR,* ser. 1, 32, pt. 1:257.

43. Hancock, *Hancock's Diary,* 322–23; Forrest report, March 8, 1864, *OR,* ser. 1, 32, pt. 1:353; Hubbard, *Notes of a Private,* 57.

44. Hancock, *Hancock's Diary,* 322–23.

45. Larson, *Sergeant Larson,* 222.

46. Isaac W. Curtis report, March 1, 1864, *OR,* ser. 1, 32, pt. 1:302; Records diary, February 22, 1864, Records Papers, ISL; Smith report, March 4, 1864, *OR,* ser. 1, 32, pt. 1:255–60; Cogley, *History of the Seventh Indiana,* 95; Larson, *Sergeant Larson,* 227; Pierce, *History of the Second Iowa,* 88; Waring, *Whip and Spur,* 119. Waring later tried to excuse the incident, saying that the officers had led the cavalrymen into believing that they faced a much superior force; thus the reason for the withdrawal to Memphis. See his statements in "Sooy Smith Expedition," 417–18.

47. Jordan and Pryor, *Campaigns,* 391; Hancock, *Hancock's Diary,* 323.

48. Smith report, March 4, 1864, *OR,* ser. 1, 32, pt. 1:255–60; Waring, *Whip and Spur,* 119; Forrest report, February 26 and March 8, 1864, *OR,* ser. 1, 32, pt. 1:350, 351–55.

49. Hancock, *Hancock's Diary,* 324–25; Waring, "Sooy Smith Expedition," 418; Dinkins, *Personal Recollections,* 134–35.

50. Dinkins, *Personal Recollections,* 135; Jordan and Pryor, *Campaigns,* 396; Morton, *Artillery of Forrest's Cavalry,* 152. Jacob Gaus was Forrest's favorite bugler.

51. Hancock, *Hancock's Diary,* 325; Forrest report, March 8, 1864, *OR,* ser. 1, 32, pt. 1:353; Jordan and Pryor, *Campaigns,* 397; Lee to Polk, February 23, 1864, *OR,* ser. 1, 32, pt. 1:341.

52. Jordan and Pryor, *Campaigns,* 398; Hancock, *Hancock's Diary,* 326.

53. Forrest report, *OR,* ser. 1, 32, pt. 1:353; Hancock, *Hancock's Diary,* 327; Wills, *A Battle from the Start,* 162; Smith report, March 4, 1864, *OR,* ser. 1, 32, pt. 1:255–60; Henry, *As They Saw Forrest,* 152.

54. Jordan and Pryor, *Campaigns,* 400; Hancock, *Hancock's Diary,* 328; Forrest report, March 8, 1864, *OR,* ser. 1, 32, pt. 1:323; Smith report, February 26 and March 4, 1864, ibid., 252–53, 257.

55. Waring, "Sooy Smith Expedition," 418; Starr, *Union Cavalry,* 388; Larson, *Sergeant Larson,* 231.

56. Forrest report, March 8, 1864, *OR,* ser. 1, 32, pt. 1:322–25; Waring, *Whip and Spur,* 120–21.

57. Starr, *Union Cavalry,* 388; Waring, *Whip and Spur,* 120–21; Forrest report, March 8, 1864, *OR,* ser. 1, 32, pt. 1:323.

58. Forrest report, March 8, 1864, and Lee to Polk, February 22, 1864, *OR,* ser. 1, 32, pt. 1:320–25, 340; Jordan and Pryor, *Campaigns,* 401–2.

59. Larson, *Sergeant Larson,* 232.

60. Forrest report, March 8, 1864, *OR,* ser. 1:32, pt. 1:353; Dinkins, *Personal Recollections,* 136; Hancock, *Hancock's Diary,* 330; Waring, "Sooy Smith Expedition," 418; Pierce, *History of the Second Iowa,* 90. Guerrilla troops attacked the column while they were trying to cross the

Tippah River, causing a stampede into the water, drowning some men and horses. For more on this see Records diary, February 24, 1864, Records Papers, ISL; and Hancock, *Hancock's Diary,* 330.

61. Grierson manuscript, p. 313, Grierson Papers, ISHL.

62. Hancock, *Hancock's Diary,* 331; Forrest report, February 26 and March 8, 1864, *OR,* ser. 1, 32, pt. 1:351, 352, 353.

63. Records diary, February 28, March 1, 1864, Records Papers, ISL; Colonel Joseph Karge report, March 16, 1864, *OR,* ser. 1, 32, pt. 1:285; S. A. Hurlbut to W. T. Clark, April 27, 1864, *OR,* ser. 1, 32, pt. 2:280; Smith report, February 26, 1864, *OR,* ser. 1, 32, pt. 1:259–60.

64. *New York Tribune,* February 29, 1864.

65. Smith report, February 26, 1864, *OR,* ser. 1, 32, pt. 1:253.

66. Quoted in Lee, "Sherman's Meridian Expedition," 56.

67. Smith report, February 26, 1864, *OR,* ser. 1, 32, pt. 1:253.

68. Benjamin Grierson to Alice Grierson, February 28, 1864, Grierson Papers, ISHL.

69. Waring, *Whip and Spur,* 116.

70. Sherman report, March 7, 1864, *OR,* ser. I, 32, pt. 1:175; Lewis, *Fighting Prophet,* 336.

71. Grant, *Memoirs,* 2:108; Forrest to Davis, February 5, 1864, *OR,* ser. 1, 32, pt. 1:346.

Chapter 8

1. Sherman report, March 7, 1864, *OR,* ser. 1, 32, pt. 1:175–76.

2. Hickenlooper memoir, February 20, 1864, Hickenlooper Papers, CHS; Howe report, March 7, 1864, *OR,* ser. 1, 32, pt. 1:236; *New York Express,* March 15, 1864.

3. Howe report, March 7, 1864, *OR,* ser. 1, 32, pt. 1:236; Hieronymous diary, February 20, 1864, Hieronymous Papers, ISHL; Underwood diary, February 20, 1864, Underwood Collection, IHS. For scarcity of rations also see Hayes, *History of the Thirty-Second Ohio,* 50.

4. Howard, *History of the 124th,* 196; Illinois soldier quoted in Draper, *History of the American Civil War,* 3:212–13; Snedeker diary, February 20, 1864, Snedeker Papers, USMHI. Hickenlooper says as many as ten thousand slaves returned to Vicksburg with the Federals; Hickenlooper memoir, March 4, 1864, Hickenlooper Papers, CHS.

5. Gebbart diary, February 20, 1864, Gebbart Papers, DUL; Hickenlooper memoir, February 20, 1864, Hickenlooper Papers, CHS; Veatch report, *OR,* ser. 1, 32, pt. 1:202.

6. Sherman report, March 7, 1864, *OR,* ser. 1, 32, pt. 1:176; Sherman to Winslow, February 22, 1864, Sherman Papers, LC.

7. Polk to Lee, February 20, 1864, *OR,* ser. 1, 32, pt. 2:781; Polk to Hardee, Hardee to Polk, and Polk to S. Hillyer, February 20, 1864, ibid., 780.

8. R. O. Perrin to Polk, February 20, 1864, ibid., 783.

9. Gebbart diary, February 21, 1864, Gebbart Papers, DUL; Griffin journal, February 21, 1864, Griffin Papers, ISHL; Snedeker diary, February 21, 1864, Snedeker Papers, USMHI.

10. Veatch report, *OR,* ser. 1, 32, pt. 1:202; Snedeker diary, February 21, 1864, Snedeker Papers, USMHI.

11. Veatch report, *OR,* ser. 1, 32, pt. 1:202; Snedeker diary, February 21, 1864, Snedeker Papers, USMHI; Westervelt diary, February 21, 1864, Westervelt Papers, USMHI.

12. Elliot diary, February 21, 1864, Elliot Collection, IHS; Hieronymous diary, February 21, 1864, Hieronymous Papers, ISHL.

13. W. F. Scott, *Story of a Cavalry Regiment,* 212–13.

14. Ibid.

15. Polk to Davis, February 21, 1864, *OR,* ser. 1, 32, pt. 1:337.

16. Polk, *Leonidas Polk,* 2:335.

17. Hickenlooper report, March 25, 1864, *OR,* ser. 1, 32, pt. 1:217; Snedeker diary, February 22, 1864, Snedeker Papers, USMHI.

18. Griffin journal, February 22, 1864, Griffin Papers, ISHL; Gebbart diary, February 22, 1864, Gebbart Papers, DUL; John Murphy Keltner diary, February 22, 1864, Leslie Anders Collection, Civil War Times Illustrated Collection, USMHI.

19. T. H. Harris to A. J. Smith, *OR,* ser. 1, 32, pt. 2:488; Underwood diary, February 22, 1864, Underwood Collection, IHS.

20. Lee, "The War in Mississippi"; Polk to S. Cooper, February 27, 1864, *OR,* ser. 1, 32, pt. 1:341.

21. Govan and Livengood, *A Different Valor,* 248–49.

22. Connelly, *Autumn of Glory,* 294; Johnston to Hardee, February 23, 1864, quoted in Symonds, *Joseph E. Johnston,* 232.

23. George H. Thomas report, *OR,* ser. 1, 32, pt. 1:6–12; Grant, *Memoirs,* 2:113–14; Govan and Livengood, *A Different Valor,* 249. See also Davis to Johnston, and Davis to Johnston, February 23, 1864, in Rowland, *Jefferson Davis,* 6:188, 189.

24. Polk to Davis, February 22, 1864, *OR,* ser. 1, 32, pt. 1:338–39.

25. Veatch report, ibid., 202–3; Hickenlooper report, March 25, 1864, ibid., 217–18; Snedeker diary, February 23, 1864, Snedeker Papers, USMHI; Hieronymous diary, February 23, 1864, Hieronymous Papers, ISHL.

26. Bettersworth, *Confederate Mississippi,* 206; Sherman to Grant, July 21, 1863, *OR,* ser. 1, 24, pt. 2:530–31; *New York World,* August 7, 1863.

27. McPherson to Potts, February 19, 1864, *OR,* ser. 1, 32, pt. 2:429–30.

28. A. H. Polk to T. F. Sevier, March 3, 1864, *OR,* ser. 1, 32, pt. 3:579–80.

29. Polk to Davis, and Polk to Davis, February 23, 1864, *OR,* ser. 1, 32, pt. 1:340.

30. Jones, *A Rebel War Clerk's Diary,* February 24, 1864.

31. Hieronymous diary, February 24, 1864, Hieronymous Papers, ISHL; Snedeker diary, February 24, 1864, Snedeker Papers, USMHI; Fike diary, February 24, 1864, Fike Papers, WHMC. See also Packard diary, February 25, 1864, Packard Papers, ISHL.

32. Elliot diary, February 26, 1864, Elliot Collection, IHS; Lucius M. Rose report, March 8, 1864, *OR,* ser. 1, 32, pt. 1:223; Westervelt diary, February 26, 1864, Westervelt Papers, USMHI; Hieronymous diary, February 26, 1864, Hieronymous Papers, ISHL.

33. Special Field Orders no. 21, February 26, 1864, *OR,* ser. 1, 32, pt. 1:188–89; Special Field Orders no. 20, February 18, 1864, ibid., 187–88.

34. E. B. Quiner letter, n.d., "Correspondence of Wisconsin Volunteers, 1861–1865," USMHI; Anonymous letter to editor, February 28, 1864, in Moore, *Rebellion Record,* 8:481.

35. J. Scott, *Story of the Thirty-second Iowa,* 123.

36. Special Field Orders no. 20, February 18, 1864, in Clinton H. Haskell Collection, William L. Clements Library, University of Michigan, Ann Arbor.

37. General Field Orders no. 4, February 19, 1864, *OR,* ser. 1, 32, pt. 2:432; Snedeker diary, February 19, 1864, Snedeker Papers, USMHI.

38. General Order no. 5, February 18, 1864, *OR,* ser. 1, 32, pt. 2:427.

39. W. F. Scott, *Story of a Cavalry Regiment,* 216. For more orders on the cessation of pillaging and burning of property see General Field Orders no. 6 and Special Field Orders no. 8, February 25, 1864, *OR,* ser. 1, 32, pt. 2:471.

40. Sherman to J. A. Rawlins, February 27, 1864, *OR,* ser. 1, 32, pt. 1:173; Sherman, *Memoirs,* 395.

41. Hickenlooper report, March 25, 1864, *OR,* ser. 1, 32, pt. 1:219; Rood, *Story of Company E,* 248; Underwood diary, March 1, 1864, Underwood Collection, IHS.

42. William Jackson report, March 21, 1864, Adams report, March 12, 1864, and Starke report, March 13, 1864, *OR,* ser. 1, 32, pt. 1:370, 374, 377.

43. Charles G. Loesch, unpublished memoir, 7, Charles G. Loesch Papers, Loesch Collection, WHMC. The Confederates captured and hanged one of the scouts the day after he left Winslow. An Arkansan, William J. Spicer of the Tenth Missouri, was denounced by a neighbor who rode with the Confederate cavalry. Without a trial, he was executed as a spy because he wore Confederate clothing.

44. Special Field Orders no. 11 and General Field Orders no. 7, February 29, 1864, *OR,* ser. 1, 32, pt. 2:501, 502; Haas, *Mountain of Fire,* 113; Veatch report, *OR,* ser. 1, 32, pt. 1:203.

45. W. B. Smith, *On Wheels and How I Came There,* 135; Rood, *Story of Company E,* 248–49.

46. Special Field Orders no. 63, March 3, 1864, and Polk to Cooper, March 4, 1864, *OR,* ser. 1, 32, pt. 1:356, 342–43.

Conclusion

1. Sherman report, March 7, 1864, *OR,* ser. 1, 32, pt. 1:177. McPherson lists his loss totals at 104, conflicting with Sherman's report, but he agrees with Sherman that 44 cavalrymen were casualties or missing. This discrepancy probably resulted because Sherman did not have McPherson's full report when he wrote his own; McPherson report, March 16, 1864, ibid., 212–13.

2. William H. Jackson report, March 21, 1864, ibid., 371. Stephen D. Lee commanded Jackson's division as his own during the Meridian campaign, although Jackson was the division commander; Lee report, April 18, 1864, ibid., 369. The total numbers exclude any casualties or soldiers involved in skirmishes at Rome, Dalton, or Mobile or on the Yazoo River.

3. Hickenlooper memoir, March 4, 1864, Hickenlooper Papers, CHS. Also see Hickenlooper report, March 25, 1864, and McPherson report, March 16, 1864, *OR,* ser. 1, 32, pt. 1:220–21, 212–13; Howard, *History of the 124th,* 205; Sherman report, March 7, 1864, *OR,* ser. 1, 32, pt. 1:177.

4. Lee, "The War in Mississippi," 53; Hattaway, *General Stephen D. Lee,* 108.

5. A. H. Polk to T. F. Sevier, March 3, 1864, *OR,* ser. 1, 32, pt. 3:579–80; Samuel Tate to L. Polk, March 8, 1864, and L. Polk to Davis, March 10, 1864, *OR,* ser. 1, 32, pt. 1:343–44, 344–45.

6. Blackwell, *Railroads of the Confederacy,* 241.

7. Draper, *History of the American Civil War,* 3:205. Sherman read everything Draper wrote before publication and offered his opinions and critiques. It is safe to say that Sherman probably felt that his Meridian campaign did affect the outcome of the Battle of Nashville. For correspondence between Draper and Sherman see John W. Draper Papers, LC.

8. Blackwell, *Railroads of the Confederacy,* 242.

9. Ibid.

10. McMurry, "Sherman's Meridian Campaign," 32.

11. Sherman report, March 7, 1864, *OR,* ser. 1, 32, pt. 1:177; Rood, *Story of Company E,* 250. See also "Another Account," February 28, 1864, in Moore, *Rebellion Record,* 8:481.

12. Bettersworth, *Confederate Mississippi,* 151.

13. Sherman report, March 7, 1864, *OR,* ser. 1, 32, pt. 1:177; Bettersworth, *Confederate Mississippi,* 206–7.

14. Alfred McNair to Brother, March 9, 1864, Alfred McNair Papers, ISHL.

15. Chambers, "My Journal," 302–3. For more on Mississippi troop desertions see Bettersworth, *Mississippi in the Confederacy,* 153.

16. Marcher quoted in Gerling, *The 117th Illinois,* 65; Sherman report, March 7, 1864, *OR,* ser. 1, 32, pt. 1:177.

Bibliography

Manuscript Collections

Champaign County Historical Archives. Urbana, Illinois
Ira Blanchard Papers
Cincinnati Historical Society. Cincinnati, Ohio
Andrew H. Hickenlooper Papers
Duke University Library. Perkins Library. Durham, North Carolina
Noah Gebbart Papers
John H. Pierce Papers
Illinois State Historical Library. Springfield, Illinois
Henry Allen Papers
Lemuel Burke Papers
Luther Frost Papers
Sarah Gregg Papers
Benjamin Grierson Papers
John A. Griffin Papers
Benjamin Hieronymous Papers
C. E. Lanstrum Papers
Alfred McNair Papers
Jacob A. Melick Diary
Jonathan Merriam Collection
John Messinger Papers
J. W. Miller Letters
Rice Mortimer Papers
Thaddeus Packard Papers
David W. Poak Papers
Walker Papers
Ezekial Thomas Willoughby Papers

Indiana Historical Society. William H. Smith Library. Indianapolis, Indiana
William S. Elliot Collection
Walter Q. Gresham Collection
Albert Underwood Collection
Indiana State Library. Indianapolis, Indiana
Wilfred B. McDonald Collection
William H. Records Papers
Library of Congress. Washington, D.C.
John W. Draper Papers
Albert Q. Porter Papers
William T. Sherman Papers
Lyman Trumbull Papers
Louisiana State University. Troy Middleton Library. Baton Rouge, Louisiana
John Carmichael Jenkins Papers
Meridian Public Library. Meridian, Mississippi
Jim Dawson. "Paths to the Past: Board of Police, 1832–1870, Board of Supervisors, 1870–1992."
"Roster of the Meridian Invincibles."
Vertical Subject File
Mississippi Department of Archives and History. Jackson, Mississippi
Business Directory of Meridian
William A. Montgomery Papers
Mitchell Memorial Library, Mississippi State University, Special Collections
Economic Research Department Mississippi Power and Light Company. "Mississippi Statistical Summary of Population, 1800–1980."
National Archives, Washington, D.C.
Hickenlooper, Andrew. "Map of Meridian Expedition, 1864." Civil War Maps, Cartography Division
Ohio Historical Society. Columbus, Ohio
Benjamin F. Hart Papers
Unknown Ohio Soldier Diary
Rice University Library. Fondren Library. Houston, Texas
David H. Reed Papers
Rutherford B. Hayes Presidential Library. Fremont, Ohio
Ralph P. Buckland Papers
Robert H. Caldwell Papers
Caldwell Family Papers
Orin O. England Papers
William S. Foerster Collection
John Hetrick Papers
James B. McPherson Papers
John B. Rice Papers
State Historical Society of Wisconsin. Madison, Wisconsin
J. Harvey Green Papers
James Proudfit Collection
E. B. Quiner Papers
G. Swain Papers

Alanson Wood Papers
United States Army Military History Institute. Carlisle, Pennsylvania
General Collections
James Bradd Papers
W. S. Featherston Papers
Philip Roesch Papers
"Correspondence of Wisconsin Volunteers, 1861–1865"
Civil War Miscellaneous Collection
"Campaigns of the 178th New York Volunteers"
George C. Burmeister Papers
J. A. Cates Papers
John A. Cato Papers
Thomas Douglas Papers
Simon Peter Duck Papers
William Stubbs Elliot Papers
Abram Fulkerson Papers
Charles H. Lutz Papers
Stephen H. Smith Papers
Charles Henry Snedeker Papers
Columbus Sykes Papers
William B. Westervelt Papers
Civil War Times Illustrated Collection
Leslie Anders Collection
Thomas J. Gundy Papers
John Murphy Keltner Papers
Frederick Pell Papers
Cyrenus Z. Russell Papers
Nehemiah Davis Starr Papers
Adolphus P. Wolfe Papers
University of Alabama. W. S. Hoole Special Collections Library. Tuscaloosa, Alabama
Duncan McCollum Papers
Alonzo Miller Papers
University of Arkansas. Mullins Library. Fayetteville, Arkansas
Harris Reynolds Daniels Papers
University of Michigan. W. L. Clements Library. Ann Arbor, Michigan
Clinton H. Haskell Collection
University of Notre Dame. South Bend, Indiana
Sherman Family Papers
University of Washington. Suzzallo Library. Seattle, Washington
Manning Ferguson Force Papers
Western Historical Manuscript Collection. University of Missouri. Columbia, Missouri
General Collections
John A. Blackwell Papers
Henry Fike Papers
Edwin Jones Papers
Bundy G. Smith Papers
Loesch Collection

Robert L. LaValle Papers
Charles G. Loesch Papers

Books and Articles

Anders, Leslie. *The Twenty-first Missouri: From Home Guard to Union Regiment.* London: Greenwood Press, 1975.

Anderson, Mary Ann, ed. *The Civil War Diary of Allen Morgan Greer: Twentieth Regiment, Illinois Volunteers.* New York: Cosmos Press, 1977.

Ash, Stephen. *When the Yankees Came: Chaos and Conflict in the Occupied South, 1860–1865.* Chapel Hill: University of North Carolina Press, 1995.

Atlas to Accompany the Campaigns of the Civil War. New York: Thomas Yoseloff, 1963.

Avery, P. O. *The Fourth Illinois Cavalry Regiment.* Humbolt, Neb.: The Enterprise: A Print Shop, 1903.

Ballard, Michael B. "Yankees in the Yard: Mississippi Women during the Vicksburg Campaign." In *Mississippi Women: Crossroads of Circumstance,* ed. Elizabeth Anne Paupe, Marjorie Spruill, and Martha Swain. Athens: University of Georgia Press, forthcoming.

Barber, Lucius W. *Army Memoirs of Lucius Barber, Company D, Fifteenth Illinois Volunteer Infantry.* Chicago: J. M. W. Jones Stationary and Printing Co., 1894.

Barnard, Harry V. *Tattered Volunteers: The Twenty-seventh Alabama Infantry Regiment.* Northport, Ala.: Hermitage Press, 1965.

Barron, S. B. *The Lone Star Defenders: A Chronicle of the Third Texas Cavalry, Ross' Brigade.* New York: Neale, 1908.

Bearss, Edwin C. "Grierson's Winter Raid on the Mobile and Ohio Railroad." *Military Affairs* 24 (Spring 1960): 20–37.

———. *The Siege of Jackson.* Baltimore: Gateway Press, 1981.

Bearss, Majorie R. *Sherman's Forgotten Campaign: The Meridian Expedition.* Baltimore: Gateway Press, 1987.

Belknap, William W., and Loren S. Tyler. *History of the Fifteenth Regiment Iowa Veteran Volunteer Infantry, from October 1861, to August, 1865, when Disbanded at the End of the War.* Keokuk, Iowa: R. B. Ogden and Son, Print., 1887.

Bettersworth, John K. *Confederate Mississippi.* Philadelphia: Porcupine Press, 1943.

———. *Mississippi in the Confederacy: As They Saw It.* Baton Rouge: Louisiana State University Press, 1961.

Bevier, R. S. *History of the First and Second Missouri Confederate Brigades.* St. Louis: Bryan, Brad, 1879.

Bishop, Judson W. *The Story of a Regiment.* St. Paul: Published by the Survivors of the Regiment, 1890.

Blackwell, Robert C., III. *Railroads of the Confederacy.* Chapel Hill: University of North Carolina Press, 1952.

Blanchard, Ira. *I Marched with Sherman: Civil War Memoirs of the Twentieth Illinois Volunteer Infantry.* Lincoln: toExcel, 1992.

Blassingame, John W. *The Slave Community: Plantation Life in the Antebellum South.* New York: Oxford University Press, 1972.

Bonney, Philip C. *The Civil War Letters of Pvt. P. C. Bonney.* Lawrenceville, Ill.: Lawrenceville Publishing Company, 1963.

Bowman, S. M., and R. B. Irwin. *Sherman and His Campaigns.* New York: C. B. Richardson, 1865.

Bowman, T. H. *Reminiscences of an Ex-Confederate Soldier or Forty Years on Crutches.* Austin: Gammel-Statesman, 1864.

Boyd, Davis F. "Gen. W. T. Sherman: His Early Life in the South and His Relations with Southern Men." *Confederate Veteran* 18 (September 1910): 409–14.

Boynton, H. V. *Sherman's Historical Raid: The Memoirs in the Light of the Record.* Cincinnati: Wilstach, Baldwin, 1875.

Brinsfield, John W. "The Military Ethics of William T. Sherman: A Reassessment." *Parameters* 12 (1983): 36–48.

Brown, Andrew. *Company K, Twentieth Regiment, Illinois Volunteer Infantry.* Yorkville, Ill.: Kendall County Record Print, 1894.

Bryner, Cloyd. *Bugles Echoes: The Story of Illinois 47th.* Springfield, Ill.: Philips Brothers, 1905.

Burton, William L. *Descriptive Bibliography of Civil War Manuscripts in Illinois.* Evanston: The Civil War Centennial Commission of Illinois and Northwestern Illinois Press, 1965.

Castel, Albert. *Decision in the West: The Atlanta Campaign of 1864.* Lawrence: University Press of Kansas, 1992.

Chalmers, James R. "General J. R. Chalmers' Address at White Sulphur Springs on Nathan Bedford Forrest." *Southern Historical Society Papers* 7 (1879): 450–76.

Chambers, William P. "My Journal: The Life of a Soldier Told by Himself." In Dunbar Rowland, *Publications of the Mississippi Historical Society,* 5:302–3.

Clarke, Hewitt. *Thunder at Meridian.* Spring, Tex.: Lone Star Press, 1995.

Clinton, Catherine. *Tara Revisited: Women, War, and the Plantation Legend.* New York: Abbeville Press, 1995.

Clinton, Catherine, and Nina Silber, eds. *Divided Houses: Gender and the Civil War.* New York: Oxford University Press, 1992.

Cogley, Thomas S. *History of the Seventh Indiana Cavalry Volunteers.* LaPorte, Ind.: Herald Company Steam Printers, 1876.

Connelly, Thomas L. *Autumn of Glory: The Army of Tennessee, 1862–1865.* Baton Rouge: Louisiana State University Press, 1971.

Cozzens, Peter. *Shipwreck of Their Hopes: The Battles for Chattanooga.* Urbana: University of Illinois Press, 1994.

Craven, Hervey. *A Brief History of the Eighty-ninth Illinois Volunteer Infantry from Its Organization August 28, 1862 to the Close of Its Term of Service, Including Official Reports, and a List of Casualties in Actions.* Wabash, Ind.: Monson-Corrie, 1899.

Crist, Lynda, and Kenneth H. Williams, eds. *The Papers of Jefferson Davis.* Vol. 10. Baton Rouge: Louisiana State University Press, 1999.

Dacus, Robert. *Reminiscences of Company "H," First Arkansas Mounted Rifles.* Dardenelle, Ark.: Post-Despatch Print, 1897.

Denney, Robert E. *The Civil War Years: A Day-by-Day Chronicle of the Life of a Nation.* New York: Sterling, 1992.

Depasquale, Steven M. "The Twentieth Illinois Infantry during the Civil War." M.A. thesis, Illinois State University, 1993.

Desha, Robert. *Business and Complete Directory of the City of Meridian.* Meridian, Miss.: Campell and Powell, 1873.

Deupree, J. G. "The Noxubee Squadron, Mississippi Cavalry." *Publications of the Mississippi Historical Society* 2 (1918): 88–89.

——. *Reminiscences of Service with the First Mississippi Cavalry.* Jackson: Publications of the Mississippi Historical Society, 1918.

Dinges, Bruce J. "The Making of a Cavalryman: Benjamin H. Grierson and the Civil War along the Mississippi, 1861–1865." M.A. thesis, Rice University, 1978.

Dinkins, James. *Personal Recollection and Experiences in the Confederate Army, by an Old Johnnie.* Dayton, Ohio: Morningside Bookshop, 1975.

Dodge, Grenville M. *Personal Recollections of President Abraham Lincoln, General Ulysses S. Grant, General William T. Sherman.* Denver: Sage, 1965.

Draper, John W. *History of the American Civil War.* 3 vols. New York: Harper, 1867–70.

Dyer, Frederick H. *A Compendium of the War of the Rebellion.* Des Moines: Dyer, 1908.

Edwards, Laura F. *Scarlett Doesn't Live Here Anymore: Southern Women in the Civil War.* Urbana: University of Illinois Press, 2000.

Eighth Census of the United States. Washington, D.C.: U.S. Census Office, 1865.

Evans, Clement A., ed. *Confederate Military History.* New York: Thomas Yoseloff, 1962.

Experiences in the War of the Great Rebellion: By a Soldier of the Eighty-first Regiment Illinois Volunteer Infantry. Carbondale, Ill.: Edmond Newsome, 1880.

Faust, Drew G. *Mothers of Invention.* Chapel Hill: University of North Carolina Press, 1996.

Fellman, Micheal. *Citizen Sherman: A Life of William Tecumseh Sherman.* New York: Random House, 1995.

Force, Manning F. *Great Commanders: General Sherman.* New York: D. Appleton, 1899.

French, Samuel. *Two Wars: An Autobiography of General Samuel G. French.* Nashville: Confederate Veteran, 1901.

Frost, Luther. *Letters of Luther and Orville Frost.* Great Bend, Kans.: M. E. VanPelt, 1988.

Fulton, Joseph Edward, ed. *From Beardstown to Andersonville: The Civil War Letters of Asa Newton Paschal and Samuel Thomas Paschal.* Bowie, Md.: Heritage Books, 1998.

Gammage, W. L. *The Camp, the Bivouac, and the Battlefield.* Little Rock: Arkansas Southern Press, 1864.

Garner, James W. *Reconstruction in Mississippi.* Baton Rouge: Louisiana State University Press, 1968.

Gault, W. P. *Ohio at Vicksburg: Report of the Ohio Battlefield Commission.* Washington, D.C.: Government Printing Office, 1906.

——. *Roster of [with diary] William P. Gault O.V.V.I.* Columbus, Ohio: Society of the 78th Regimental Association, 1901.

Gebbart, Carl Dean. "The Eleventh Illinois Infantry Regiment in the Civil War." M.A. thesis, Western Illinois University, 1968.

Geer, Walter. *Campaigns of the Civil War.* New York: Brentano's, 1926.

Genovese, Eugene. *Roll Jordan Roll: The World the Slaves Made.* New York: Pantheon Books, 1974.

Gerling, Edwin G. *The 117th Illinois Infantry Volunteers (The McKenzie Regiment) 1862–1865.* Highland, Ill.: n.p., 1992.

Gladieux, Rolland J. *The Fourteenth Indiana Light Artillery Battery.* Kenmore, N.Y.: Work Experience Press, 1978.

Glatthaar, Joseph T. *March to the Sea and Beyond: Sherman's Troops in the Savannah and Carolina Campaigns.* New York: New York University Press, 1985.

Govan, Gilbert E., and James W. Livengood. *A Different Valor: The Story of General Joseph E. Johnston C.S.A.* New York: Bobbs-Merrill, 1956.

Grant, Ulysses S. *Personal Memoirs of U.S. Grant.* New York: Charles L. Webster, 1886.

Grimsley, Mark. *The Hard Hand of War: Union Military Policy toward Southern Civilians, 1861–1865.* New York: Cambridge University Press, 1995.

Haas, Garland. *To the Mountain of Fire and Beyond: The Fifty-third Indiana Regiment from Corinth to Glory.* Carmel: Guild Press of Indiana, 1997.

Hale, Douglas. *The Third Texas Cavalry in the Civil War.* Norman: University of Oklahoma Press, 1993.

Halleck, Henry W. *International Law; or, Rules Regulating the Intercourse of States in Peace and War.* New York: D. Van Nostrand, 1861.

Hancock, R. R. *Hancock's Diary: A History of the Second Tennessee Confederate Cavalry.* Dayton, Ohio: Press of Morningside Bookshop, 1981.

Hattaway, Herman. *General Stephen D. Lee.* Jackson: University Press of Mississippi, 1976.

Hattaway, Herman, and Archer Jones. *How the North Won the War: A Military History of the Civil War.* Chicago: University of Illinois Press, 1983.

Hayes, E. Z. *History of the Thirty-second Ohio Veteran Volunteer Infantry Regiment.* Columbus: Cott and Evans, 1896.

Heidler, David S., and Jeanne T. Heidler, eds. *Encyclopedia of the American Civil War.* 5 vols. Santa Barbara: ABC-CLIO, 2000.

Henry, Robert S., ed. *As They Saw Forrest.* Jackson, Tenn.: McCowat-Mercer Press, 1956.

Hirchson, Stanley P. *The White Tecumseh: A Biography of General William T. Sherman.* New York: Wiley, 1997.

Hobart, Edwin. *Semi-History of a Boy-Veteran of the Twenty-eighth Regiment Illinois Infantry Volunteers, in a Black Regiment.* Denver, 1909.

Horn, Stanley F. *The Army of Tennessee.* New York: Bobbs-Merrill, 1941.

Houp, Randall. *The Twenty-fourth Missouri Volunteer Infantry.* Alma, Ark.: J. Randall Houp, 1997.

Howard, Richard L. *History of the 124th Regiment Illinois Volunteer, Otherwise Known as the "Hundred and Two Dozen" from August 1862 to August 1865.* Springfield, Ill.: H. W. Rokker, 1880.

Howe, M. A. DeWolfe, ed. *Home Letters of William T. Sherman.* New York: Scribner's, 1909.

Hubbard, John M. *Notes of a Private.* St. Louis: Nixon-Jones, 1913.

Hurst, Jack. *Nathan Bedford Forrest: A Biography.* New York: Knopf, 1993.

Illinois in the Civil War. Urbana: University of Illinois Press, 1966.

Janda, Lance, "Shutting the Gates of Mercy: The American Origins of Total War, 1860–1880." *Journal of Military History* 59 (January 1995): 7–26.

Johnson, Ludwell H. *Red River Campaign: Politics and Cotton in the Civil War.* Kent, Ohio: Kent State University Press, 1993.

Johnston, Joseph E. *Narrative of Military Operations.* Bloomington: Indiana University Press, 1959.

Joiner, Gary. *One Damn Blunder from Beginning to End: The Red River Campaign of 1864.* Wilmington, Del.: Scholarly Resources, 2003.

Jomini, Antoine Henri, Baron de. *The Art of War.* Philadelphia: Lippincott, 1862.

Jones, J. B. *A Rebel Clerk's Diary at the Confederate State Capital.* 2 vols. New York: Old Hickory Bookshop, 1935.

Jordan, Thomas, and J. P. Pryor. *The Campaigns of Lieut.-Gen. N. B. Forrest, and of Forrest's Cavalry.* Dayton, Ohio: Morningside Bookshop, 1977.

Keim, Randolph De B. *Sherman: A Memorial.* In *Art, Oratory, and Literature by the Society of the Army of Tennessee with the Aid of the Congress of the United States of America.* Washington, D.C.: Government Printing Office, 1904.

Kellogg, Frederic Henry. *From Your Affectionate Son: The Civil War Letters of Frederic Henry Kellogg.* Cripple Creek, Colo.: Columbine Press, 1996.

Kennedy, Joseph C. G. *Agriculture of the United States: Compiled from the Original Returns of the Eighth Census.* Washington, D.C.: Government Printing Office, 1864.

Kennett, Lee. *Marching through Georgia: The Story of Soldiers and Civilians during Sherman's Campaign.* New York: Harper Collins, 1995.

———. *Sherman: A Soldier's Life.* New York: Harper Collins, 2001.

Kerr, Homer L., ed. *Fighting with Ross' Texas Cavalry Brigade C.S.A.* Hillsboro: Hill Jr. College Press, 1976.

Kilian, Kerwin C. "Common Valor: A History of the Twentieth Wisconsin Infantry." M.A. thesis, St. Cloud State University, 1999.

Larson, James. *Sergeant Larson Fourth Cavalry.* San Antonio: Southern Literary Institute, 1935.

Lash, Jeffery N. *A Politician Turned General: The Civil War Career of Stephen Augustus Hurlbut.* Kent, Ohio: Kent State University Press, 2003.

Leckie, William H., and Shirley A. Leckie. *Unlikely Warriors: General Benjamin H. Grierson and His Family.* Norman: University of Oklahoma Press, 1984.

Lee, Stephen D. "Operations of the Cavalry in Mississippi from January to March, 1864." *Southern Historical Society Papers* 9 (1881): 97–102.

———. "Sherman's Expedition from Vicksburg to Meridian, February 3 to March 6, 1864." *Southern Historical Society Papers* 12 (1904): 310–19.

———. "Sherman's Meridian Expedition and Sooy Smith's Raid to West Point." *Southern Historical Society Papers* 8 (1880): 49–62.

———. "The War in Mississippi after the Fall of Vicksburg, July 4, 1863." *Publications of the Mississippi Historical Society* 10 (1909): 47–62.

Lewis, Lloyd. *Sherman, Fighting Prophet.* New York: Harcourt Brace, 1958.

Liddell Hart, B. H. "Sherman—Modern Warrior." *American Heritage* 13 (August 1972): 21–23, 102–6.

———. *Sherman: Soldier, Realist, American.* New York: Dodd, Mead, 1929.

Lytle, Andrew Nelson. *Bedford Forrest and His Critter Company.* Seminole, Fla.: Green Key Press, 1931.

Mahan, Alfred T. *Naval Strategy, Compared and Contrasted with the Principles and Practice of Military Operations on Land.* Boston: Little, Brown, 1900.

Marszalek, John F. *Sherman: A Soldier's Passion for Order.* New York: The Free Press, 1993.

———. *Sherman's Other War: The General and the Civil War Press.* Rev. ed. Kent, Ohio: Kent State University Press, 1999.

Massey, Mary E. *Refugee Life in the Confederacy.* Baton Rouge: Louisiana State University Press, 1964.

———. *Women in the Civil War.* Lincoln: University of Nebraska Press, 1966.

Maury, D. H. "Remarks of General Maury." *Southern Historical Society Papers* 7 (1879): 448–50.

McCall, D. *Three Years in the Service: A Record of the Doings of the 11th Regimental Missouri Volunteers.* Springfield, Mo.: Steam Press of Baker and Phillips, 1864.

McDonough, James Lee. *Chattanooga: Death Grip on the Confederacy.* Knoxville: University of Tennessee, 1985.

McGee, B. F. *History of the Seventy-second Indiana Volunteer Infantry of the Mounted Light Brigade.* LaFayette, Ind.: S. Vater, 1882.

McMurry, Richard M. "Sherman's Meridian Campaign." *Civil War Times Illustrated* 14 (May 1975): 24–32.

McPherson, James M. *For Cause and Comrades: Why Men Fought in the Civil War.* New York: Oxford University Press, 1997.

Merrill, James M. *William Tecumseh Sherman.* Chicago: Rand McNally, 1971.

Mieyal, Timothy. "A Story of Valor: The Seventh Ohio Volunteer Infantry." M.A. thesis, Kent State University, 1998.

Miller, Francis T. *The Photographic History of the Civil War.* New York: Review of Reviews, 1911.

Mitchell, Reid. *Civil War Soldiers.* New York: Viking, 1988.

Mohr, Clarence L. *On the Threshold of Freedom: Masters and Slaves in Civil War Georgia.* Athens: University of Georgia Press, 1986.

Montgomery, Frank A. *Reminiscences of a Mississippian in Peace and War.* Cincinnati: Robert Clark Company Press, 1901.

Moore, Frank, ed. *Rebellion Record: A Diary of American Events.* 8 vols. New York: D. Van Nostrand, 1865.

Morris, W. S., ed. *History of the Thirty-first Regiment Illinois Volunteers.* Carbondale: Southern Illinois Press, 1902.

Morse, F. W. *Personal Experiences in the War of the Great Rebellion from December, 1862 to July, 1865.* Albany: Musell, 1866.

Morton, John W. *The Artillery of Nathan Bedford Forrest's Cavalry.* Nashville: M. F. Church, 1909.

Newsome, F. W. *Personal Experiences in the War of the Great Rebellion from December, 1862 to July, 1865.* Carbondale, Ill.: E. Newsome, 1879.

Parks, Joseph H. "A Confederate Trade Center under Federal Occupation: Memphis, 1862 to 1865." *Journal of Southern History* 7 (August 1941): 289–314.

———. *General Leonidas Polk, C.S.A.: The Fighting Bishop.* Baton Rouge: Louisiana State University Press, 1962.

Pierce, Lyman B. *History of the Second Iowa Cavalry.* Burlington, Iowa: Hawk-Eye Steam Book and Job Printing Establishment, 1865.

Polk, William M. *Leonidas Polk, Bishop and General.* 2 vols. New York: Longmans Green, 1915.

Quiner, E. B. *The Military History of Wisconsin: A Record of the Civil and Military Patriotism of the State, in the War of the Union.* Chicago: Clarke and Co., 1866.

Raab, James W. *W. W. Loring: Florida's Forgotten General.* Manhattan, Kans.: Sunflower United Press, 1996.

Roark, James L. *Masters without Slaves: Southern Planters in the Civil War and Reconstruction.* New York: Norton, 1977.

Roesch, Phillip. *Memorandum of Phillip Roesch, Co. H., Twenty-fifth Regiment, Wisconsin Volunteers: Kept during My Service, August 6, 1862, to June 11, 1865.* Midland, Mich.: Richard K. Long, 1979.

Rood, Hosea W. *Story of the Service of Company E, and of the Twelfth Wisconsin Regiment, Veteran Volunteer Infantry, in the War of the Rebellion.* Milwaukee: Swain and Tate, 1893.

Roth, Margaret Brobst, ed. *Well Mary: Civil War Letters of A Wisconsin Volunteer.* Madison: University of Wisconsin Press, 1960.

Rowland, Dunbar. *Jefferson Davis, Constitutionalist: His Letters, Papers, and Speeches.* 10 vols. Jackson: Mississippi Department of Archives and History, 1923.

———. *Military History of Mississippi, 1803–1898.* Spartanburg, S.C.: The Reprint Company, 1988.

Royster, Charles. *The Destructive War.* New York: Knopf, 1991.

Rusling, James F. *Men and Things I Saw in Civil War Days.* Cincinnati: Curts and Jennings, 1899.

Scott, John. *Story of the Thirty-second Iowa Infantry Volunteers.* Nevada, Iowa: John Scott, 1896.

Scott, William Forse. *The Story of a Cavalry Regiment: The Career of the Fourth Iowa Veteran Volunteers.* New York: Putnam, 1893.

Shank, George K., Jr. "Meridian: A Mississippi City at Birth, during the Civil War, and in Reconstruction." M.A. thesis, Mississippi State University, 1961.

———. "Meridian: A Mississippi City at Birth, during the Civil War, and in Reconstruction." *Journal of Mississippi History* 24 (November 1964): 275–82.

Sherman, William T. *The Memoirs of William T. Sherman.* Bloomington: Indiana University Press, 1957.

Sifakis, Stewart. *Who Was Who in the Civil War.* New York: Facts on File, 1998.

Simkins, Francis B., and James W. Patton. *Women of the Confederacy.* New York: Garrett and Massie, 1936.

Simon, John Y., ed. *The Papers of Ulysses S. Grant.* Carbondale: Southern Illinois University Press, 1982.

Simpson, Brooks D., and Jean V. Berlin, eds. *Sherman's Civil War: Selected Correspondence of William T. Sherman, 1860–1865.* Chapel Hill: University of North Carolina Press, 1999.

Slave Narratives: Oklahoma and Mississippi Narratives. St. Clair, Mich.: Scholarly Press, 1976.

Smith, W. B. *On Wheels and How I Came There: A Real Story for Real Boys and Girls.* New York: Hunt and Eaton, 1893.

Smith, Walter G. *The Life and Letters of Thomas Kilby Smith.* New York: Putnam, 1898.

Starke, P. B. "Sherman's Advance on Meridian." *Southern Historical Society Papers* 9 (April 1881).

Starr, Stephen Z. *The Union Cavalry in the Civil War.* Baton Rouge: Louisiana State University Press, 1985.

Stevenson, Thomas M. *History of the Seventy-eighth Regiment of O.V.I.I., from Its "Muster-In" to Its "Muster-Out": Comprising Its Organization, Marches, Campaigns, Battles, and Skirmishes.* Zanesville, Ohio: Hugh Dunne, 1865.

Stover, John F. *The Railroads of the South, 1865–1900.* Chapel Hill: University of North Carolina Press, 1955.

Sutherland, Daniel E. "Abraham Lincoln, John Pope, and the Origins of Total War." *Journal of Military History* 56 (October 1992): 567–86.

Sword, Wiley. *Southern Invincibility.* New York: St. Martin's Griffin, 1999.

Symonds, Craig. *Joseph E. Johnston: A Civil War Biography.* New York: Norton, 1992.

Taylor, F. Jay, ed. *The Reluctant Rebel: The Secret Diary of Robert Patrick.* Baton Rouge: Louisiana State University Press, 1959.

Thomas, Wilbur. *General George H. Thomas: The Indomitable Warrior.* New York: Exposition Press, 1964.

Thorndike, Rachel Sherman. ed. *The Sherman Letters.* New York: Scribner, 1894.

U.S. War Department. *Official Records of the Union and Confederate Navies in the War of the Rebellion.* 30 vols. Washington, D.C.: Government Printing Office, 1894–1922.

———. *The War of the Rebellion: A Compilation of the Official Records of the Union and Confederate Armies.* 128 vols. Washington, D.C.: Government Printing Office, 1880–1901.

Vandiver, Frank E. "Joseph Eggleston Johnston." In *Leaders of the American Civil War,* ed. Charles F. Ritter and Jon L. Wakelyn, 217–18. Westport, Conn.: Greenwood Press, 1998.

Victor, Orville James. *The History, Civil, Political, and Military, of the Southern Rebellion, from Its Incipient Stages to Its Close.* 4 vols. New York: J. D. Torrey, 1861–68.

Walker, Francis A. *The Statistics of the Wealth and Industry of the United States.* Washington, D.C.: Government Printing Office, 1872.

Walters, John B. "General Sherman and Total War." *Journal of Southern History* 14 (1948): 448–62.

———. "General William T. Sherman and Total War." Ph.D. diss., Vanderbilt University, 1947.

———. *Merchant of Terror: General Sherman and Total War.* Indianapolis: Bobbs-Merrill, 1973.

Waring, George E., Jr. "The Sooy Smith Expedition." In *Battles and Leaders of the Civil War,* ed. Robert Underwood Johnson and Clarence Clough Buel, 4:417–18. New York: The Century Company.

———. *Whip and Spur.* New York: Doubleday, Page, 1897.

Warner, Ezra. *Generals in Gray: Lives of the Confederate Commanders.* Baton Rouge: Louisiana State University, 1959.

———. "General William T. Sherman and Total War." *Journal of Southern History* 14 (November 1948): 447–80.

Welcher, Frank. *The Union Army, 1861–1865: Organization and Operations.* Indianapolis: Indiana University Press, 1989.

Wessells, William W. *Born to Be a Soldier: The Military Career of William Wing Loring of St. Augustine, Florida.* Ft. Worth: Texas Christian University Press, 1971.

West, Emmet C. *History and Reminiscences of the Second Wisconsin Cavalry Regiment.* Portage, Wisc.: State Register Print, 1904.

Westervelt, Wm. B. *Light and Shadows of Army Life.* Marlboro, N.Y.: C. H. Cochrane, 1886.

Westwood, Howard C. "After Vicksburg, What of Mobile?" *Military Affairs* 48 (October 1984): 169–73.

Whaley, Elizabeth J. *Forgotten Hero, General James B. McPherson: The Biography of a Civil War General.* New York: Exposition Press, 1955.

Wills, Brian Steel. *A Battle from the Start: The Life of Nathan Bedford Forrest.* New York: Harper Collins, 1992.

Wood, Alanson. "History of Thirty-second Regiment, Wisconsin Infantry." The State Historical Society of Wisconsin, 1888.

Woodward, C. Vann, ed. *Mary Chestnut's Civil War.* New Haven: Yale University Press, 1981.

Worley, Ted R. *The War Memoirs of Captain John W. Lavender, C.S.A.* Pine Bluff, Ark.: The Southern Press, 1956.

Wyeth, John A. *That Devil Forrest: Life of General Nathan Bedford Forrest.* New York: Harper, 1959.

Young, J. P. *The Seventh Tennessee Cavalry.* Nashville: M. E. Church, South, 1890.

Index